The Incompleat
Eco-Philosopher

SUNY series in Environmental Philosophy and Ethics

J. Baird Callicott and John van Buren, editors

The Incompleat Eco-Philosopher

Essays from the Edges of Environmental Ethics

Anthony Weston

Cover photo: "Panorama of Mars," courtesy of Stocktrek Images/Collection Mix: Subjects/Getty Images.

Published by
State University of New York Press, Albany

© 2009 State University of New York

For information, contact State University of New York Press, Albany, NY
www.sunypress.edu

Production by Eileen Meehan
Marketing by Anne M. Valentine

Library of Congress Cataloging-in-Publication Data

Weston, Anthony, 1954–
   The incompleat eco-philosopher : essays from the edges of
environmental ethics / Anthony Weston.
       p. cm.
   Includes bibliographical references and index.
   ISBN 978-0-7914-7669-7 (hardcover : alk. paper)
   1. Environmental ethics.   2. Environmental responsibility.   I. Title.

GE42.W478 2009
179'.1—dc22   2008024990

10 9 8 7 6 5 4 3 2 1

This book is dedicated to Jim Cheney and Tom Birch,
best of companions in all kinds of wildernesses.

Contents

Preface   ix

1   Introduction   1

2   Before Environmental Ethics   23

3   Self-Validating Reduction: Toward a Theory of
     Environmental Devaluation   45

4   Environmental Ethics as Environmental Etiquette:
     Towards an Ethics-Based Epistemology in
     Environmental Philosophy (with Jim Cheney)   65

5   Multicentrism: A Manifesto   89

6   De-Anthropocentrizing the World: Environmental
     Ethics as a Design Challenge   109

7   What If Teaching Went Wild?   131

8   Galapagos Stories: Evolution, Creation, and the
     Odyssey of Species   149

9   Eco-Philosophy in Space   163

Appendix: Complete Publication List   187

Index   193

Preface

This book is a selection from my work in environmental philosophy over the past fifteen years or so: essays that explicitly address the question of method in environmental ethics and this moment in environmental philosophy. The opening essay, new to this volume, sketches the overarching themes and introduces each essay in context. Eight essays follow, with brief introductory notes, and there is an accounting of all of my work in the field at the end.

True to its title, this book is incomplete in a variety of ways. My work is ongoing, and anyway only some of it appears here. More scandalously, the work of environmental ethics itself, in the view I wish to advance, is necessarily and fundamentally incomplete. We speak of what may be one of the most profound ethical shifts in millennia, at least for the West, and it is, after all, *barely begun.* It is still young, still unformed, still bears the deep marks of its ancestry, its long and uncertain gestation, its labor to be born. As with any other kind of newborn and delicate thing, we cannot even begin to glimpse the shape of a settled more-than-human ethics without a far wider range of ethical experiments and remade practices, all tested in turn by time and as yet barely foreseen events.

Thus in many ways we still stand, as one of my titles goes, "Before Environmental Ethics." *All* eco-philosophy is radically incomplete. But this moment of beginnings is also—precisely as such—a moment at which we can make an immense difference. Certain philosophical and personal practices are discouraged, yes. Certain traditional aspirations are neither achievable, in my view, nor desirable. By the same token, though, other truly inviting and "edgy" new possibilities open up, both in and beyond environmental ethics and for a transformative philosophical practice in other keys. Take this collection as a sort of imaginative guidebook, a first survey of the new country, and an invitation to explore it further yourself.

My previous books in the field got away from me in this regard. For better or worse, they did not hang around arguing about the usual conceptual boundary-markers, but ended up already a bend or two of the trail farther along (perhaps taking the markers along with them, a trick

I learned in the actual wilderness from the venerable Tom Birch). When I began the book that eventually appeared as *Back to Earth: Tomorrow's Environmentalism* (Temple University Press, 1994), I really did mean to address methodological and conceptual issues as an integral part of the project. In the end, though, *Back to Earth* barely speaks to the usual philosophical debates and categories at all. Instead it devotes itself to exploring the world's possibilities, sensuous and magical, beyond the wholly human; to understanding how we have managed to so thoroughly obscure those depths from ourselves (simply overpowering and destroying them is only the crudest way); and to seeking out some specific paths, partial and modest enough in their ways but radical still, to recover them, to reconnect. I came to see that this kind of exploration was quite enough (was more than enough, in fact could itself only be sketched in the barest way) without also having to bushwhack through all the usual methodological brambles so very far off-road, as it were, to what after all is still only a starting point. Instead I simply found myself speaking from a different place, never mind how I got there.

A few years later I edited a small collection called *An Invitation to Environmental Philosophy* (Oxford University Press, 1999), but here again the main project was more to embody or enact an alternative kind of philosophy—actually, to model of whole set of them, with varied friends and fellow travelers—than to make its presuppositions explicit and try to defend them against the usual (and also usually implicit) expectations.

Yet part of my hope, and a central part of my work, has always been to contend with and for philosophy itself. Here I part from my friend and wilderness companion Jim Cheney, who holds that we free spirits should just re-christen ourselves "ex-philosophers" and head into the high country with much lighter backpacks. Often enough I am right beside him. But not always. There is another side. Why cede Philosophy Itself to the most heavily laden? Why should philosophy be a burden at all? Isn't it also a necessary task to make an alternative visible *philosophically?* The struggle for a truly environmental philosophy, in the long run, may also be a struggle for the soul of philosophy itself.

In my essays, then, I have also been writing, right along, *in* "the field," struggling to make alternative ethical and philosophical presuppositions explicit and to defend them against the usual expectations. This work has mostly appeared in professional and other journals, however, and consequently is somewhat scattered over both time and space. Four of these essays reprinted here first appeared in the journal *Environmental Ethics.* Some of these essays have been regularly anthologized in turn. Others have been published much farther afield—*The Canadian Journal of Environmental Education*; the multidisciplinary journal *Soundings*; and

Jobs for Philosophers, my self-published "little book of heresies"—and the last and farthest afield of all, "Eco-Philosophy in Space," has only been circulated to (mostly disbelieving) colleagues.

Until now I have not tried to bring these more methodological and conceptual pieces together in one place. Always there was the next piece, another trip, some other form in which an idea could be put. In the last few years, though, a few things have changed. For one thing, I finally attained the age at which Plato thought one could actually become a philosopher, so perhaps a certain kind of prelude is over. There is a practical impulse too. Students and colleagues, as well as I myself, are finding it increasingly difficult to relocate and recopy articles or find reprints from back issues of a variety of journals in order to put together readers for students or to pass on the most helpful or provocative materials to other researchers and writers. This part of my work has grown and diversified in its own right but remains too scattered for easy use by others. I am gratified that others share my feeling that these essays are *alive*; that together they lay out the possibility of a dramatically different and still barely suspected way of thinking about environmental values. But each separate essay needs to add its piece. It is time they were drawn together in a single place, next to each other at last.

I want to say for the record that I did not enter the field of environmental philosophy with any inkling that it might in time take me into so many wild lands around the world or bring me such dear friends. Yet it is so, and I am grateful beyond words.

My greatest debt of gratitude is to the land, this land, almost any land, to the country that sustains and welcomes, wherever it may be, even right next door. For me, at least, it is an old debt, the original impulse, all the way back to those long summers I spent on the prairie as a boy playing in the woods and cornfields. Long nights under the stars, so captivating that my first professional ambition was to be an astronomer. A series of wild companions opened up wider lands for me, starting with my father when I was freshly minted from high school, whose idea of celebrating my coming of age was to go backpacking through the Great Smoky Mountains, though neither of us had ever dreamed of such a thing before. Ridge trails snaking through high meadow grasses, vanishing into forests beyond; the blue afternoon mists of those hills; strange birdcalls that later became as familiar as the plants in my garden—here was the trailhead of many of my later paths.

Meanwhile environmental consciousness was rising—this was the early 1970s—so much so that my second serious professional ambition was to be an environmental lawyer. But barely embarked on that path I found philosophy, though it was still some time before my philosophical thinking found, or rather remembered, the larger-than-human world. Philosophy itself is proudly and persistently "on the edge" in certain ways, but eventually you begin to realize, when you think from the point of view of the more-than-human world, that most official philosophy still follows narrowly circumscribed paths, and that even the country that lies over the first range of low hills just beyond philosophy's usual thoroughfares may be quite different and far more fabulous than what shows up along the usual routes, or even on the maps.

A few years ago, backpacking in the Beaverhead Mountains in southwest Montana, a friend and I scrambled up a steep talus slope to the very edge of a ridge—there forming the Continental Divide—to find not only a still more precipitous drop-away into a stunning country of conical peaks and ragged valleys, but also a massive thunderstorm rushing up the nearest cleft practically upon us. It had sounded much farther away from the other side. You never know. In any case, I am wholly convinced that only by actually going into such wild country can you also begin to enter, as it were, this particular wild country of the mind. Scrambling half a mile down mountaintop scree with the lightning sizzling all around us, as we did that day; tracking up (another trip) through the rising mists and snow clouds to a rippling little lake along the Eastern front of the Rockies on the occasion of the first (September!) snow of the season; waking on bird time, well before dawn, morning after morning, deep in the woods somewhere; or simply spending time alone in the larger world, anywhere beyond the world of mostly human sounds and sights—you inhabit a different world as a result, everything is different, and from then on your struggle is to stay true to it in the rest of your work and life: to give it a kind of voice, to re-inhabit it more deeply, and to keep going back.

And what good fortune to have found such intrepid and generous companions! Jim Cheney and Tom Birch of ZenLite Philosophical Expeditions fame, first of all, my companions for a decade and a half all over the edges and high mountain meadows of Montana and Idaho and farther afield, sometimes even in my dreams, and through a good bit of environmental and classical philosophy as well. Bob Jickling, Yukon philosopher of education and intrepid guide to the land of the midnight sun. The Australians: Val Plumwood, sharpest of thinkers on "environmental culture"—Forest Lover, Live Forever!; Freya Mathews, panpsychist; and Patsy Hallen and the students with whom we trekked along the Bibbulmun Track and through the Pilbara, aboriginal lands, in 2004. Teacher-activist-writer-dreamer extraordinaire, Patsy invited me to co-teach an eco-philosophy course she organized out of Perth's Murdoch University around two long backpack trips into the Australian outback. Thus it was that my fiftieth year found me quite literally all the way around the world from my Carolina home, traipsing overland with students through the red desert and along the shores of the tumultuous Southern Ocean, sleeping under the shimmering unfamiliar stars, and later car-camping with my family up and down the west coast and among the great monoliths of the Red Center and in the rain forests of the Northern Territory. So much from "the bush" seems to hover just on the other side of perception, an invitation to something immense and powerful but seemingly just out of reach. I began to wonder if that kind of enigmatic depth isn't a feature of the world in general, just more visible in the bush, closer to the surface. Australia came back home with me like an unanswered question, and stays with me still.

My thanks as well to so many other friends and colleagues: to all of the above not just for their companionship but also very specifically for comments and suggestions on many of the papers included here; to my colleagues and co-teachers in the Elon University Department of Philosophy, especially John Sullivan; to Frithjof Bergmann, Jennifer Church, and David Abram for long-standing inspiration of many sorts; to Carolyn Toben and her beautifully conceived Center for Education, Imagination, and the Natural World; to Irene Klaver, Dexter Roberts, Patti Cruickshank-Schott, Rick Kool, Holmes Rolston III, Greg Haenel, and Tom Regan; and to my running-mate Amy Halberstadt and our lovely children Anna Ruth and Molly, who have now become such good wilderness companions of their own.

For permission to reprint this material here I am grateful to Gene Hargrove, founder and longtime editor of *Environmental Ethics*; Bob Jickling, founder and editor of *The Canadian Journal of Environmental Education*; and the editors at *Soundings*. Anonymous reviewers for all of these publications were helpful as well. J. Baird Callicott, with whom I disagree philosophically about nearly everything, nonetheless was the soul of generosity in shepherding this book toward publication, and Jane Bunker and her colleagues at the State University of New York Press have been supportive at every step. Heartfelt thanks to you all.

Anthony Weston
Durham, North Carolina
Summer Solstice, 2007

Chapter 1

Introduction

You might have thought that environmental ethics would enthusiastically embrace a naturalistic view of values. When the whole effort is to rejoin the human enterprise to the encompassing world, mustn't values be accorded an organic place in that world as well? How else to picture value except as deeply rooted in embodied perception, coalesced around desire, need, and susceptibility, and tuned to more-than-human as well as human rhythms?

Such a picture has another immense attraction too: it does not make value, as such, a *problem*. Values so understood do not need to be "grounded," at least in the sense that without certain sorts of philosophical self-accounting they would have no foothold in the world at all. They may need more fertility, reconstruction, and redirection; they may need criticism, deepening, and change; but the bottom line, regardless, is that they are already *here*, quite gloriously here—all of them, of course, the congenial along with less congenial. Values are not fragile or rare or delicate or endangered. We do not live in an axiological desert but in a rain forest. Everywhere the air is thick with them.

Most readers will know, however, that contemporary environmental ethics has followed a very different path—so far, at least. In the field as we find it, naturalism is widely mistrusted, and the very existence of environmental values *is* taken to be a problem, indeed the most fundamental and intractable of problems. We are invited to "ground" our ethical claims on some independent and philosophically locked-down "intrinsic value," or on an ethical theory of a more traditional sort awkwardly retrofitted for broader-than-human scope. This, for better or worse, is what seems natural to most philosophers—so natural, indeed, that its methodological commitments often are not even articulated but are simply left without saying. And so not only do we learn to live in the thin air: we also come to imagine that it is, so to speak, the only kind of atmosphere there could be.

This book is, among other things, a plea to reconsider. The essays presented here aim to recover and elaborate a systematic alternative to

1

this entire conception of the proper tasks and methods of environmental ethics. Environmental ethics emerges here in another key; in radically different axiological biome, as it were, with thicker air and life already abundant; and two-footedly "grounded" on the *actual* ground. Correspondingly, this book also offers a kind of methodological complement to other work in the field—mine and others'—already in this alternative key. The necessary sort of work is already underway. The challenge is partly to learn to see it as such.

Fully embraced, moreover, a thoroughgoing naturalism leads us much further. I want to suggest that it points to a vision of philosophical engagement as "reconstructive" in the Deweyan sense—and not just of environmental philosophy but of the environment itself. The familiar question of anthropocentrism, for example—of human-centeredness as a doctrine—appears in an entirely different light. I argue that the root of the problem is not a doctrine at all, but an actual process: anthropocentri*zation*, the narrowing and relentless humanizing of the actual world, a world that we *make* and that pervasively remakes itself both experientially and conceptually. Typically we suppose that we must determine what the philosophically mandated "nonanthropocentrism" must look like and then rebuild the world to suit. From a pragmatic perspective the actual challenge is the other way around: to remake—or more pointedly to de-anthropocentrize—the actual world in such a way that a new ethic, only barely conceivable now, might *evolve*.

"Nonanthropocentrism," after all, is only a placeholder, a refusal without content. We know that we want to escape, but only in the vaguest way where we need to go. Instead, the task must be to enable the emergence of a new ethic—by the kinds of settings we create, by the larger-than-human invitations we offer both in our own bearing and through the patterns of attention and the possibilities of encounter we build into the world. We need an environmental *etiquette,* then, as much as an ethic. Its development will be a *process,* an ongoing evolution rather than some form of theoretical exertion. And it must be a genuinely *multicentric* process, in place of the usual moral extensionisms that, however well-intended, still end up making ourselves the touchstones and "centers" of an "expanded circle." This book offers one path in those directions.

Pragmatism

Environmental ethics' fundamental complaint is supposed to be that the dominant attitude toward nature reduces the entire more-than-human world to no more than a means to human ends, and indeed only to a few of those: to commercially provided consumption opportunities, more or less immediate and supposedly consequence-less. This crassly self-centered value system is often labeled *pragmatism*, which naturally makes it hard to imagine that the philosophical movement called Pragmatism in any way could be encouraging to environmental ethics.

This, though, is only the crudest and most journalistic sense of the word "pragmatism." John Dewey's distinctly American philosophy actually offers something radically different and, in my view, radically more promising. It is on this point that my work in the field began, now twenty-five years ago.

Notice first that only a few short and seemingly completely natural philosophical steps lead the familiar line of environmental-ethical argument from the rejection of that crass instrumentalism directly into a familiar and very specific paradigm. If you think that the problem is that we reduce everything to means to human ends, to resources for our use, then what could be more obvious than to defend natural values by making them *intrinsic* rather than "merely" instrumental? Somehow, we conclude, they must represent another kind of value: ends rather than means; values entirely outside of the give-and-take of everyday making-do.

It seems obvious enough. Yet the result is that a vast amount of energy and ingenuity is spent imagining what such intrinsic values in nature could be, how they can be kept pure and isolated from anything instrumental, and how they might finally be "grounded." Strenuous and lavishly outfitted overland expeditions continue to be launched to link them up to everything from self-interest to a variety of new ontologies. Massive philosophical resources go into rearguard actions to defend them against various critics and skeptics—though, for all that, the bottom-line argument all too often is still only some re-invocation of the original bugbear: "Well then, is nature to be left only a mere means to our ends?"

My first article in the field took issue with all of this. "Beyond Intrinsic Value"[1] argued that Dewey's pragmatism points toward a far richer and more workable understanding of values. Dewey calls us "to embrace the richness and diversity of our actual values and then to make full use of that richness and diversity to open up a new sense of possibility in practical action. Pragmatism so understood represents a pluralistic, integrative, even experimental approach to ethics, at once almost an ordinary kind of practical wisdom and a philosophically self-conscious alternative in ethics."[2] On a Deweyan view, both means *and* ends can *already* be found everywhere: what we really need is to articulate and re-integrate those now overlooked and marginalized.

Instead of the familiar insistence on "grounding" intrinsic values in nature, then, I say that our real challenge is to develop something more like an *ecology of values*: to situate natural values in their contexts, understand their dynamics, and bring them into fuller attention and wider play. Even the most precious experiences in and of nature, barely noticeable to so many others and desperately needing wider play, are already as "grounded" as they need to be, thank you. They are rooted deep in the interplay of experience and the larger world. What they really need is more visibility: more loving elaboration, new and recovered kinds of language, as well as more intentional and systematic design for their readier emergence in experience.

Put another way: just as the first task of environmentalism proper is to bring forth a richer sense of where we actually live, of how deeply intertwined we are and must be with the Earth, so, I argue, one of the first tasks of environmental ethics is to bring forth a richer sense of what we *do* value: of how value, down to earth, actually goes. Even those kinds of ethics that seem on the surface so relentlessly human-centered often bring the Earth in the back door, and a wide and mostly unguarded back door at that. Think of our susceptibility to animals, both domestic and wild. Think of our fascination with stars and storms. Think of the hundred million or so Americans who claim to be gardeners, the tens of millions who belong to a wide range of environmental organizations. Think of the great nature poets, from Wordsworth to Wendell Berry. Think of fundamentalist Creationists, for God's sake, who celebrate this world as Creation, though not a very dynamic one, I guess. Think even of our very own professional selves, who would not be so desperately in search of intrinsic values in nature in the first place if we were not *already* persuaded that nature is (to put it in a less ontologically suggestive way) precious in its own right. We are trying to create (what we will then describe as "discover") the sources and underpinnings of (what we will then describe as a "justification for") values and perceptions that we in fact held long before we felt the need for such philosophical exertions. Maybe it is time to widen the lens. Environmental ethics may have much more leverage than we usually imagine, right where we already are.

Social Contingency and its Implications

Along with situating values in the sphere of desire I also want to bring them emphatically into the orbit of social construction. If value is, as I propose, deeply rooted in embodied perception and coalesced around desire, need, and susceptibility, then particular values and indeed the whole shape of value-systems are also—yes—contingent. They are not "givens," not some kind of timeless essences, but socially and culturally shaped, and thus open to reshaping as well. I will add right away that for me this contingency—indeed, pragmatism's embrace of a kind of deconstructive method, seeking out and even celebrating contingency, foolhardy as it too may seem to many in environmental ethics—is in fact a methodological touchstone. It is what provokes and enables the fundamentally *re*constructive turn that gives my work whatever distinctiveness it may have. But it is also, I know, a rather unsettling path, whose implications will need to be drawn out slowly in this essay and throughout this book.

Take for instance the supposed problem of self-centeredness again—or, more broadly, as Alan Watts famously put it, the "skin-encapsulated ego." As we know all too well, egoism is often supposed to be a sort of default human condition. Indeed, from Hobbes through the theory of the "Moral Point of View," such a pessimism about human nature has been made into the rationale for ethics itself. Dewey would argue, though, that self-centeredness is no more natural or essential than its opposite. Human nature, in general, is *plastic*. People have and have had many different "natures," and likely will have still others in times to come. Nonetheless it *may* be the case that that human selves are markedly involuted or fortified in our time. From a social-constructionist angle, still, this fact, so far as it really is a fact, is not an invitation to keep debating about "true human nature," but reappears instead in another and more challenging guise. Maybe the real danger is that this is what we are *becoming*. Egoism and the crasser utilitarianisms, so far from somehow being the default human condition, might therefore better be pictured as radical reductions of it, end results of a long and militant process of self-desiccation. But it is not too late to change directions. Marx may after all have been right when he said that the real task is not to solve certain philosophical problems but to change the world so that such problems do not arise in the first place. It's not that the problems are unreal—they can be quite real, and may even have solutions, of a sort anyway—but rather that they are unnecessary.[3] The universe does not compel us to drive ourselves, either individually or as a species, ever deeper into our hard little shells. There are other ways, and once again perhaps quite close beside us.

Broadly deconstructive themes arise first in my essay "Before Environmental Ethics" (Chapter 2 of this book). Its specific project is to argue that that contemporary nonanthropocentric environmental ethics is profoundly shaped by the very anthropocentrism that it aims to transcend, and therefore that we may have to go much farther afield than we have so far imagined if we are to (eventually) truly transcend anthropocentrism. Consider, for example, the question that contemporary environmental philosophers take as fundamental: whether "we" should open the gates of moral considerability to "other" animals (sometimes just: "animals"), and to the likes of rivers and mountains. "Before Environmental Ethics" comments:

> [This] phrasing of "the" question may seem neutral and un-exceptionable. Actually, however, it is not neutral at all. The called-for arguments address all and only humans on behalf of "the natural world." Environmental ethics therefore is invited to begin by *positing*, not questioning, a sharp divide that "we" must somehow cross, taking that "we" unproblematically to denote all humans. To invoke such a divide, however, is already to take one ethical position among others.[4]

For one thing, this entire frame of reference is largely peculiar to modern Western cultures. Other cultures have felt no compulsion to divide the entire world between all humans on the one hand and all nature on the other. Even our own immediate predecessor societies lived in *mixed communities*, to use Mary Midgley's apt term. "The" question above may be *our* question, of course: the urbanized, modern, Westerner's question. But that is just the point. "The" very question that frames contemporary environmental ethics presupposes a particular cultural and historical situation, not at all the only human possibility, and which is itself perhaps precisely the problem.

We could even reconsider the supposedly fundamental means/end distinction in this light. Everyday experience suggests that most values exist in the middle: *both* means and ends, or *between* means and ends, as I put it in another early article, "Between Means and Ends."[5] Dewey writes of "immediate" values; I speak of "values-as-parts-of-patterns," invoking a holistic view in place of the linearity of means-end relations. In general, the simplest point is that nearly everything has both aspects. Every value both takes its place in a long—indeed endless—chain of means and also has its own gratifications in itself. Contrariwise, if we are losing this two-sidedness—in particular, if more and more of the multiple and modest natural values next to us are being simplified down to mere means, a dramatically simplified "ecology of values"—then, once again, we have a *problem*. Albert Borgmann and others have perceptively argued that precisely this is the distinctive malaise of modern industrialism.[6]

With these last points you already begin to see, I hope, that there is life after deconstruction: that the specific contingencies of the present structure of values also open up specific avenues and strategies for change. This theme especially will take time to unfold, and there are others that come first, but at this point we should at least note that precisely this contingency also undercuts the supposed conceptual barriers to environmental ethics that are sometimes invoked from outside the field.

Take a familiar kind of linguistic or conceptual objection. Still widely argued is that it is conceptually confused to hold that a mountain or forest might have some kind of right against dynamiting or clearcutting, or that nonconscious beings have moral interests or other any kind of independent standing against whatever we might wish to do to them. It is part of the very meaning of *rights* or *interests*, many critics say, that you cannot have them without awareness or at least feeling. Therefore, inanimate nature cannot have moral standing, and the whole project of an environmental ethics—valuing nature for its own sake—is simply confused, mistaken, misconceived. But it is a curiously rigid and self-congratulatory argument. Surely the very same premise—that environmental values are not readily conceivable in present terms—might much more sensibly be taken to imply that present concepts must be *changed*. In a world whose fundamental self-understandings are in flux, why ever suppose that such a particular conception of interests is somehow fixed, secure, and timelessly given, let alone somehow accessible to philosophers in the solitude of their studies or classrooms? This concept of interests, and indeed the conception of moral consideration that ties it to interests in the first place, is an artifact of a very specific legal system—and there is nothing wrong with that, either, but it is certainly not the whole story, or any kind of necessity. Such systems are *created*, they evolve, and they always must expect re-creation as well.

And we could add: *of course* the proposed reconceptions will look "confused." How else would they look to the guardians of the established order? That is more like a sign that they are actually getting somewhere.[7]

Self-Validating Reduction

A step further into the coevolution of values and world and we begin to notice some deeper and trickier dynamics. These are the theme of "Self-Validating Reduction: A Theory of the Devaluation of Nature" (Chapter 3 of this book).

Often enough we encounter a world that has an apparently "given" character. And often enough, to be honest, the values for which environmental ethics wishes to speak—indeed, the values for which ethics in general wishes to speak—are genuinely hard to *see* in that world. The animal inmates of factory farms are bred for such docility and stupidity, and raised in conditions so inimical to any remaining social or communicative instinct, that the resulting creatures are pretty poor candidates for rights or any other kind of moral consideration. Likewise, most of the places of power revered in the pagan world are gone—often deliberately destroyed by command of the new, self-describedly "jealous Gods." But as even the faintest remnants of the great natural world's sacredness are degraded and even the whispers silenced, it becomes progressively harder, sometimes even for us environmentalists, to see what all the fuss is about.

The familiar consequence is that environmental ethics (and often ethics in general) is often perceived, even by its advocates, as sentimental, "nostalgic," lost in some realm of abstraction and idealization only tangentially related to "the real world." Sometimes, I am sure, it is. But this entire set of expectations, I argue, is also flawed to its core. The reduced world is not somehow the limit of reality itself. It is a world we have *made*—not the only possibility.

Moreover, it is a world we have made in a peculiarly self-reinforcing way. At work here is a kind of self-fulfilling prophecy that I call "self-validating reduction." Those animals in factory farms, for instance: having reduced them to mere shadows of what their ancestors once were, we then can look at them and genuinely find any sort of moral claim unbelievable. "See? They really *are* stupid, dirty, dysfunctional, pitiable." But then even more drastic kinds of devaluation and exploitation become possible. Already the genetic engineers speak of chickens with no heads at all. The circle closes completely. And the same story can be told, of course, of the reduction of so many particular places and of the land in general.

The implications are dramatic. For one thing, it follows that the environmental crisis is not fundamentally the result of some kind of error in reasoning, essentially to be engaged on the philosophical level. Instead, it is "a slow downward spiral, a reduction in fact as well as in thought, in which our ideas are as much influenced by the reduced state of the world as vice versa, and . . . each stage is impeccably rational."[8] Philosophical conceptions are not merely epiphenomenal in this process, but they *are* part of a larger dynamic in which material factors also make a difference.

For another thing—again, and crucially—this world is no kind of given. The way things are, right now, is not the way they must be. We are not stuck defending the world as it is or simply trying to read values off the world we now see before us. "The world as it is" is itself a production of multiple and sustained reductions. It is in flow, and open to change. Ethics speaks, instead and in addition, to *possibilities*—sometimes to thoroughly hidden possibilities, if need be, but possibilities nonetheless. Part of the very outrage is that they remain so hidden, that they are so insistently reduced. Ethics' fundamental effort, then, is to find ways to bring those possibilities forth. Its voice cannot be one of mere reportage, justification, or "defense." No: it must be a call, an *invitation*—to assist, and join, the self-unveiling of a different kind of world.

Environmental Etiquette

"Self-validating reduction" is the first of a series of concepts that together begin to offer a new sort of conceptual toolbox for environmental ethics. Two more are introduced in "Environmental Ethics as Environmental Etiquette" (Chapter 4 of this book), an essay with my philosophical and backwoods co-adventurer Jim Cheney. Here self-validating reduction finds its complement in "self-validating invitation," while environmental ethics finds its more challenging opposite in what Cheney and I call "environmental etiquette."

There are musicians, now, who paddle out to the orca in open ocean in canoes trailing underwater mikes and speakers, inviting them to jam, working out new musical forms together. You can order the CDs on the Internet.[9] There are animal trainers whose "ways of moving fit into the spaces shaped by the animals' awareness," as Vicki Hearne elegantly puts it—and "fit" not so much consciously as instinctively. Then and only then do the animals respond. There is a self-validating dynamic here too, then, except headed in the other direction. On the usual ethical epistemology,

> we must first know what animals are capable of and then decide on that basis whether and how we are to consider them ethically. On the alternative view, we will have no idea of what other animals are actually capable of —we will not readily understand them—until we *already* have approached them ethically: that is, until we have offered them the space and time, the occasion, and the acknowledgment necessary to enter into relationship.[10]

If the world is a collection of more or less fixed facts to which we must respond, then the task of ethics is to systematize and unify our responses. This is the expected view, once again so taken for granted as to scarcely even appear as a "view" at all. Epistemology is prior to ethics. Responding to the world follows upon knowing it—and what could be more sensible or responsible than that? If the world is *not* "given," though—if the world is what it seems to be in part because we have *made* it that way, as I have been suggesting, and if therefore the process of inviting its further possibilities into the light is fundamental to ethics itself—then our very knowledge of the world, of the possibilities of other animals and the land and even ourselves in relation to them, follows upon "invitation," and ethics must come *first*. Ethics is prior to epistemology—or, as Cheney and I do not say in the paper but probably should have said, what really emerges is another kind of epistemology—"etiquette," in our specific sense, *as* epistemology.

But then of course we are also speaking of something sharply different from "ethics" as usually understood. We are asked not for a set of well-defended general moral commitments in advance, but rather for something more visceral and instinctual, a mode of comportment more than a mode of commitment, more fleshy and more vulnerable. Etiquette so understood requires us to take risks, to offer trust before we know whether or how the offer will be received, and to move with awareness, civility, and grace in a world we understand to be capable of response. Thus Cheney and I conclude that ethical action itself must be "first and foremost an attempt to open up possibilities, to enrich the world" rather than primarily an attempt to respond to the world as already known.

Cheney, true to his nature, also takes the argument on a more strenuous path, exploring indigenous views of ceremony and ritual. Once again the question of epistemology turns out to be central. Euro-Americans, Cheney says, want to know what beliefs are encoded in the utterances of indigenous peoples. We treat their utterances as propositional representations of Indigenous worlds. But what if these utterances function, instead, primarily to *produce* these worlds? Cheney cites the indigenous scholar Sam Gill on the fundamentally performative function of language. When Gill asks Navajo elders what prayers *mean,* he reports, they tell him "not what messages prayers carry, but what prayers *do.*" More generally, Gill asserts that "the importance of religion as it is practiced by the great body of religious persons for whom religion is a way of life [is] a way of creating, discovering, and communicating worlds of meaning largely through ordinary and common actions and behavior."[11]

What then, Cheney and I ask, if this performative dimension of language is fundamental not just in indigenous or obviously religious settings, but generally? How we speak, how we move, how we carry on, all the time, also literally brings all sorts of worlds into being—and thus, again, the ethical challenge put mindful speech, care, and respect *first*. Indeed we would now go even further. Here it is not so much that epistemology comes first but that, in truth, it simply fades away. The argument is not the usual suggestion that the West has misunderstood the world, got it wrong, and that we now need to "go back" to the Indians to get it right. Cheney is arguing that understanding the world is not really the point in the first place. We are not playing a truth game at all. What matters is how we relate to things, not what things are in themselves. Front, center, and always, the world *responds*. The great task is not knowledge but *relationship*.

Multicentrism

By now we have moved far indeed from the usual frames of reference in environmental ethics, at least as an academic and philosophical field. Yet it remains my concern to stay in dialogue—indeed, dialectic—with that field. Not only is the line of thought unfolding here meant itself as a "position" of sorts *in* that field, but it also suggests a systematic critique of and alternative to the field's usual theories and conceptual categories. Moreover, in my view, it is a very widely shared critique and alternative—much more widely shared, and in fact much more specific and systematic, than currently recognized. "Multicentrism: A Manifesto" (Chapter 5 in this book) is an attempt to give it an explicit and inclusive shape—and a name.

We know that the challenge of finding an alternative to "anthropocentrism" has multiplied "centrisms" all over the map. Insisting that more than humans alone matter—that the "center" must be bigger, indeed far bigger, than us—we are offered ethical systems that focus on suffering or self-awareness, and so "center" on certain forms of consciousness in many, possibly all, other animals. Beyond these lie "*bio*centrism" (life-centered ethics) or "*eco*centrism" (ecosystem-centered ethics), again in many varieties. Beyond these in turn lie Gaian ethics, where the whole Earth moves in its own right into the great circle of moral consideration.

Arguments between these views sometimes are taken to practically exhaust the field itself. Yet all of these views, whatever their divergences, take for granted a very specific set of theoretical demands. They all start from the supposition that the post-anthropocentric task is to expand the moral universe by highlighting some single feature, now supposed to be more inclusive than anything just human, that can plausibly be argued to justify or "ground" moral status as such. In this sense they are all, as I put it, forms of *mono*centrism. We imagine larger and larger circles, but what lies within them and what justifies moral extension across them is supposed to be—of necessity—one sort of thing.

One problem, I argue, is that in an unnoticed but also almost tautological sense, this project remains ineradicably *human*-centered, despite its generous intentions. Not only is *our* standing never in question, but moral standing is extended to others by analogy to our own precious selves: to animals, maybe, on the grounds that they suffer as we do.

But here is the most fundamental worry: Can an ethic of relationship actually remain so monocentric, homogeneous, single-featured? Might we not even wonder whether monocentrism almost by definition militates *against* real relationship? The eco-theologian Thomas Berry has declared that the essential task of environmental ethics is "to move from a world of objects to a community of subjects." Berry's almost Buberian language of subject-hood is not much heard in the environmental ethics we know. The phrase may call us up short. A true community of subjects must be an interacting whole of distinctive, nonhomogenized parts, in which no one set of members arrogates to themselves alone the right to gate-keep or even merely to welcome, however generously, moral newcomers. We are all "in" to start with. Thus Berry might be read as calling not merely for an alternative to anthropocentrism but for an alternative to the entire homogenizing framework of "centrism" itself. And this invitation, arguably, has very little to do with the received project of "expanding the circle" of moral consideration. What we actually need is a vision of multiple "circles," including the whole of the world from the start.

What I propose to call *multi*centrism thus envisions a world of irreducibly diverse and multiple centers of being and value—not one single moral realm, however expansive, but *many* realms, as particular as may be, partly overlapping, each with its own center. Human "circles," then, do not necessarily invite expansion or extension, but rather augmentation and addition. In a similar pluralistic vein, William James challenges us to imagine this world not as a *uni*verse but as a "*multi*verse," and thus a world that calls for (and, we might hope, calls *forth*) an entirely different set of skills—even, perhaps, something more like improvisation and etiquette, once again, in the all-too-serious place usually accorded ethics. Certainly it would have to be a world in which etiquette is in play: where collective understandings are *negotiated* rather than devised and imposed, however sympathetically, by one group of participants on the others.

All of these themes, I believe, are emerging from a wide variety of work both within and outside academic environmental ethics. My own emerging emphasis on the responsiveness of the world, and correspondingly how much a responsive world can be reduced by unresponsiveness on the other side; Cheney's insistence on the constitutive role of what he calls "bioregional narrative," co-constituted between human and more-than-human; our mutual friend Tom Birch's argument for "universal consideration," according to which moral "consideration" itself must, of necessity, keep itself considerately and carefully open to everything (*there's* universality for you!). Many strands in ecofeminism, from a persistent and overdue attention to actual patterns and failures of human-animal relationships to Val Plumwood's incisive exposure of the whole seamy conceptual underpinnings of "centering," whether it be on and by males or Europeans or humans as a whole. Thomas Berry, David Abram, Gary Snyder, Paul Shepard, Sean Kane, and many others, cited and drawn upon in this paper, all speak of the human relation to nature in terms of *negotiation* and *covenant* rather than the philosophical unilateralism we have learned to expect.

There is a *movement* here, in short: much more than a collection of scattered, hard-to-categorize complaints and idiosyncratic, extraphilosophical views, but a shared alternative vision of the world—and of the tasks of anything rightly called an "environmental ethic." "Multicentrism" is not the perfect name for it—the chapter explores this problem too—but for the moment I think it will have to do.

De–Anthropocentrizing the World

One more conceptual renovation completes the alternative conceptual toolbox I have been advancing in this set of essays. To introduce it, we may begin by returning to the closing themes of "Before Environmental Ethics."

I argue, in that essay and elsewhere, that there is no leapfrogging the culture in thought, as if we could think our way to a thoroughly post-anthropocentric ethic from the very midst of a thoroughly anthropocentrized culture. Thinking by itself will not get us out of this mess. In fact, we live in a dramatically "reduced" world in which our very ethics is implicated both as sometime agent of reduction (anthropocentrism, in its many guises, dismisses and disvalues the natural world) and as one of its many *effects* (for what philosophy is more natural to "read off" a wholly humanized world?). In truth we cannot even begin to imagine what a truly nonanthropocentric ethic would be like. As I put it elsewhere:

A thoroughly humanized language; the commercially colonized imagination; even the physical settings in which the
question of post-anthropocentrism comes up—all of these
inevitably give our supposed post-anthropocentrisms a profoundly and necessarily anthropocentric cast, though often
enough, and naturally enough, well below the threshold
of awareness.[12]

Whatever finally succeeds anthropocentrism will even not be called
anything like "nonanthropocentrism." Not-X, for any X, is simply a
negation. The term itself is only a reflex of our present reaction, not a
program but more like a hedged and partial form of refusal. Anthropocentrism's successor will in fact be about *something else*—and, like any
ethic, about something else in *particular*, one or a few of the infinity
of possibilities always before us. But what can we say about it? How
can we even get going? And what can philosophy—environmental ethics
or any other part of philosophy—actually contribute?

It is already quite clear, I am sure, that in my view the task is
emphatically *not* a matter of completing the systematization or cautious
extension of the ethical systems we already happen to have.

Today we are too used to that easy division of labor that
leaves ethics only the systematic tasks of "expressing" a set of
values that is already established, and abandons the originary
questions to the social sciences. The result, however, is to
incapacitate philosophical ethics when it comes to dealing with
values that are only now entering an originary stage. Even
when it is out of its depth, we continue to imagine that systematic ethics . . . is the only kind of ethics there is. We continue
to regard the contingency, open-endedness, and uncertainty
of "new" values as an objection to them, ruling them out
of ethical court entirely, or else as a kind of embarrassment
to be quickly papered over with an ethical theory.[13]

In fact, however, the situation of environmental ethics, at least,
calls for something entirely different, or so I claim. Here we stand
at an originary stage, and the challenge is not so much to discover or
report or defend a kind of ethic that already exists, but to construct
or reconstruct something far more ambitious and new. If values co-evolve
with entire cultural systems, the co-evolution of new values is more like
a cultural *project* than any form of philosophical discovery.

Philosophical method, then, along with our conceptual toolbox, must be revised and repointed. Though we continue to imagine that the true virtues of an ethical philosopher are the all too familiar precision, lucidity, literalness, seriousness, and theoretical unity—all good, systematic virtues—the truth is that at stages closer to the beginning, to the moments of origin, the appropriate style and standards are closer to the opposite, to the genuinely youthful. Here we can only be exploratory, experimental, unsystematic, open-ended, imaginative, metaphorical.[14] In ethics at such a formative stage, virtues for system-*making* or -remaking are required: improvisation, curiosity, risk taking, susceptibility. Inventiveness is key; a willingness to follow out unexpected lines of thought; and multicentric pluralism: welcoming multiple voices, expecting and encouraging them, quite likely speaking in multiple voices oneself. Etiquette, as Cheney and I argue, is crucial: that is, the reconstitution and deepening of multiple relationships, and the exploration of new possible relationships. Art, not science. Genuine experiments, open-ended, in our own persons, and perhaps over lifetimes.

We must also take the project of "reconstruction" in its absolutely most literal sense. To say it again: the key thing, the unacknowledged bulk of the problem, on my view, is not the ideology, not some sort of philosophical mistake that an appropriate critique can somehow correct, but rather anthropocentrism's underlying, cultural preconditions, its own quite literal "environment": the pervasive embodiment and ongoing self-reproduction of the ever-more-thoroughly humanized world that underlies and underwrites it. It is here that change work is most urgently needed—and is most inviting and in some places already well underway. Following out this line of thought, the character of the actual built world figures more and more centrally. I propose therefore to shift the conceptual focus from anthropocentr*ism* to what I call anthropocentri*zation*, and correspondingly from somehow "refuting" anthropocentr*ism* or advancing nonanthropocentrism to literally rebuilding—or, more exactly, *de*-anthropocen*trizing*—the world.

This is the thrust of "De-Anthropocentrizing the World: Environmental Ethics as a Design Challenge" (Chapter 6 in this book).

Tomorrow belongs to the designers. Tomorrow belongs to those who are beginning to remake our ways of living, yes, and of eating, building, celebrating, keeping time, sharing a world with other creatures. [I] offer here a philosophical prolegomenon to their work, then, and more: a philosophical claim to it. Here lies a different kind of invitation to philosophy, a different kind of philosophical dialectic and task: "breaking the spell of the actual" not in the service of some already-theorized post-anthropocentric alternative, but precisely in the service of finding our way to it.[15]

And the essay goes on to advance actual proposals for remaking the culture: new kinds of architecture, of agriculture, of music-making and art; even new, or re-understood, holidays.

De-anthropocentrizing re-designers are already seriously at work. Large-scale and inventive "cultural tinkerers" such as Stewart Brand, for example, with his plans for ten-thousand-year clocks and other ways of inviting us to live in a longer—indeed vastly longer—"Now," much as, he says, the first Apollo photographs of Earth from Moon invited us to live in a much larger "Here." They became icons of global awareness out of a more parochial time—a function Brand also energetically promoted (*before* Apollo, which he declares was worth every penny of its (then) $25 billion cost just for that one photo) and still promotes. And so too, for Brand, our cultural nearsightedness, our self-reduction to the purview of a few moments or the next business quarter, is most fundamentally a *design problem*, not an invitation to begin by rethinking our philosophical categories. We need to devise and enact cultural forms that lengthen our view.

Multiply this approach many times over, vary its goals to speak to every aspect of our narrowed and hyper-anthropocentrized world, and you have a new and wild vision of the possibilities for what currently takes itself to be a small academic speciality. Reconnecting with animals; re-designing neighborhoods for contact, maximizing the margins and "edges" where encounters are more likely; honoring and deepening "mixed community"; re-localizing food-growing; re-contextualizing the old holidays within the great cycles of light and dark, and generating new holidays as well (imagine that: suppose we invented an insistently *celebratory* environmentalism) . . . here we have not only an entirely unexpected and surely far more compelling and inviting cultural program than environmental philosophy offers at present, but also a radical path to the reconstruction of environmental philosophy itself.

Environmental Education

We know that all is not well in the schools. What is puzzling is that, even so, environmentalists have so readily acquiesced in—indeed have plumped hard for—the institutionalization of "environmental education," a new subject that, entirely predictably, quickly became human-centered in both its epistemological orientation and its normative assumptions, not to mention firmly anchored within the managerial structures of school itself: preset curricula, testable and technical skills, the works. School as we know it is a leading standard-bearer and exemplification of both anthropocentrism and, more pointedly, anthropocentrization. "Literacy," for instance, in the form of the widely promoted goal of "ecological literacy," the excuse for it all, is clearly a schoolish skill. But should it not make us a little uneasy to remember that pretty much the only people who have so far managed to live sustainably on this earth have been *il*literate? David Abram provocatively argues that the very phonetic alphabet, of all things, is a prime agent of anthropocentrization, cutting us off from the voices of the more-than-human all around us. We need to have more doubts.

My first essay in this area was "Instead of Environmental Education,"[16] a kind of companion and follow-up to "Before Environmental Ethics," indeed arriving at much the same place. The impetus and energy for reconnection, for love for the Earth, I argue, primarily lies *outside* of school: in the life of the family, community, and ideally the practice of a whole society, as well as in its ways of building, growing food, celebrating, birthing and marrying and dying. This is where the juice is, a set of practices that school at its best can augment and support but cannot create on its own out of whole cloth. "Environmental education" cannot somehow succeed by itself, any more than stand-alone ethical reconceptions, as if a philosophical reorientation could ground all others. *Both* require systematically transformed cultural practices. In such a transformed world, teaching can be dynamite. In the world as we know it, teaching can still provoke and unsettle and suggest—I sketch some ways to do this, too—but cannot turn the corner on its own.

This challenge, and puzzle, is also close to our own everyday practice, since most environmental philosophers are themselves university teachers. As a teacher I am constantly challenged to rethink my pedagogy along the lines of my unfolding environmental philosophy—a challenge indeed, as environmental philosophy in my view diverges ever farther from the sort of "content area" that fits most readily with the traditional conception of teaching as the transfer of information. Environmentalism in my thinking is taking a very different direction—but how then to teach it? Even for more mainline environmental ethics, the challenge arises. Almost by necessity, school cuts us off from the experience of a larger world: from natural rhythms, natural beings, more-than-human flows of knowledge and inspiration. In fact, we could hardly design a *worse* setting for environmental education. What to do?

"What If Teaching Went Wild?" (Chapter 7 in this book) is the beginning of my answer. I begin by echoing the above set of concerns—the need for something vastly more ambitious than environmental education—and then turn quickly to the classroom teacher, firmly situated within school and our times. Us, after all. Can teaching "go wild"—can we begin to reconnect—even here? I argue that we can. Indeed I argue that it may even be possible to make a foil of school's hyper-humanized setting to this very end: we can force anthropocentrism to reveal itself, in silhouette as it were, and to begin to draw forth alternatives not merely "somewhere else" but right in the very belly of the beast. But the required pedagogy is much more personally demanding and unnerving than the usual sorts of pedagogical innovations.

> To be willing to remake the very space of a classroom, to invite a kind of more-than-human wildness into a space that started out so neat, bodiless, wholly anthropocentrized, and in control, you must be attentive in a bodily way to the very shape and feel of space itself. . . . You yourself must experience the human/other-than-human boundary as more permeable than our culture teaches us it is.[17]

In the end the advice is practical: students end up eating flowers, combing the room for spiders, and even rediscovering their own selves as animal—for the great wild world is, in at least one important sense, *right here*. Not incidentally, you get a sense here for what a multicentric environmental etiquette might look like in entirely achievable practice. Even, after all, in school!

Farther Afield

The last two essays in this book range farther afield—through the evolution-creation debate, and then, of all places, into outer space—with the same set of concerns and conceptual tools.

In January of 2003 my biologist colleague Gregory Haenel invited me to co-lead his course studying evolution in mainland Ecuador and the Galapagos Islands. The course begins on the mainland coast of Ecuador, with its rain forests and ragged sandstone promontories, where the great oceanic currents last brush land before angling out across 700 miles of water to those tiny volcanic islands on the equator, another kind of edge. All of the life that colonized the Galapagos had to fly or swim or float there, most of it from here. Our students did their forest and shore plant and animal inventories, waded out into the surf to toss in a variety of seeds to see which might have a chance of floating, built up their hypotheses of what they might find on the Islands.

Then we went to see. So many stunning, unique, immensely trusting animals. Days spent traipsing over the bare lava or through thick brush; nights seasick on the small boat on the open sea, examining the logbooks in which previous guests express all kinds of thoughts, profound doubts as well as deep appreciation; arguing with Greg into the wee hours in our little cabin—I too was provoked. I came home realizing that even here, even at the place of Darwinism's own origins, there is a kind of creativity at work not captured by the familiar mechanistic metaphors of traditional Darwinism. There are other ways to think about adaptation—there is more room to recognize spontaneity, improvisation, intelligence—within Darwinism itself. But this is certainly no brief for Creationism either, which simply does not engage the complex inter-relations and dynamics of life also so evident here (and, as Greg always insisted, in fact evident *everywhere* to the trained eye).

Even the current, seemingly a priori standoff between evolution and creationism may shortly yield to a quite different set of antago-nists, as a vision of a far more dynamic, catastrophic, and perhaps also short-lived Earth history is coming into view—with, of course, its own characteristic pattern of insights and oversights. The Great Mystery once again eludes us.

Thus my essay "Galapagos Stories" (Chapter 8 of this book), an attempt to recast the evolution debate toward, once again, a deeper love for the Earth itself and a deeper appreciation for its dynamism. We are not, in fact, in the end-game of a battle to the death between a goliath called "Evolution" and another called "Creation." It may be that the real challenge of our time is very different: to find more productive and revealing ways to speak to the impulses that drive both, and newly emerging alternatives too. Again—we live in originary times.

Chapter 9 concludes this collection by going up to, and probably over, another sort of radical edge. It pays to remember that it was the space program that gave us our first true vision of Earth as a single, fragile whole. Maybe it is no accident that the first Earth Day so closely followed the first Moon landing. Likewise, the continuing and possibly soon-to-be-reinvigorated space program opens philosophical doors that have barely yet even been imagined. We are already engaged in deep space exploration that frames not just the Earth as a single whole, but the entire solar system, or even larger wholes. Profound challenges to established ways of thinking—now including environmentalism itself—arise once again, as we begin to recognize ourselves not merely as Earthlings but as "Solarians," or maybe "plain cosmic citizens."

For one thing, the vast horizons of space offer a sort of express trip beyond anthropocentrism—not so easy a voyage to get off, either physically or conceptually. (Test case: what were/are your reactions when you realize(d) that this book's cover photo is in fact from Mars?) We are also reminded that Earth's "environment" is not a closed system. It may turn out that we are only a local corner of a cosmic ecosystem. How would our systems of Earth-centered ethics, themselves only recently and so very laboriously won, look then? If, on the other hand, life is rare in the universe, maybe it is our very own task to spread it to the stars. Could we even imagine genetically engineered living forms, trees maybe, inhabited by myriads of still others, pushed by the vast "solar sails" already being tested—giant wooden sailing ships again going forth to unknown adventure? How will environmental philosophy, or its successors, rise to this challenge?

You see, anyway, that thinking about space may lead us to contemplate unexpected provocations well beyond environmentalism itself, not to mention a return to (hu)manned space exploration in, perhaps, a wildly different key. Happy to think ourselves at the very edge of radicalism in ethics, we may still be unprepared for the sheer spaciousness of the philosophical challenges posed by "space." How can we assume, for example, that an Earth-centered ethics is somehow the end of the line, as inclusive as ethics can get? Suppose environmental ethics itself is only a station on the way to somewhere else? Thus a book that begins with a chapter called "Before Environmental Ethics" ends, in a sense, with the question of what comes *after* environmental ethics.

But then too: might not environmental philosophy also make its own distinctive contribution to this most momentous of reconceptions, as humans imagine stepping off the home planet in earnest? If the exploration of space may transform environmental philosophy, so environmental philosophy may also transform the exploration of space, again in real and deeply engaging ways. This too is part of our task, our challenge, and the fascination of our times and work. I don't say that any of it is probable. In fact, nothing is particularly probable once we are thinking out a few centuries, let alone a millennium or two. But it is *possible*, aye—and who would have thought it? Marinate space exploration in eco-philosophy for a few centuries, and who knows what either one will end up looking like. The only safe bet is that we are in for a wild ride.

Notes

1. "Beyond Intrinsic Value: Pragmatism in Environmental Ethics," *Environmental Ethics* 7 (1985), pp. 321–39, reprinted in *Environmental Prag-*

matism, edited by Andrew Light and Eric Katz (London: Routledge, 1995) and *Environmental Philosophy: Critical Concepts*, edited by J. B. Callicott and Clare Palmer (London: Routledge, 2004). Eric Katz wrote a reply to this article, titled "Searching for Intrinsic Value," *Environmental Ethics* 9 (1987), to which I published a reply in turn ("Unfair to Swamps," *Environmental Ethics* 10 [1988], also reprinted in *Environmental Pragmatism*). For another version of the argument, see my book *Toward Better Problems* (Philadelphia: Temple University Press, 1992), chapter 5.

2. This is how I put it in an early work on method in ethics: *Toward Better Problems*, p. ix.

3. So unfamiliar is this way of thinking that it was a struggle to get the emphatically Deweyan title of my early monograph, *Toward Better Problems*, past the publisher (Temple University Press). Yet it is, in my view, a precise capsule of what a pragmatic or deconstructive approach offers on the constructive side: a sense that not only solutions but also problems themselves can be reshaped.

4. P. 24, this book.

5. "Between Means and Ends," *Monist* 75 (1992), pp. 236–49.

6. Albert Borgmann, *Technology and the Character of Contemporary Life* (Chicago: University of Chicago Press, 1984).

7. For a celebration of this point, see Inge Anderegg, "On the Natural History of *On the Natural History of Values*," in Anthony Weston, *Jobs for Philosophers* (Philadelphia: Xlibris, 2004), chapter 5. Lovely as it would be to have philosophical bedfellows of this sort, I have to admit that Inge Anderegg is only one of my alter egos. For more on *Jobs for Philosophers*, see in the introduction to chapter 6 of this book.

8. P. 59, this book.

9. Check out www.interspecies.com.

10. P. 68, this book.

11. Sam Gill, "One, Two, Three: The Interpretation of Religious Action," in Gill, *Native American Religious Action: A Performance Approach to Religion* (Columbia: University of South Carolina Press, 1987), pp. 162–63, 151.

12. P. 110, this book. Another pseudonymous selection, this time a manifesto, from *Jobs for Philosophers*.

13. Pp. 32–33, this book.

14. This argument is much elaborated in Anderegg, "On the Natural History of *On The Natural History of Values*."

15. P. 110, this book.

16. "Instead of Environmental Education," in Bob Jickling, ed., *Proceedings of the Yukon College Symposium on Ethics, Environment, and Education* (Whitehorse, YT: Yukon College, 1996), and subsequently reprinted as "Deschooling Environmental Education" in *Canadian Journal of Environmental Education* I (1996).

17. P. 146, this book.

Chapter 2

Before Environmental Ethics

I. Introduction

To think "ecologically," in a broad sense, is to think in terms of the
evolution of an interlinked system over time rather than in terms of
separate and one-way causal interactions. It is a general habit of mind.
Ideas, for example, not just ecosystems, can be viewed in this way. Ethical ideas, in particular, are deeply interwoven with and dependent on
multiple contexts: other prevailing ideas and values, cultural institutions
and practices, a vast range of experiences, and natural settings as well. An
enormous body of work, stretching from history through the "sociology
of knowledge" and back into philosophy, now insists on this point.[1]

It is curious that environmental ethics has not yet viewed itself in
this way. Or perhaps not so curious: for the results are unsettling. Certain theories, in particular, claim to have transcended anthropocentrism
in thought. Yet such theories arise within a world that is profoundly
and beguilingly anthropocentrized.[2] From an "ecological" point of
view, transcending this context so easily seems improbable. In part II
of this paper, I argue that even the best nonanthropocentric theories in
contemporary environmental ethics are still profoundly shaped by and
indebted to the anthropocentrism that they officially oppose.

I do not mean that anthropocentrism is inevitable, or even that
nonanthropocentric speculation has no place in current thinking. Rather,
as I argue in part III, the aim of my critique is to bring into focus
the slow process of culturally constituting and consolidating values that
underlies philosophical ethics as we know it. The aim is to broaden our
conception of the nature and tasks of ethics, so that we can begin to
recognize the "ecology," so to speak, of environmental ethics itself, and

"Before Environmental Ethics" first appeared in *Environmental Ethics* 14 (1992), pp.
323–40, and was subsequently reprinted in a variety of teaching anthologies in environmental ethics.

thus begin to recognize the true conditions under which anthropocentrism might be overcome.

One implication is that we must rethink the practice of environmental ethics. In part IV, I ask how ethics should comport itself at early stages of the process of constituting and consolidating new values. I then apply the conclusions directly to environmental ethics. In particular, the co-evolution of values with cultural institutions, practices, and experience emerges as an appropriately "ecological" alternative to the project of somehow trying to leapfrog the entire culture in thought. In part V, finally, I offer one model of a co-evolutionary approach to environmental philosophy, what I call "enabling environmental practice."

II. Contemporary Nonanthropocentrism

I begin by arguing that contemporary nonanthropocentric environmental ethics remains deeply dependent on the thoroughly anthropocentrized setting in which it arises. Elsewhere I develop this argument in detail.[3] Here there is only room to sketch some highlights.

For a first example, consider the very phrasing of the question that most contemporary environmental philosophers take as basic: whether "we" should open the gates of moral considerability to "other" animals (sometimes just: "animals"), and/or to such things as rivers and mountains. The opening line of Paul Taylor's *Respect for Nature*, for example, invokes such a model. Environmental ethics, Taylor writes, "is concerned with the moral relations that hold between humans and the natural world."[4]

Taylor's phrasing of "the" question may seem neutral and unexceptionable. Actually, however, it is not neutral at all. The called-for arguments address all humans, and only humans, on behalf of "the natural world." Environmental ethics therefore is invited to begin by *positing*, not questioning, a sharp divide that "we" must somehow cross, taking that "we" unproblematically to denote all and only humans. To invoke such a divide, however, is already to take one ethical position among others. For one thing, it is largely peculiar to modern Western cultures. Historically, when humans said "we," they hardly ever meant to include all other humans, while they often did mean to include some individuals of other species. Mary Midgley emphasizes that almost all of the ancient life patterns were "mixed communities" of humans and an enormous variety of other creatures, from dogs (our relation with whom she calls "symbiotic"), to reindeer, weasels, elephants, shags, horses, and pigs.[5] One's identifications and loyalties lay not with the extended human species (extended, usually, in both space and time: a striking abstraction) but with a local and concretely realized network of relationships involving many different species.

Taylor might respond that his question is at least *our* question: the urbanized, modern, Westerner's question. So it is. But it is precisely this recognition of cultural relativity that is crucial. "The" very question that frames contemporary environmental ethics appears to presuppose a particular cultural and historical situation, not at all the only human possibility, and itself perhaps precisely the problem. Cross-species identifications, or a more variegated sense of "the natural world," arise awkwardly, if at all.

Consider a second example. A defining feature of almost all recent nonanthropocentrisms is some appeal to "intrinsic values" in nature. Once again, however, this kind of appeal is actually no more neutral or timelessly relevant than an appeal to all and only humans on behalf of the rest of the world. Intrinsic values in nature are so urgently sought at precisely the moment that the *instrumentalization* of the world—at least according to a certain sociological tradition[6]—has reached a fever pitch. It is because we now perceive nature as thoroughly reduced to a set of "means" to human ends that an insistence on nature as an "end in itself" seems the only possible response. We may even be right. Still, under other cultural conditions, unthreatened by such a relentless reduction of everything to "mere means," it at least might not seem so *obvious* that we must aspire to a kind of healing that salvages a few nontraditional sorts of "ends" while consigning everything else to mere resourcehood. Instead we might challenge the underlying "means"-"ends" divide itself, turning toward a more pragmatic sense of the interconnectedness of all of our values.[7]

Also, unthreatened in this way, we might not be tempted to metaphysical turns in defense of the values we cherish. Jim Cheney has suggested that the turn to metaphysics in some varieties of contemporary environmental ethics represents, like the ancient Stoics' turn to metaphysics, a desperate self-defense rather than a revelation of a genuine nonanthropocentrism. Cheney charges in particular that a certain kind of radical environmentalism, which he dubs "Ecosophy S," has been tempted into a "neostoic" philosophy—an identification with nature on the level of the universe as a whole—because neostoicism offers a way to identify with nature without actually giving up control. Abstract arguments become a kind of philosophical substitute for "real encounter" with nature.[8]

Cheney is arguing in part that Ecosophy S reflects a profoundly contemporary psychological dynamic. I want to suggest that it also reflects the diminished character of the world in which we live. The experiences for which Ecosophy S is trying to speak are inevitably marginalized in a thoroughly anthropocentrized culture. They are simply not accessible to most people or even understandable to many. Wild experience may actually *be* the starting point for "Ecosophy S," then, but there are only a few, ritualized, and hackneyed ways to actually speak for it in a culture that does not share it. Thus—again, under present circumstances—environmental ethics may be literally *driven* to abstraction.

Once again, it may even be true that abstraction is *our* only option. Nonetheless, in a different world, truly beyond anthropocentrism, we might hope for a much less abstract way of speaking for and of wild experience—for enough sharing of at least the glimmers of wild experience that we can speak of it directly, even perhaps invoking a kind of love. But such a change, once again, would leave contemporary nonanthropocentric environmental ethics—whether neostoic or just theoretical—far behind.

As a third and final example, consider the apparently simple matter of what sorts of criticism are generally regarded as "responsible" and what sorts of alternatives are generally regarded as "realistic." The contemporary anthropocentrized world, in fact the product of an immense project of world-reconstruction that has reached a frenzy in the modern age, has become simply the taken-for-granted reference point for what is "real," for what must be accepted by any responsible criticism. The absolute pervasiveness of internal combustion engines, for example, is utterly new, confined to the last century and mostly to the last generation. By now very few Westerners ever get out of earshot of internal combustion engines for more than a few hours at a time. The environmental consequences are staggering, the long-term effects of constant noise on "mental health" are clearly worrisome, and so on. And yet all of this has so thoroughly embedded itself in our lives that even mild proposals to restrict internal combustion engines seem impossibly radical. This suddenly transmuted world, the stuff of science fiction only fifty years ago, now just as suddenly defines the very limits of imagination. When we think of "alternatives," all we can imagine are carpools and buses.

Something similar occurs in philosophical contexts. Many of our philosophical colleagues take a careful, neutral, critical style as a point of pride. But in actual practice this style is only careful, neutral, and critical in certain directions. Suggest anything *different* and prejudgments kick in galore. The project of going beyond anthropocentrism still looks wild, incautious, intellectually overexcited. Most of our colleagues are still far more comfortable exploring ways in which we might gerrymander a somewhat more environmentally sensitive ethic that does not "go so far" as to actually contemplate ethical connections to the nonhuman world. Of course, they may be right. Notice, however, that anthropocentrism itself is almost never scrutinized in the same way. Apparently it just forms part of the "neutral" background: it seems no more than what the careful, critical thinker can *presuppose*. Thus, it is the slow excavation and logical "refutation" of anthropocentrism that, perforce, occupy our time—rather than, just for example, a much less encumbered, more imaginative exploration of other possibilities, less fearful of the disapproval of the Guardians of Reason, or, for another example, a psychological exploration of anthropocentrism itself, taking it to be more like a kind of lovelessness or blindness than a serious philosophical position needing to be "refuted." Anthropocentrism still fills the screen, still dominates our energies. It delimits what is "realistic" because in many ways it still delimits "reality" itself.

III. Ethics in Social Context

The conclusion of the argument so far might only seem to be that we need better nonanthropocentrisms: theories that rethink Taylor's basic question, theories that are not so easily seduced by intrinsic values, and so on. These would be useful. But the argument just offered also points toward a much more fundamental conclusion, one upon which very large questions of method hang. If the most rigorous and sustained attempts to transcend anthropocentrism still end up in its orbit, profoundly shaped by the thought and practices of the anthropocentrized culture within which they arise, then we may begin to wonder whether the project of transcending culture in ethical thought is, in fact, workable *at all*. Perhaps ethics requires a very different self-conception.

Here, moreover, is a surprising fact: ethics generally—beyond the borders of environmental ethics—*has* a very different self-conception. Most "mainstream" ethical philosophers now readily acknowledge that the values they attempt to systematize are indeed deeply embedded in and co-evolved with social institutions and practices. John Rawls, for example, who at earlier moments appeared to be the very incarnation of the philosophical drive toward what he himself called an "Archimedean point" beyond culture, now explicitly justifies his theory only by reference to its "congruence with our deeper understanding of ourselves and our aspirations, and our realization that, given our history and the traditions embedded in our public life, it is the most reasonable doctrine for us." For *us*: it answers "our" questions. "We are not," he says, "trying to find a conception of justice suitable for all societies regardless of their social or historical circumstances." Instead, the theory "is intended simply as a useful basis of agreement in our society."[9] The same conclusion is also the burden, of course, of an enormous body of criticism supposing Rawls to be making a less culturally dependent claim.

Rawls, in other words, does not transcend his social context at all. Rather, his theory is, to adapt a phrase that Nietzsche uses about Kant, a particularly scholarly way of *expressing* an already established set of values. That contemporary nonanthropocentric environmental ethics does not transcend *its* social context, therefore, becomes much less surprising. At least it is in good company.

Similarly, John Arras, in an article surveying Jonsen and Toulmin's revival of casuistry, as well as the Rawls-Walzer debate, remarks almost in passing that all of these philosophers agree that "there is no escape from the task of interpreting the meanings embedded in our social practices, institutions, and history."[10] Michael Walzer argues for a plurality of justice values rooted in the varied "cultural meanings" of different goods.[11] Alasdair MacIntyre makes the rootedness of values in "traditions" and "practices" central to his reconception of ethics.[12] Charles Taylor localizes the appeal to rights within philosophical, theological, and even aesthetic movements in the modern West.[13] Sabina Lovibond updates Wittgensteinian "form of life" ethics along sociologically informed "expressivist" lines.[14]

It may seem shocking that the "Archimedean" aspirations for ethics have been abandoned with so little fanfare. From the point of view of what we might call the "theology of ethics," it probably is. Day to day, however, and within the familiar ethics of persons, justice, and rights practiced by most of these philosophers just cited, it is less surprising. Operating within a culture in which certain basic values are acknowledged, at least verbally, by nearly everyone, there is no practical need to raise the question of the ultimate origins or warrants of values. Because the issue remains metaphilosophical and marginal to what are supposed to be the more systematic tasks of ethics, we can acquiesce in a convenient division of labor with the social sciences, ceding to them most of the historical and cultural questions about the evolution of values while keeping the project of systematizing and applying values for our own. "Scholarly forms of expression" of those values—or at least systematic forms of expression, "rules to live by"—are then precisely what we want.

It now seems entirely natural, for example to view persons as "centers of autonomous choice and valuation," in Paul Taylor's words, "giving direction to their lives on the basis of their own values," having a sense of identity over time, and so on. It also seems natural to point to this "belief-system" to ground respect for persons, as Taylor also points out. He does *not* ask how such a belief-system came into being and managed to rearrange human lives around itself. He does not *need* to ask. But we need at least to remember that these are real and complex questions. It is only such processes, running their courses, that make possible the consensus behind the contemporary values in the first place. Weber traces our belief-system about persons, in part, to Calvinist notions about the inscrutability of fate, paradoxically leading to an outwardly calculating possessiveness coupled with rigid "inner asceticism," both self-preoccupied in a fundamentally new way. In addition, he traces it to the development of a system of increasingly impersonal commercial transactions that disabled and disconnected older, more communal ties between people.[15] The cultural relativity of the notion of persons is highlighted, meanwhile, by its derivation from the Greek dramatic "personae," perhaps the first emergence of the idea of a unique and irreplaceable individual. A tribal African or Native American would never think of herself in this way.[16]

It will no doubt be objected that to stress the interdependence of ethical ideas with cultural institutions, practices, and experience simply reduces ethical ideas to epiphenomena of such factors. However, the actual result is quite different. The flaw lies with the objection's crude (indeed, truly "vulgar," as in "vulgar Marxist") model of causation. Simple, mechanical, one-way linkages between clearly demarcated "causes" and "effects" do not characterize cultural phenomena (or, for that matter, *any* phenomena). So the question is emphatically *not* whether ethical ideas are "cause" or "effect" in cultural systems, as if the only alternative to being purely a cause is to be purely an effect. Causation in complex, interdependent, and evolving systems with multiple feedback loops—that is, precisely an "ecological" conception of causation—is a far better model.[17]

One implication of such a model, moreover, is that fundamental change (at least constructive, noncatastrophic change) is likely to be slow. Practices, habits, institutions, arts, ideas all must evolve in some coordinated way. Even the physical structure of the world changes. The development of individualism and its associated ideas of privacy, for example, accompanied a revolution in home and furniture design.[18] Thus it may not even be that visionary ethical ideas (or anything else visionary, e.g., revolutionary architecture) are simply impossible at any given cultural stage, but rather that such ideas simply will not be recognized or understood, given all of the existing practices alongside which they have to be put and the fact that they cannot be immediately applied in ways that will contribute to their development and improvement.[19] To use Darwinian metaphors, all manner of "mutations" may be produced at any evolutionary stage, but conditions will be favorable for only a few of them to be "selected" and passed on.[20]

It will also be objected that any such view is hopelessly "relativistic." Though the term "relativism" now seems to be so confused and ambiguous as to be nearly hopeless itself, there is a genuine concern here: that if values are thoroughly relativized to culture, rational criticism of values may become impossible. In fact, however, rational criticism remains entirely possible—only its "standpoint" is internal to the culture it challenges, rather than (as in the Archimedean image) external to it. Much of what we tend to regard as radical social criticism reinvokes old, even central, values of a culture rather than requiring us to somehow transcend the culture in thought. Weber, for example, reread Luther's conception of the individual's relation to God as an extension of the already old and even revered monastic ideal to society at large. Likewise, the challenges of the 1960s in America arguably appealed not to new values but to some of the oldest and most deeply embedded values of our culture. The Students for a Democratic Society's "Port Huron Statement" persistently speaks in biblical language; the Black Panthers invoke the Declaration of Independence; the Civil Rights Movement was firmly grounded in Christianity. In his 1981 encyclical "Laborem Exercens," Pope John Paul II appealed to Genesis to ground a stunning critique of work in industrial societies reminiscent of the early Marx.[21]

In general, those who worry about the implications of social-scientific "relativism" for the rationality of ethics should be reassured by Richard Bernstein's delineation of a kind of rationality "beyond objectivism and relativism": a much more pragmatic and processual model of reason built on the historical and social embeddedness and evolution of ideas.[22] Those who worry that "relative" values will be less serious than values that can claim absolute allegiance might be reassured by the argument that it is precisely the profound embeddedness of our ethical ideas within their cultural contexts that marks their seriousness. For *us*, of course. But that is who we speak of, and to.

Although these last remarks are very sketchy, they at least serve to suggest that a sociological or "evolutionary" view of values is not somehow the death knell of ethics. Instead, again, such a view seems to be almost the enabling condition of modern philosophical ethics. At the same time, however, "mainstream" ethics does not need to be, and certainly *has* not been, explicit on this point. The actual origins of values are seldom explored at all, and the usual labels—like Lovibond's "expressivism" and even MacIntyre's "traditions"—only indirectly suggest any social provenance. But it is time to be more explicit. As I argue below, large issues outside the mainstream may depend on it.

IV. The Practice of Ethics at Originary Stages

In order to begin to draw some of the necessary conclusions from this "evolutionary" view of values, let us turn our attention to the appropriate comportment for ethics at what we might call the "originary stages" of the development of values: stages at which new values are only beginning to be constituted and consolidated. In the case of the ethics of persons, for example, we must try to place ourselves back at the time when respect for persons, and indeed persons themselves, were far less secure—not fixed or familiar or "natural" as they now seem, but rather strange, forced, truncated, the way they must have seemed to, say, Calvin's contemporaries. How then should—how *could*—a proto-ethics of persons proceed in such a situation?

First, such early stages in the development of a new set of values stages require a great deal of exploration and metaphor. Only later the new ethical notions later harden into analytic categories. For example, although the concept of "rights" of persons now may be invoked with a fair degree of rigor, through most of its history it played a much more open-ended role, allowing the possibility of treating whole new classes of people as rights holders—slaves, foreigners, the propertyless, women—in ways previously unheard of, and in ways that, literally, were misuses of the concept. (" 'Barbarian rights'? But the very *concept* of 'barbarian' precludes being one of 'us,' i.e., Greeks, i.e., rights-holders . . .") This malleable rhetoric of rights also in part *created* "rights-holders." To persuade someone that they have a right to something, for example, or to persuade a whole class or group that their rights have been violated, may dramatically change their behavior, and ultimately reconstructs their belief-systems and experiences of themselves as well. Even now the creative and rhetorical possibilities of the concept of rights are not exhausted. We might read the sweeping and inclusive notion of rights in *The United Nations Declaration of Human Rights* in this light, for instance, rather than dismissing it, as do more legalistic thinkers, as conceptually confused.[23]

Moreover, the process of co-evolving values and practices at originary stages is seldom a smooth process of progressively filling in and instantiating earlier outlines. Instead, we see a variety of fairly incompatible half-sketches coupled with a wide range of proto-practices, even social experiments of various sorts, all contributing to a kind of cultural working-through of a new set of possibilities. The process *seems* smooth in retrospect only because the values and practices that ultimately win out rewrite the history of the others so that the less successful practices and experiments are eventually obscured—much as successful scientific paradigms, according to Kuhn, rewrite their own pasts so that in retrospect their evolution seems much smoother, more necessary, and more univocal than it actually was. Great moments in the canonical history of rights, for example, include the Declaration of Independence and the Declaration of the Rights of Man, capitalism's institutionalization of rights to property and wealth, and now the persistent defense of a nonpositivistic notion of rights for international export. *Not* included are the utopian socialists' many experimental communities, for example, which often explicitly embraced (what *became*) nonstandard, even anticapitalistic notions of rights, or such sustained and massive struggles as the labor movement's organization around working persons' rights and the various modern attempts by most social democracies to institutionalize rights to health care.

A long period of experimentation and uncertainty, then, ought to be expected and indeed welcomed in the originary stages of any new ethics. Again, as I suggested above, even the most familiar aspects of personhood co-evolved with a particular, complex, and even wildly improbable set of ideas and practices. Protestantism, for instance, contributed not just a theology, and not just Calvin's peculiar and (if Weber is right) peculiarly world-historical "inner-world asceticism," but also such seemingly simple projects as an accessible Bible in the vernacular. Imagine the extraordinary impact of reading the holy text oneself, of being offered or pushed into an individual relation to God after centuries of only the most mediated access. Imagine the extraordinary self-preoccupation created by having to choose for the first time between rival versions of the same revelation, with not only one's eternal soul in the balance but often one's earthly life as well. Only against such a background of practice did it become possible to begin to experience oneself as an individual, separate from others, beholden to inner voices and "one's own values," "giving direction to one's life" oneself, as Paul Taylor puts it, and bearing the responsibility for one's choices.

Since we now look at the evolution of the values of persons mostly from the far side, it is easy to miss the fundamental contingency of those values and their dependence on practices, institutions, and experiences that were for their time genuinely uncertain and exploratory. Today we are too used to that easy division of labor that leaves ethics only the systematic task of "expressing" a set of values that is already established, and abandons the originary questions to the social sciences. As a result, ethics is incapacitated when it comes to dealing with values that are *now* entering an originary stage. Even when it is out of its depth, we continue to imagine that systematic ethics, such as the ethics of the person, is the only kind of ethics there is. We continue to regard the contingency, open-endedness, and uncertainty of "new" values as an objection to them, ruling them out of ethical court entirely, or else as a kind of embarassment to be quickly papered over with an ethical theory.

This discussion applies directly to environmental ethics. First and fundamentally, if environmental ethics is indeed at an originary stage, we can have only the barest sense of what ethics for a culture truly beyond anthropocentrism would actually look like. The Renaissance and the Reformation did not simply actualize some preexisting, easily anticipated notion of persons, but rather played a part in the *co-evolution* of respect for persons. What would emerge could only be imagined in advance in the dimmest of ways, or not imagined at all. Similarly, we are only now embarking on an attempt to move beyond anthropocentrism, and we simply cannot predict in advance where even another century, say, will take us.

Indeed, when anthropocentrism is finally cut down to size, there is no reason to think that what we will have or need in its place is something called "*non*anthropocentrism"—as if that characterization would even begin to be useful in a culture for which anthropocentrism were indeed transcended. Indeed it may not be any kind of "centrism" whatsoever, that is, some form of hierarchically structured ethics. It is already clear that hierarchy is by no means the only option.[24]

Second and correlatively, at this stage exploration and metaphor become crucial in environmental ethics. Only later can we harden originary notions into precise analytic categories. Any attempt to appropriate the moral force of rights language for (much of) the trans-human world, for example, ought to be expected from the start to be *im*precise, literally "confused." (" 'Animal rights'? But the very *concept* of 'animal' precludes being one of 'us,' i.e., persons, i.e., rights-holders . . .") It need not be meant as a description of prevailing practice, but should be read instead as an attempt to *change* the prevailing practice. Christopher Stone's book *Should Trees Have Standing? Toward Legal Rights for Natural Objects*, for example, is making a revisionist proposal about legal arrangements, not offering an analysis of the existing concept of rights.[25]

Something similar should be understood when we are invited to conceive not only animals or trees as rights holders, but also the land as a community and the planet as a person. Such arguments should be understood to be rhetorical, in a nonpejorative, pragmatic sense: they are suggestive and open-ended sorts of challenges, even proposals for Deweyan kinds of social reconstruction, rather than attempts to demonstrate particular conclusions on the basis of premises supposed to be already accepted.[26] The force of these arguments lies in the way they open up the possibility of new connections, not in the way they settle or "close" any questions. Their work is much more formative than summative, more prospective than retrospective. Their chief function is to provoke, to loosen up the language and correspondingly our thinking, to fire the imagination: to *open* questions, not to settle them.

I suggest that the founders of environmental ethics were explorers along these lines. Here I want, in particular, to reclaim Aldo Leopold from the theorists. Bryan Norton reminds us, for example, that Leopold's widely cited appeal to the "integrity, stability, and beauty of the biotic community" occurs in the midst of a discussion of purely economic constructions of the land. It is best read, Norton says, as a kind of counterbalance and challenge to the excesses of pure commercialism, rather than as a criterion for moral action all by itself. Similarly, John Rodman has argued that Leopold's work then should be read as an environmental ethic *in process*, complicating the anthropocentric picture more or less from within, rather than as a kind of proto-system, simplifying and unifying an entirely new picture, that can be progressively refined in the way that utilitarian and deontological theories have been refined over the last century.[27] This is the Leopold who insists, after all, that

> the land ethic [is] a *product of social evolution* . . . Only the most superficial student of history supposes that Moses "write" the Decalogue; it evolved in the mind [and surely also in the practices] of the thinking community, and Moses wrote a tentative summary of it. . . . I say "tentative" because evolution never stops.[28]

It might be better to read Leopold not as purveying a general ethical theory at all, but rather simply as opening some questions, unsettling some assumptions, and prying the window open just far enough to lead, in time, to much wilder and certain more diverse suggestions or "criteria."

Third and more generally, as I put it above, the process of evolving values and practices at originary stages is seldom a smooth process of progressively filling in and instantiating earlier outlines. At originary stages we should instead expect a variety of fairly incompatible outlines coupled with a wide range of proto-practices, even social experiments of various sorts, all contributing to a kind of cultural working-through of a new set of possibilities. In environmental ethics, we arrive at exactly the opposite view from J. Baird Callicott, for example, who insists that we attempt to formulate, right now, a complete, unified, even "closed" (his term) theory of environmental ethics. Callicott even argues that contemporary environmental ethics should not tolerate more than one basic type of value, insisting on a "univocal" environmental ethic.[29] In fact, however, as I argued above, originary stages are the worst possible times to demand that we all speak with one voice. Once a set of values is culturally consolidated, it may well be possible, perhaps even necessary, to reduce them to some kind of consistency. But environmental values are unlikely to be in such a position for a very long time. The necessary period of ferment, cultural experimentation, and thus *multi*-vocality is only *beginning*. Although Callicott may be right about the demands of systematic ethical theory at later cultural stages, he is wrong—indeed, I suggest, wildly wrong—about what stage environmental values have actually reached.

V. Enabling Environmental Practice

Space for some analogues to the familiar theories does remain in the alternative environmental ethics envisioned here. Although I have argued that they are unreliable guides to the ethical future, they might well be viewed as another kind of ethical experiment or proposal, rather like, for example, the work of the utopian socialists. However unrealistic, they may nonetheless play a historical and transitional role, highlighting new possibilities, inspiring reconstructive experiments, even perhaps eventually provoking environmental ethics' equivalent of a Marx.

It should be clear, though, that the kind of constructive activity suggested by the argument offered here goes far beyond the familiar theories as well. Rather than systematizing environmental values, again, the overall project at this stage should be to begin to *co-evolve* those values with practices and institutions that make them even *un*systematically possible. In this section I want to develop one specific example of such a co-evolutionary practice. It is by no means the only example. Indeed the best thing that could be hoped, in my view, is the emergence of many others. But it is *one* example, and it may be a good example to help clarify how such approaches might look, and thus to clear the way for more.

A central part of the challenge is to create the social, psychological, and phenomenological preconditions—the conceptual, experiential, or even quite literal "space"—for new or stronger environmental values

to evolve. Because such creation will "enable" such values, I call such
a practical project *enabling environmental practice.*

Consider the attempt to create actual, physical spaces for the emergence of trans-human experience: *places* within which some return to
the experience of and immersion in natural settings is possible. Suppose
that certain places are set aside as quiet zones: places where automobile
engines, lawnmowers, and low-flying airplanes are not allowed, and yet
places where people will still live. On one level, the aim is modest: simply
to make it possible to hear the birds, the winds, and the silence once
again. If bright outside lights were also banned, one could see the stars
at night and feel the slow pulsations of the light over the seasons. A
little creative zoning, in short, could make space for increasingly divergent styles of living on the land: experiments in recycling and energy
self-sufficiency, for example; Midgleyan mixed communities of humans
and other species, serious "re-inhabitation" (though perhaps with more
emphasis on place and community than on the individual re-inhabitors),
the "ecosteries" that have been proposed on the model of monasteries;
or other possibilities not yet even imagined.[30]

This is not a utopian proposal. Unplug a few outdoor lights,
reroute some roads, and in some places of the country we would easily have a first approximation right now. In gardening, meanwhile, we
already experience some semblance of mixed communities. Practices
like bee-keeping already model a symbiotic relation with the "biotic
community." It is not hard to work out policies to protect and extend
such practices.

Enabling environmental practice is of course a *practice.* It does not
follow that it is not also philosophical. Theory and practice interpenetrate
here. In the abstract, for example, the concept of "natural settings," just
invoked, has been acrimoniously debated, and the best-known positions
are unfortunately more or less the extremes. Social Ecologists insist that
no environment is ever purely natural, that human beings have already
remade the entire world, and that the challenge is really to get the process
under socially progressive and politically inclusive control. Some Deep
Ecologists, by contrast, argue that only wilderness is the "real world."[31]
Both views have something to offer. But it may be that only within the
context of a new practice, even so simple a practice as the attempt to
create "quiet places," will we finally achieve the necessary distance to
take what we can from the purely philosophical debate and also to go
beyond it toward a better set of questions and answers.

Both views, for example, unjustly discount "encounter." On the one
hand, nonanthropocentrism should not become anti-anthropocentrism:

the aim is not to push humans out of the picture entirely, but rather to open up the possibility of reciprocity *between* humans and the rest of nature. But reciprocity does require a space not wholly permeated by humans either. What we need to explore are possible realms of *interaction*. Neither the wilderness nor the city (as we know it) are "the real world," if we must talk in such terms. We might take as the most "real" places the places where humans and other creatures, honored in their wildness and potential reciprocity, can come together, perhaps warily but at least openly.

The work of Wendell Berry is paradigmatic of this kind of philosophical engagement. Berry writes, for example, of what he calls "the phenomenon of edge or margin, that we know to be one of the powerful attractions of a diversified landscape, both to wildlife and to humans." "Margins" are places where domesticity and wildness meet. Mowing his small hayfield with a team of horses, Berry encounters a hawk who lands close to him, watching carefully but without fear. The hawk comes, he says,

> because of the conjunction of the small pasture and its wooded borders, of open hunting ground and the security of trees . . . The human eye itself seems drawn to such margins, hungering for the difference made in the countryside by a hedgy fencerow, a stream, or a grove of trees. These margins are biologically rich, the meeting of two kinds of habitat . . .[32]

The hawk would not have come, he says, if the field had been larger, or if there had been no trees, or if he had been plowing with a tractor. Interaction is a fragile thing, and we need to pay careful attention to its preconditions. As Berry shows, this is a deeply philosophical and phenomenological project as well as a "practical" one—but nonetheless it always revolves around and refers back to practice. Without actually maintaining a farm, he would know very little of what he knows, and that the hawk would not—*could* not—have come to him.

Margins are, of course, only one example. They cannot be the whole story. Many creatures avoid them. It is for this reason that the spotted owl's survival depends on large tracts of old-growth forests. Nonetheless, they are still *part* of the story—a part given particularly short shrift, it seems, by all sides in the current debate.

It is not possible in a short article to develop the kind of philosophy of "practice" that would be necessary to work out these points fully.

However, I can at least note two opposite pitfalls in speaking of practice. First, again, it is not as if we come to this practice already knowing what values we will find or exemplify there. Too often the notion of practice in contemporary philosophy has degenerated into "application," that is, of prior principles or theories. At best it might include a space for feedback from practice to principle or theory. I mean something more radical here. Practice is the opening of the "space" for interaction, for the re-emergence of a larger world. It is a kind of exploration. We do not know in advance what we will find. Berry had to *learn*, for example, about "margins." Gary Snyder and others propose Buddhist terms to describe the necessary attitude: a kind of mindfulness, attentiveness. Tom Birch calls it the "primary sense" of the notion of "consideration."[33]

On the other hand, this sort of open-ended practice does not mean reducing our own activity to zero, as in some form of quietism. I do not mean that we must simply "open, and it will come." There is not likely to be any single and simple set of values that somehow emerges once we merely get out of the way. Berry's view is that a more open-ended and respectful relation to nature requires constant and creative *activity*—in his case, constant presence in nature, constant interaction with his own animals, maintenance of a place that maximizes margins. Others will, of course, choose other ways. The crucial thing is that humans must neither monopolize the picture entirely nor absent ourselves from it completely, but rather to try to live in interaction, to create a space for genuine encounter as part of our ongoing reconstruction of our own lives and practices. What will come of such encounters, what will emerge from such sustained interactions, again, we cannot yet say.

No doubt it will be argued that Berry is necessarily an exception, that small unmechanized farms are utterly anachronistic and that any real maintenance of margins or space for encounter is unrealistic in mass society. Perhaps. But these automatically accepted commonplaces are also open to argumentation and experiment. Christopher Alexander and his colleagues, in *A Pattern Language* and elsewhere, make clear how profoundly even the simplest architectural features of houses, streets, and cities structure our experience of nature—and that they can be consciously redesigned to change those experiences. Windows on two sides of a room make it possible for natural light to suffice for daytime illumination. If buildings are built on those parts of the land that are in the worst condition, not the best, we thereby leave the most healthy and beautiful parts, alone while improving the worst parts. On a variety of grounds, Alexander and his colleagues argue for the presence of still and moving water throughout the city, for extensive common land, "accessible green," sacred sites and burial grounds within the city, and so on. If we built mindfully, they argue, maintaining and even expanding margins is not only possible but easy, even with high human population densities.[34]

VI. Conclusion

The last section offers only the barest sketch of enabling environmental practice: a few examples, not even a general typology. To attempt a more systematic typology of its possible forms at this point seems to me premature, partly because ethics has hitherto paid so little attention to the cultural constitution of values that we have no such typology, and partly because the originary stage of environmental values is barely underway.

Moreover, enabling environmental practice is itself only one example of the broader range of philosophical activities invited by what I have called a co-evolutionary view of values. I have not denied that even theories of rights, for instance, have a place in environmental ethics. However, it is not the only place there is, and rights themselves, at least when invoked beyond the sphere of persons, must be understood (so I argued) in a much more metaphorical and exploratory sense than usual. This has been argued by many others, of course, but usually with the intention of ruling rights-talk out of environmental ethics altogether. A pluralistic project is far more tolerant and inclusive. Indeed it is surely an advantage of the sort of umbrella conception of environmental ethics suggested here that nearly all of the current approaches may find a place in it.

Enabling environmental practice is closest to my own heart. I therefore struggle with the temptation to make it the whole story. It is not. Given the prevailing attitudes, though, we continue to need to insist that it is *part* of the story. Of course we might still have to argue at length about just whether and how far enabling environmental practice is "philosophical" or "ethical." My own view, along pragmatic lines, is that it is both, deeply and essentially. Indeed, for Dewey, the sustained practice of social reconstruction—experimental, improvisatory, and pluralistic—is the most central ethical practice of all. But that is an argument for another time. In any case it is one of the most central tasks that now calls to us.

Notes

1. Some landmarks of this body of work come into view in the later discussion. For a general overview of work on ethical ideas in particular from

this perspective, see Maria Ossowska, *Social Determinants of Moral Ideas* (Philadelphia: University of Pennsylvania, 1970).

2. I distinguish "anthropocentrism," as a philosophical position issuing in an ethics, from the practices and institutions in which it is embodied, which I call "anthropocen*trized.*"

3. "Non-Anthropocentrism in a Thoroughly Anthropocentrized World," *The Trumpeter* 8 (1991): 108–12.

4. Paul Taylor, *Respect for Nature* (Princeton: Princeton University Press, 1986), p. 3.

5. Mary Midgley, *Animals and Why They Matter* (Athens: University of Georgia Press, 1983), p. 118. See also Arne Naess, "Self-Realization in Mixed Communities of Humans, Bears, Sheep, and Wolves," *Inquiry* 22 (1979): 231–41.

6. A tradition beginning with Max Weber's *The Protestant Ethic and the Spirit of Capitalism*, trans. Talcott Parsons (New York: Scribner's, 1958) and *Economy and Society*, ed. G. Roth and C. Wittich (Berkeley: University of California Press, 1978), and carried into the present in different ways by (e.g.) Morris Berman, *The Reenchantment of the World* (Ithaca: Cornell University Press, 1981) and Albert Borgmann, *Technology and the Character of Contemporary Life* (Chicago: University of Chicago Press, 1984).

7. Anthony Weston, "Beyond Intrinsic Value: Pragmatism in Environmental Ethics," *Environmental Ethics* 7:4 (Winter 1985): 321–39.

8. Jim Cheney, "The Neo-Stoicism of Radical Environmentalism," *Environmental Ethics* 11:4 (Winter 1989): 293–325.

9. John Rawls, "Kantian Constructivism in Moral Theory," *Journal of Philosophy* 77 (1980), p. 318; and "Justice as Fairness: Political not Metaphysical," *Philosophy and Public Affairs* 14 (1985), p. 228.

10. John Arras, "The Revival of Casuistry in Bioethics," *Journal of Medicine and Philosophy* 16 (1991), p. 44.

11. *Spheres of Justice* (New York: Basic Books, 1983).

12. *After Virtue* (Notre Dame: University of Notre Dame Press, 1981).

13. In his aptly named *Sources of the Self* (Cambridge: Harvard University Press, 1989).

14. *Realism and Imagination in Ethics* (Minneapolis: University of Minnesota Press, 1983).

15. Weber, op. cit.

16. For classic examples of selves in other keys, see Louis Dumont, *Homo Hierarchichus* (Chicago: University of Chicago Press, 1980) and Colin Turnbull, *The Forest People* (New York: Simon and Schuster, 1961).

17. Unavoidable here is the Kantian objection that ethical values actually offer "reasons" rather than anything in the merely "causal" universe. My dogmatic response is that, despite its patina of logical necessity, this insistence on seceding from the phenomenal world actually derives from the same misconception of causal stories criticized in the text. While I am dogmatizing, let me add that, in my view, the idea that one can somehow understand and systematize ethical values in ignorance of their origins and social dynamics also partakes of the spectacular overconfidence in Philosophical Reason implicitly criticized in

this paper as a whole. For some support on this point, see Kai Nielsen, "On Transforming the Teaching of Moral Philosophy," *APA Newsletter on Teaching Philosophy*, November 1987, pp. 3–7.

18. Witold Rybczynski, *Home: A Short History of an Idea* (New York: Viking, 1986).

19. I do not mean to deny that rapid change (both cultural and biological) occasionally does happen, perhaps precipitated by unpredictable but radical events. Drastic global warming or a Chernobyl-style accident outside of Washington, DC might well precipitate a drastic change in our environmental practices. Still, even in moments of crisis we can only respond using the tools that we then have. From deep within our anthropocentrized world it remains hard to see how we could respond without resorting either to some kind of "enlightened" anthropocentrism or to a reflex rejection of it, still on anthropocentrism's own terms. Thus when I speak of "fundamental" change, I mean change in the entire system of values, beliefs, practices, and social institutions—not just in immediate practices forced on us by various emergencies.

20. For this way of putting the matter I am indebted to Rom Harre.

21. In general, the possibility of invoking dissonant strands in a complex culture is part of the reason that radical social criticism is possible in the first place. Cf Lovibond, *Realism and Imagination in Ethics*; Walzer, *Interpretation and Social Criticism* (Cambridge: Harvard University Press, 1987); and my *Toward Better Problems: Pragmatic Imperatives in Practical Ethics* (Philadelphia: Temple University Press, 1992), pp. 167–74.

22. Richard Bernstein, *Beyond Objectivism and Relativism* (Philadelphia: University of Pennsylvania Press, 1983).

23. While Hugo Bedau (in "International Human Rights," in Tom Regan and Donald Vandeveer, eds., *And Justice Toward All: New Essays in Philosophy and Public Policy* (Totowa, NJ: Rowman and Littlefield, 1982) calls the *Declaration* "the triumphant product of several centuries of political, legal, and moral inquiry into . . . 'the dignity and worth of the human person' " (p. 298), he goes on to assert that "It is . . . doubtful whether the General Assembly that proclaimed the UN Declaration understood what a human right is," since in the document rights are often stated loosely and in many different modalities, such as "ideals, purposes, or aspirations" rather than just "as rights," and at the same time the Declaration allows considerations of general welfare to limit rights, which seems to undercut their function as protectors of individuals against such rationales (p. 302n). *Contra* Bedau, though, I am suggesting that the General Assembly understood very well what rights are. Rights language is a broad-based moral language with multiple purposes and constituencies: in some contexts a counterweight to the typically self-serving utilitarian rhetoric of the powers that be; in others a provocation to think seriously about even such much-mocked ideas as a right to a paid vacation; and so on.

24. See, for example, Bernard Williams, *Ethics and the Limits of Philosophy* (Cambridge: Harvard University Press, 1985); Walzer's *Spheres of Justice* again; and Karen Warren, "The Power and Promise of Ecofeminism," *Environmental Ethics* 12:2 (Summer 1990): 125–46.

25. Christopher Stone, *Should Trees Have Standing? Toward Legal Rights for Natural Objects* (Los Altos: Wm Kaufmann, 1974). G. E. Varner, in "Do Species Have Standing?" *Environmental Ethics* 9:1 (Spring 1987): 57–72, points out that the creation of new legal rights—as for example in the Endangered Species Act—helps expand what W. D. Lamont calls our "stock of ethical ideas—the mental capital, so to speak, with which [one] begins the business of living." There is no reason that the law must merely reflect "growth" that has already occurred, as opposed to motivating some growth itself.

26. See Chaim Perelman, *The Realm of Rhetoric* (Notre Dame: University of Notre Dame Press, 1982) and Ch. Perelman and L. Olbrechts-Tyteca, *The New Rhetoric* (Notre Dame: University of Notre Dame Press, 1969) for an account of rhetoric that resists the usual Platonic disparagement.

27. Norton, "Conservation and Preservation: A Conceptual Rehabilitation," *Environmental Ethics* 8:3 (Fall, 1986): 195–220; Rodman, "Four Forms of Ecological Consciousness Reconsidered," in Donald Scherer and Thomas Attig, *Ethics and the Environment* (Englewood Cliffs, NJ: Prentice-Hall, 1983): 89–92. Remember also that Leopold insists that ethics are "products of social evolution" and that "nothing so important as an ethic is ever 'written' "—which again suggests that we ought to rethink the usual reading of Leopold as an environmental-ethical theorist with a grand criterion for ethical action.

28. Aldo Leopold, *A Sand County Almanac* (New York: Oxford University Press, 1949), p. 225.

29. J. Baird Callicott, "The Case Against Moral Pluralism," *Environmental Ethics* 12:2 (Summer 1990): 99–124.

30. On "ecosteries," see Alan Drengson, "The Ecostery Foundation of North America: Statement of Philosophy," *The Trumpeter* 7:1 (Winter, 1990), pp. 12–16. On "re-inhabitation" a good starting-point is Peter Berg, "What Is Bioregionalism?," *The Trumpeter* 8:1 (Winter 1991), 6–12.

31. See, for instance, Dave Foreman, "Reinhabitation, Biocentrism, and Self-Defense," *Earth First!*, 1 August 1987; Murray Bookchin,. "Which Way for the US Greens?," *New Politics* 11:2 (Winter 1989); and Bill Devall, "Deep Ecology and Its Critics," *Earth First!*, 22 December 1987.

32. Wendell Berry, "Getting Along with Nature," in *Home Economics* (San Francisco: North Point Press, 1987), p. 13.

33. Gary Snyder, "Good, Wild, Sacred," in *The Practice of the Wild* (San Francisco: North Point Press, 1990); Tom Birch, "Universal Consideration," paper presented for the International Society for Environmental Ethics, American Philosophical Association, 27 December 1990 [subsequently published in as "Moral Considerability and Universal Consideration," in *Environmental Ethics* 15 (Winter 1993): 313–32]; and Jim Cheney, "Ecofeminism and Deep Ecology," *Environmental Ethics* 9:2 (1987): 115–45. Snyder also speaks of "grace" as the primary "practice of the wild"; Doug Peacock, in *The Grizzly Years* (New York: Henry Holt and Company, 1990), insists on "inter-specific tact"; Berry writes of an "etiquette" of nature; and Birch of "generosity of spirit" and "considerateness." All of these terms have their home in a discourse of manners and personal bearing, rather than moral discourse as usually conceived by ethical

philosophers. We are not speaking of some universal categorical obligation, but rather of something much closer to us, bound up with who we are and how we immediately bear ourselves in the world—though not necessarily any more "optional" for all that.

34. Christopher Alexander, et al., *A Pattern Language* (New York: Oxford University Press, 1977). On windows, see sections 239, 159, and 107; on "site repair," section 104; on water in the city, sections 25, 64, and 71; on "accessible green," sections 51 and 60; on "holy ground," sections 24, 66, and 70.

Chapter 3

Self-Validating Reduction

Toward a Theory of Environmental Devaluation

I. Self-Validating Reduction

Let us begin in a familiar place: with the notion of a self-fulfilling prophecy. "Certain expectations," as Thomas Schelling puts it in a classic essay, "are of such a character that they induce the kind of behavior that will cause the expectations to be fulfilled."[1] A respected stock brokerage predicts a strong showing for a certain company's stock: the result is that many buyers buy the stock, creating the very success the brokerage predicted. Rumors of failure can destroy banks: the rumor itself may create a panic that makes the prediction come true. The charms and rituals used by warriors before battle may produce just the confidence and mass excitement that lead to victory. A teacher betrays certain expectations for a student, thus discouraging or encouraging the student and producing the performance that justifies the original expectations.

Something similar happens in ethics. Prejudiced views of other people, for one example, readily become self-fulfilling. Sexist attitudes, for instance, can shape and diminish a woman's response to the man holding them—which then, of course, may seem to confirm those very attitudes. As Marilyn Frye writes:

> one cannot . . . manifest certain kinds of intelligence in inter-
> actions with a person who enters [the conversation] with a
> prior conviction of one's stupidity, lack of insight, absence of

"Self-Validating Reduction: A Theory of the Devaluation of Nature" appeared in *Environmental Ethics* 18 (1996), pp. 115–32. The theme emerged first in *Back to Earth*, chapter 5, and in some of my popular writing such as "Listening to the Earth," *Tikkun* 5 (March/April 1990), pp. 50–54 (reprinted in Michael Lerner, ed., *Tikkun Anthology* [Tikkun Books, 1992]). It is most fully developed in "The Hidden Possibilities of Things," chapter 3 of my *Jobs for Philosophers* (Xlibris, 2004), along with the same book's chapter 4, "Second Comings."

wit; one cannot manifest sensitivity or loyalty in interactions with someone who is distrustful and will not share relevant information . . . [Thus the misogynist] can in one fell swoop avoid seeing the critical central range of a woman's . . . abilities simply by being uncooperative and uncommunicative, and can do it without knowing he has done it by self-deceptively believing he has been cooperative and communicative.[2]

The misogynist never notices. Because his own intelligence and loyalty are, of course, not in question, when the result of an interaction is some kind of failure, the fault *must* lie with the other person. He cannot imagine that he produced it himself. Meanwhile, though, it has indisputably been produced. The promise of certain interactions has not been fulfilled. Therefore the woman, more questionable than he from the start under patriarchy, is indeed constructed as incapable and unintelligent.

It is crucial to see that this process goes far beyond simple blindness on the misogynist's part. Mere blindness can be self-fulfilling too. Some people expect to see only decadence in a certain kind of art, for example, and so they do. The art itself is not changed as a result. Women *are* changed, however, by the kind of misogyny Frye describes. Women begin to feel excluded, unappreciated. They may become more alienated and withdrawn, finding their creative outlets, not surprisingly, lying elsewhere, or their creativity drying up, until in the end they may become genuinely incapable and uncreative at work—and then, probably, out of work. Thus the beliefs of the misogynist become true not merely "for him"—that would be the mere blindness, or the perspectivism, of it—but also genuinely true, true in the world. Women are changed. Women's incapacity becomes *real*. The misogynist is only blind to his role in creating it.

Racism works in analogous ways. Frederick Douglass, campaigning against slavery in 1854, argued:

Ignorance and depravity, and the inability to arise from degradation to civilization and respectability, are the most usual allegations against the oppressed. The evils most fostered by slavery and oppression are precisely those which slaveholders and oppressors would transfer from their system to the inherent character of their victims. Thus the very crimes of slavery become slavery's best defense. By making the enslaved a character fit only for slavery, they excuse themselves for failing to make the slave a freeman.[3]

Again, it is not merely that racism blinded the slaveholder. Racism was not simply an expectation so dear to the slaveholder that he could see in a black person nothing but a slave, regardless of what the person really was. Rather, when effectively practiced, slavery deadened the slaves with work, denied them any education, and ferociously punished any independence of mind. In short, it functioned to *reduce* many slaves *to*—as Douglass put it—"characters fit only for slavery." People were deeply and fundamentally changed. As in Frye's example, the affected person's alleged incapacity became real. It is in this sense that "the very crimes of slavery become slavery's best defense." The slaveholder was only blind to his own role in perpetrating them.

At work here is a specific kind of self-fulfilling prophecy: a self-fulfilling prophecy in which one of the main effects of the "prophecy" is to *reduce* someone (or, as we shall later see, something) in the world—to make that person or thing less than they or it are or could be, to diminish some part of the world's richness and depth and promise—and in which this reduction in turn feeds back not only to justify the original "prophecy" but also to perpetuate it.[4] This reducing kind of "prophecy" or prejudice I propose to call *disvaluing*. The actual reduction—the real-world destruction, defacement, devastation—I propose to call *devaluing*. In these terms, then, what I am describing is a process in which *dis*valuing someone or something also *de*values the disvalued persons or things themselves, directly and/or indirectly, and in such a way that this devaluation comes to justify the initial disvaluation, and therefore to perpetuate the cycle. The cycle as a whole I propose to call *self-validating reduction*.

I cannot stress enough that self-validating reduction is a cycle. Disvaluing and devaluing intertwine and depend upon each other. It is not as though, in some hitherto unaffected world, a prejudice or "prophecy" somehow enters, which only later has specific and discernible effects, after which the story is over. No: the disvaluation already reflects a reduced reality; and the resulting devaluation naturally leads to more disvaluation. Both disvaluation and devaluation are gifts that keep on giving.

In this sense, self-validating reduction is a feedback loop, and here a slightly more technical vocabulary is available. Cyberneticists distinguish two kinds of feedback loops. In *negative* feedback loops, the system works to dampen any new stimulus and re-equilibrate the system. The classic example is a thermostat. A drop in temperature turns on the heat; a rise in temperature turns off the heat. In *positive* feedback loops, the system works to augment and reinforce any new stimulus, further disequilibrating the system. Despite the positive associations of the word "positive," positive-feedback systems are the more troublesome and tricky ones. This is why few mechanical systems are built for positive feedback: the best examples are systems that self-destruct. Atomic bombs, for instance: the widening chain reaction is a positive feedback loop. An analogue in human affairs is the all-too-familiar transformation of certain neighborhoods. As Schelling describes it: "certain old residential areas are deteriorating; they are deteriorating because the people who keep their homes attractive are leaving; they are leaving because the neighborhood is deteriorating because people like them are leaving because the neighborhood is deteriorating . . ."[5] Neither atomic reactions nor the deterioration of neighborhoods are unstoppable (up to a point), of course, but there certainly can be a strong and self-reinforcing downward spiral.

Self-validating reduction is a positive feedback system. Both poles of the cycle augment and reinforce the other. A small "reduction" of another person or class of people—say, the exclusion of some discriminated-against class of persons from certain activities or places—disempowers or isolates them to the point that further exclusions and reductions become natural. Then the original disvaluation—the prejudice, the slander—becomes easier to sustain. Counterevidence is harder to come by, and people are progressively blinded to what remains. Then exclusion and reduction only deepen and worsen, until the combination of desperation and anger on the part of the discriminated-against class and distance and fear on the other side makes the situation volatile, undiscussable, and in the end lethal.[6]

For a less dramatic example, think of the rise of competition and selfishness as a mode of human relationship. This also seems to be a self-validating cycle. Each betrayal of deeper communal ties causes individuals to withdraw into their selves and reduce their own communal instincts a little further—and each such withdrawal makes it more natural for other people to reduce *their* communality a little further. And so it goes. In the end it may actually become true that "everyone is selfish"—not because "that's human nature," but because, sometimes, we make it so.

Self-validating reduction may also be deliberately planned. Bruno Bettleheim argues that the Nazi concentration camps were designed to *make* the inmates subhuman, thus confirming the Nazis' prejudices and making systematic murder possible.[7] Starved, terrorized, stripped of everything that marked them as individuals in the outside world, and set against each other, the inmates no longer seemed human to the guards, and then anything was possible. Here the reduction was deliberate, carefully planned, in the expectation that once in place it would perpetuate itself. That is also a measure of the depth of the Nazi evil—though, again, we also need to remember that many of the same processes and same results are possible without any master plan at all. We can fall into self-validating reduction almost by accident, and by the time we notice, the task of resistance and reversal may well be enormous.

II. Other Animals

There is much more to say about self-validating reduction on the human side. Indeed I think that further exploration of self-validating reduction is a crucial task for ethics generally. My chief concern in this chapter, however, is with the transhuman: with the self-validating reduction of other animals and the land. I also suspect that even if our primary interest were with the human realm, self-validating reduction is easier to recognize when we ourselves are not directly at stake. In any case, a turn to the transhuman is now essential. Let us consider first the case of other animals.

We know that factory farms "reduce" the animals made to live in them. For one thing, the very confinement of the animals makes their natural development impossible. Confinement also usually pushes the animals past the point at which their social instincts can offer them emotional and social equilibrium. Caged chickens are cut off from any social relations whatsoever, while others, raised one hundred thousand to a giant shed, are "debeaked" (have their beaks cut off) so that they cannot peck each other to death in their fury and confusion.[8] All "stock" are bred for maximum weight gain. Pigs are often so bloated that they cannot even copulate without human help, and since, not surprisingly, this tends to spoil their mood, artificial insemination is coming into vogue.[9] There are already chickens who gain weight so fast that they cannot walk, and deformities and unexplained deaths abound. Research veterinarians argue that chickens already "have been bred to grow so fast that they are on the verge of structural collapse"[10]—while genetic engineers speak with enthusiasm about soon breeding chickens that have no heads at all.[11]

These facts no longer come as a surprise. Their peculiar outrageousness, however, and perhaps their moral force as well, has yet to be fully felt. I think that it may help to view them in terms of the self-validating cycles I have been describing.

The general process is this. Certain animals are reduced, partly on account of our own prejudices and needs, to the barest shadows of what they might be and once were. After all, they are "just animals," and besides we need them for food. In this way they are, in the terms proposed above, "devalued." Then we look at their present condition—the condition we have made, but a responsibility that at the moment we conveniently forget—and we can only say "See? They really *are* stupid, dirty, dysfunctional, pitiful." Reduction, once carried out, justifies itself. Treating these animals as if they were no more than raw material for our needs comes to seem, after the fact, perfectly justified. And then they are even more deformed and instrumentalized, even more under-developed, so even more drastic and complete kinds of exploitation become conceivable. We end up precisely with headless chickens. The circle closes completely: they are disvalued and then devalued; devalued and then disvalued.

Notice also how marginal and "sentimental" any attempt to speak for such animals then is made to seem. Headless chickens, or dogs bred for viciousness, are not going to be plausible candidates for animal rights. The insistently reduced animals of all sorts in our present factory farms are seldom considered at all by philosophers and activists speaking for wild animals. That is the beauty, so to speak, of self-validating reduc-tion. Once confinement, radical under- or overstimulation, and breeding have done their work, nearly everyone thinks that the stupid, psychotic, sickly, slothful, or vicious results are in fact what those animals are really like. Chickens, for instance, live about seven years naturally; the typical battery broiler lives seven *weeks*.[12] The result is that infantile animals are all we know. And in general, the better we know such creatures, the worse for them. Only the people who do *not* know them are left to raise their voices against the reduction—and then of course their ignorance can be held against them.

To speak for such insistently reduced animals in this way *is* inevitably "sentimental" ("romantic," "nostalgic"). Still, we have no alternative. Indeed, precisely that is the outrage. Reduction has proceeded so far that we have so lost sight of what it was that this reduction reduced: we have so thoroughly invested in the reduction of animals to meat even when alive that now the deeper and fuller possibilities of those creatures can only be invoked indirectly and "nostalgically." To recognize that fact is at least a first step in the other direction.

For quite a different kind of example, consider some seemingly sympathetic animal research. Jim Nollman writes of visiting an etho-logical research station in the rain forest at which howler monkeys are being studied. Nollman is informed that the monkeys are fundamentally unsociable, retreating to the forest canopy whenever humans are around. This is an objective behavioral description: that in fact is what they do. On further inquiry, however, Nollman learns that the zoologists study the monkeys by attaching radio transmitters to their necks. To attach the transmitters they tranquilize the monkeys. To tranquilize the monkeys they shoot them with tranquilizer guns, which causes them to drop out of the canopy a hundred feet or more to the forest floor.[13]

The zoologists consider this technique unproblematic, "objective," purely scientific, and they treat Nollman, a musician who tries to use music to create a shared space between humans and animals, as a sentimental and unscientific meddler. Surely, though, what looks like a genuine discovery about the monkeys' sociability is more likely a distortion imposed on them by the almost unbelievably antisocial strategy of the researchers themselves. Any creature with a modicum of intelligence would stay away from them. The scientists' "objectivity" only succeeds in reducing the monkeys to unsociable animals, which can then be reported as fact.

The monkeys are emphatically *not* approached as co-inhabitants of the world, or as in any sense kin. They are treated as objects from the start, and thus to objects they are quickly reduced. It seems unlikely that these researchers ever asked themselves how *they* would feel being shot out of the trees like these monkeys, or how they would react if, like two elephants in a recent UCLA study, they were given near-lethal doses of LSD daily for two months.[14] So the only socially sensitive behavior left to the monkeys is to act socially insensitive: to leave. The drugged elephants finally charged the researcher (who, of course, labelled this behavior "inappropriate"). Thus, just as the misogynist's misogyny ultimately not only disvalues but *de*values women, so these scientists' "objectivity" ultimately not only refuses the very connection to animals it allegedly seeks, but also finally undercuts and destroys its very possibility. The animals, reduced to distance and insensitivity, appear distant and insensitive, and maybe also dangerous. Their reduction becomes, precisely, self-validating.

Other wild animals are reduced in similarly self-validating ways. Animals that were originally indifferent or even friendly to humans can be and have been *made* hostile and "aggressive." For example, habitat destruction pushes wolves and bears into competition with humans. Hunting, naturally, creates fear and anger. Even polar bears apparently coexisted easily with aboriginal peoples and were not hostile to the first whites in the Arctic.[15] Likewise, whalers called gray whales the "devilfish" because those whales had the gall to try to kill the humans who were trying to kill them—which then, of course, made their slaughter seem all the more justified.[16] They really *were* devilish. In such ways we *make* other animals monsters, we create their hostility—and then take their hostility, now an indisputable fact about the world, to confirm our own.

Cause and effect are reversed, and our own contribution to the sorry outcome is obscured and ignored.

The classic source on "making monsters" is Mary Wollstonecraft Shelley's *Frankenstein*. We suppose, normally, that the true "making" of that monster was Victor Frankenstein's original assembly and animation of the Creature. If we reread the novel with the cycle of self-validating reduction in mind, however, a very different picture emerges. The Creature is truly made a monster not in the original act of creation, but rather by the reception he then received, first from Frankenstein himself and then from other humans. Abandoned at the very moment he comes to consciousness, driven away, hunted down, he finally *becomes* a monster. Making the Creature was not at all the same act as making the Creature a monster. Yet, strikingly, *this* reading of *Frankenstein*, in which a deeply sensitive creature is slowly reduced to monstrosity by incomprehension and insensitivity (and even then retains a moral sense: note that the Creature's vengefulness never touches anyone unconnected with his creator), is barely hinted at in the vast literature and iconography of Frankenstein, including the classic movie. Perhaps self-validating reduction is still too unfamiliar. Or perhaps it is all too familiar, and we do not want to be reminded.

The United States Navy allegedly tried to train dolphins—whose goodwill toward humans is legendary, who played with Greek children in antiquity[17] and according to my students still do—to kill "enemy" divers and swimmers. Did anyone pause to think what would have happened had such behaviors caught on among the highly social dolphins? Perhaps the making of Frankensteins goes on. Barry Lopez cites Nunamiut hunters speculating about the evolution of new behaviors among wolves, and concludes: "If social animals evolve, then what you learn today may not apply tomorrow. . . . In striving to create a generalized static animal you have lost the real, dynamic animal."[18] Such social animals may evolve new social forms, just as we do. Perhaps lethal ones, as the dolphins might have done, or, again, perhaps just less complex and intelligent ones, more suited to the humanized environments within which these animals willy-nilly find themselves. Either way, the result is a genuine loss of probably irrecoverable possibilities. Here too, then, we devalue other animals, reducing them to the mere "animals," vicious, stupid, or slavish, that we began by imagining they were.

III. The Land

We come next to the self-validating reduction of natural places and the land. Here too, in a sense, familiar facts are invoked, but once again, crucially, the kind of trap they create, the cycle of devaluation they perpetuate, has remained invisible and unappreciated.

In one version of the Ten Commandments, Israel is commanded to "tear down the [pagan] altars, break their images, cut down their groves."[19] Sacredness, on the new, monotheistic, transcendental view, did not dwell in this world. God is separate, the real life of the spirit is elsewhere. Therefore, precisely in order to make this radically new and radically separate sense of sacredness plausible, the sacred spots in this world had to be destroyed. In our terms: the new transcendentalism's *dis*valuation of what Christians derisively called "this" world had to be made plausible by the deliberate destruction—the *de*valuation—of the numinous places that did in fact exist in the ancient world. Paul Shepard calls this "the evangelical desacralizing of place." Christianity carried the same reduction well into medieval times; James Watt, perhaps, into the present. Spirit is *made* to flee this world, and then the transcendent realm is the only place it can go. The original denial of sacredness to this world becomes self-fulfilling. This world is reduced to "this" world.

Remember too that Christianity's world-disvaluation itself arose in a region that had in many ways been degraded already. Again, the process is cyclical. Long before the birth of Jesus, the great juniper forests of Persia were gone, the cedars of Lebanon were going, and the Tigris and Euphrates Rivers, having nourished the cradles of civilization, were carrying massive silt loads from failed irrigation projects. The hills of the entire Mediterranean region were stripped and eroded. Homer's Odysseus got his scar from a boar that surprised him while hunting on Mount Parnassus. The woods were so thick that he got too close. By the Golden Age, Parnassus was, as it is is now, nothing but rock: no trees, no boar, nothing. The Greeks needed the trees for their navies. The newly exposed topsoil ran down to the sea, where it created the marshes that sustained the mosquitoes that sustained the malaria that plagued the ancient world. In short, even by the time of Jesus, the reduction of the Mediterranean region was already an accomplished fact. The world—the actual physical world, the health of the land—already was in decline. Christianity both expressed that sense of decline and contributed to it, speeding up its tempo and eventually exporting it to ecologically richer and more innocent places.[20]

As we all know, similar cycles of disvaluation and devaluation continue, on a massive scale, right now. Some kinds of environmentalism attempt to recover a sense of the land as somehow sacred, or at least, in Leopoldian terms, as a kind of community of which humans are only a part, "plain biotic citizens." Both notions are opposed to the commercial, anthropocentric view of land as essentially a subdividable and consumable commodity. Yet the commercial, anthropocentric view

is hardly just a "view." In most places it is *true*. The land has been
divided and consumed in accord with it. And I mean that it is "true"
quite literally, just as it may have been true quite literally that the inmates
of concentration camps were reduced to something less than human.
It is not just that the land *seems* dead. The reduction is real. The land
is dead, for example when a parking lot replaces a woodland. Or it is
radically degraded, as when chemical-intensive monocultures replace the
old mixed-community farms in which weeds were tolerated and insect
pests kept within ecological limits (and fed on the weeds) or when it is
laid out, mile after square mile, in an unvarying grid pattern, nearly all
vegetation gone except at the edges of roads, the rest plowed under and
planted in the same crop. So much of the land is now boring, simple,
homogenous, "all the same"—so we have *made* it.

Technological forms of devaluation also remake the land. The
demand for progressively faster speeds produces a demand for progressively more massive rearrangement of the land to suit the needs of
automobiles. Little one-lane, hedgerow-lined roads, like those of the
English countryside, often worn well below the surface and consequently
nearly invisible and inaudible until you practically fall into them, are
replaced by larger and larger roads until we have eight-lane superhigh-
ways whose noise and visual presence dominate whole valleys. Along the
Connecticut secondary roads I used to drive, "developers" are taking
bulldozers to whole hillsides, rearranging them to suit someone's idea
of what a hillside should look like, and to suit the structural needs of
the enormous houses that follow, and the needs of the cars that come
with them. The land becomes no more than a setting for suburbia and
its automotive needs.

Noise remakes the land. Even in the wilderness you seldom can
go very long without hearing engines. The human world insistently
reintroduces itself: rarely can we feel, even for a moment, the sheer *difference* of the wild. But then it is a perfectly natural reaction to wonder
what is so special or different about wilderness. In much the same way,
light remakes the land. Much of our countryside is being turned into
an extended dimly lit suburb. All of the neighboring farms back in the
Wisconsin countryside where I grew up (twenty-odd miles from Leopold's
shack) now have bright outdoor fluorescents. Here the "reduction" of
the sense-world is staggering: it is, as it were, immediately cut in half.
Few teenagers now can go out, as I could, to watch the Milky Way and
the Northern Lights. The wilder animals who depend on the dark for
cover or adaptation die, or move. Air pollution is reducing the acuity
of daytime vision too. Visibility in the eastern United States has been
reduced by an astonishing 80 percent, from ninety miles to fifteen, even

in the countryside.[21] What we are creating, then, is a world of dim sights and dim lights; once again a world that is progressively less interesting, less rich and deep, less engaging, and therefore less deserving of protection from further devaluation. The cycle continues. The land is devalued, disvalued, then devalued again.

There is, finally, the most modern form of world-reduction: what the French philosopher Jean Baudrillard and other critics call "simulation."[22] Here the land is not obviously destroyed outright, but is, instead, turned into a kind of surface facsimile of some preexisting, media-generated image of "nature," while its real depth is eradicated precisely in order to ensure that the simulacra meet our expectations: a pleasant consumer experience.

In Grand Teton National Park, reports Jack Turner,

> 93% of the visitors never visit the backcountry. If visitors do make other stops, it is at designated picturesque "scenes" or educational exhibits presenting interesting facts—the names of peaks, a bit of history—or, very occasionally, for passive recreation, a ride in a boat or an organized nature walk. . . .[23]

The effect is to reduce the land to scenery. Albert Borgmann, writing of what he calls "the widespread and easy acceptance of equivalence between commodities and things even when the experiential differences are palpable," goes on:

> People who have traveled through Glacier Park in an airconditioned motor home, listening to soft background music and having a cup of coffee, would probably answer affirmatively when asked if they knew the park, had been in the park, or had been through the park. Such people have not felt the wind of the mountains, have not smelled the pines, have not heard the red-tailed hawk, have not sensed the slopes in their legs and lungs, have not experienced the cycle of day and night in the wilderness. . . .[24]

Of the motor home visit, Borgmann complains: "The experience has not been richer than one gained from a well-made film viewed in suburban Chicago." That, however, is precisely the point. The video kind of experience is all that we are now offered as "knowing nature." Nothing else would be either expected, or welcome, or even assimilable.

Nature, in short, is reduced to what the logging companies call a "beauty strip": like the thin strip of trees separating a road from a clear-cut. Unless they look carefully—or actually stop, God forbid, and walk back through the trees—drivers will never know that most of the forest has been devastated. The beauty strip is only a simulacrum of a forest, but we no longer know (and, more frightening, perhaps no longer care about) the difference. Veiled in this ignorance, what is left of real nature can be ever more readily reduced *to* a beauty strip. Only a weak constituency will organize and act against clear-cutting or strip-mining out of view of the main roads.

These days the sacred groves are not cut. Instead they are turned into another tourist attraction, with the usual resource extraction continuing just barely out of sight. In case this seems like merely another alarmist fantasy, consider the following recent news report. Egypt has been planning a tourist hotel and casino on top of Mount Sinai, including a lighted walkway to the spot where Moses met God.[25] So now the tourist class will be able to "experience" the site of one of humankind's most profound religious experiences, then stroll back to the Marriott for an evening of blackjack and maybe shrimp scampi. The Greek Orthodox monastary at the foot of Sinai, cradling the skulls of fourteen centuries of its dead monks in its charnel house, and sheltering what tradition says was the Burning Bush, an olive tree that has been putting out fresh green shoots for three thousand years, may be overrun and destroyed. Or perhaps the Egyptian government could charge admission? Unemployed ex-nomads could be hired to impersonate the monks. A plastic olive tree would take less tending. In any case, yet another numinous spot will be gone, and once again we will hardly know the difference. When everything is reduced to a commodity, the commodification of the world seems only natural. Nothing else even seems understandable. In this way, once again, even the most spectacular reduction can not only validate itself but finally even seems perfectly unremarkable. After all, Egypt needs the money. . . .

IV. Anthropocentrism as a Self-Validating System

Next I want to examine the extent to which all of these individual processes of reduction also reinforce and validate each other. That is, I suspect that self-validating reduction has a systematic aspect too. It has, as it were, a threshold level, after which every reduction of nature has the effect of augmenting and reinforcing all the others. After the threshold level has been reached, instead of speaking in the plural—self-validating reductions—we would speak more accurately in the singular. It becomes one process rather than many.

For example, we no longer draw much distinction between different kinds of animals when we speak derogatively about them. The concept "animal" is now used both to cover *all* other creatures—conveniently leaving ourselves out, as usual, of course—and to convey a general dismissal and distance. Once so many of the animals we see are reduced to pets, meat, or roadkill (we ignore the few that aren't, like the birds all around us), it becomes difficult and finally impossible to see animals—*any* animals—in any way other than as instruments for our use and pleasure. They are progressively reduced to infantile, simple, totally dependent creatures. Paul Shepard sketches the image of animal life that sets in once domestication passes a certain threshold: "Life is inevitably physical deformity and limitation, mindless frolic and alarms, bluntness, following and being herded, being fertile when called upon. . . ."[26] The final effect of all of the various forms of human reconstruction of animal nature is that there are almost no other models of animals around. In this way our civilization-long project of domesticating all other life-forms may finally be close to validating itself.

Something parallel can be said about the land—all land, land as such. Here too domestication has proceeded so far that very few of us ever experience the wildness or otherness or mystery of the land. "Land" becomes just what goes by as we drive the freeway, and increasingly even what we drive by are just shopping centers and suburbs. So then why *wouldn't* it seem a perfectly natural place for more shopping centers and suburbs? It is hard to imagine any other uses for the land, or modes of inhabitation that are not "uses" at all, even for those people who recognize that more suburbs and malls are not a good idea. Even the reasons we usually give against more suburbs or "malling" are economic or agricultural: in short, anthropocentric. Once again, then, we have a kind of self-validating reduction, but once again also a kind of reduction that is sweeping and systematic. After a certain threshold, long ago passed for most of us, the reduction of the land affects not just particular pieces of land but *all* land. The land has been so thoroughly anthropocen*trized*—made over to suit our needs and purposes—that even our resistance to the most fashionable forms of anthropocentrization still is reduced to anthropocentric appeals.

A certain degree of reduction becomes self-validating even for those of us who think we are attuned to the larger living world, because even in the realm of imagination, domestication has succeeded in removing any real alternatives to itself. It is sobering to remember that for a long time even Aldo Leopold, working as a forester and conservationist in the New Mexico deserts, took himself to be defending pristine wilderness. It was not until a trip to Mexico in 1930 that he came to recognize that his New Mexican lands were in fact already radically reduced—in his later words, already "sick land."[27] Prior to that trip, without a comparison, "sick land" was his only model of health. There was no way to tell that it was "sick." The question is: Where can today's Leopolds go for such a reality check? Possibly the answer is: nowhere at all. Critical distance takes *actual* distance, but today even our wildernesses are so thoroughly anthropocentrized—by noise, light, visitors, acid rain, climate changes, and even, as Tom Birch argues, by the political act of their "incarceration" itself[28]—that little or no distance is really possible. In short, today's reduction reaches deep into our *imagination*.

Let me conclude with one more and perhaps simpler example. Leopold speaks of the land as a living community. To the extent that we begin to feel this, we also recognize ever more forcibly how much of that living community has been destroyed. Other parts do still remain. Still, the very possibility of destruction—the contemporary scope of destruction—irrevocably changes our relation even to those fragments of relatively untouched land that remain. It becomes something else: *so far* untouched land. Nothing is safe. Once I know that any such land might be destroyed, I can no longer commit myself to it wholeheartedly. One of my consolations for the past several years has been to run or walk or just meditate in a forested tract in the very heart of the Research Triangle: a state park adjacent to North Carolina State University forestland. As I write, the state Department of Transportation is pushing hard to put a four-lane road right between the two areas. Even if the road is stopped this year, my overall feeling in that area now is one of greater distance, and pain too: it all seems to me to exist in so uncertain and temporary a state. Perhaps I am unwilling to expose myself more fully to the pain. Even to know that the preservation of a certain region or forest may depend on our action, my letter-writing or your persuasiveness at certain public meetings, undercuts a more open-ended and reciprocal relation. The more-than-human comes to depend on us. Thus, again, even specific reductions of natural places, multiplied many times over, have effects beyond themselves. Destruction on any significant scale puts *all* of nature under the sign of contingency.

V. Some Implications for Environmental Ethics

I have argued that self-validating reduction underlies the crisis that environmental ethics aims to address. If I am right, we need to ask what difference an understanding of self-validating reduction might make in environmental ethics. Are we pointed toward sharply different approaches? I think we are. I want in the briefest way to sketch a new picture here.

Precisely because environmental ethics hopes to respond to the current disvaluation and devaluation of nature, an account of the *origins* of these phenomena is crucial to the self-location of our discipline. What is at stake is a kind of disvaluation that we consider a profound kind of mistake: a pathology, a dysfunction. Like good doctors, who do not venture to treat a disease without some understanding of its origins, we too need to know how the pathology or dysfunction with which we are concerned arose. Only then do we know what response, and more fundamentally what *kind* of response, the devaluation of nature actually calls for.

Approached with this kind of question in mind, the theory of self-validating reduction has radical implications. For one thing, it implies that the "environmental crisis" is not fundamentally the result of some error in reasoning, which incisive philosophical argument could somehow put right. Instead it is a slow (sometimes not so slow) downward spiral, a reduction in fact as well as in thought, in which our ideas are as much influenced by the state of the world as vice versa,[29] and—crucially—each stage is impeccably rational. Broiler chickens are not plausible candidates for animal rights; twice-logged kudzu-clogged woods are not plausible candidates for intrinsic value; Mount Sinai with a casino is no longer numinous; and so on.[30] Each new devaluation validates the next disvaluation, and vice versa.

From this perspective it is no surprise that philosophical arguments in environmental ethics have failed to gain much of a grip outside (and barely even inside) the philosophical community. This too is a symptom of the pathology. There is no denying that we live in a devalued world. We are called, I think, to a different kind of engagement and critique. As Part II of this paper points out, any voice raised in objection to the prevailing reductions necessarily will be "unrealistic" to the extent that the prevailing reductions are self-validating. So let us embrace unrealism. We *do* speak for realities and possibilities that are systematically being driven into the ground, or destroyed outright. We *are* deliberately stepping out of the cycle of dis- and devaluation. Looked at from the perspective of the account offered here, breaking out of that cycle is part of the very point of ethics. "Unrealism"—in this sense—is not somehow an objection to ethics, but rather part of ethics' very calling.

In this way, then, understanding the dynamics of self-validating reduction uncovers the pathology of the present in a practical and useful way—it insists that our job is to break the cycle, a process with two sides and not just one—while at the same time it also uncovers the peculiar necessity of our own task as ethical philosophers. All of us who teach ethics know that there are many times when the voice of ethics seems to be unrealistic. Even to ourselves, and especially to our students, we sound sentimental, romantic, softheaded, and utopian. My current suggestion is that we *should*. We speak for what the world might be, perhaps for what it once was—not necessarily for what it is right now.

Our epistemological position is correspondingly different too. If ethics is in some ways necessarily "unrealistic"—if the peculiar calling of ethics is to refuse the narrowly circumscribed options offered to us by a social system hell-bent on reduction—then ethics is necessarily open-ended. It is not as though ethical imperatives can be "read off" the world if we only could figure out where to look. Once and for all we might lay to rest the idea that ethical imperatives ultimately rest on some kind of objective and timeless "fact," like intrinsic values or essences and all their cousins. The world, the very "facts," are constantly being reconstructed right under our feet—and now, in particular, the world is being devalued all around us. Our attention ought to be directed toward re-valuational *possibilities*, toward overlooked openings, toward the manifold hidden possibilities of things. We object to the reduction and destruction precisely of that open-endedness and diversity.

Objectivism has been much argued over in environmental ethics as well as in ethics generally. Perhaps a different way of putting things would be helpful. Classical empiricism, we now believe, is too passive in its relation to the world. Modern empiricism, modeled on science, insists that to understand the world it is necessary to try things, to pose questions: to experiment. Certainly classical empiricism is too passive in a world of self-validating reduction. Again, one cannot "read" the possibilities of things "off the world" when so much energy is being devoted to destroying those very possibilities. The "facts" are up for grabs, and we are losing. Instead, the very idea of "experimenting" must become more radical. We must begin to try to *draw out* the hidden possibilities of things. That is the kind of "experiment" we need. Experiment in relationship is not a notion we are yet well-equipped to understand—the experimental method as science now knows it is crippled by a enthusiastically reductivist methodology—but nonetheless, that more radical kind of experiment is what is now asked of us.

Ethics so conceived, finally, becomes as much a form of *action* as a form of analysis. The hidden possibilities of things cannot be discerned a priori. How might we relate to other animals if they were not being mass-produced for our consumption all around us? How might a parking lot regrow into woods or prairie, recapitulating ecological succession with its cement cover broken to bits and slowly returning to soil? What might we learn from whales or condors or jumping spiders if we sought out their media for "communication" (like music, for whales and dolphins, as musicians like Nollman are attempting to do)? In advance, there is not much to say. There is no way to answer. Critique is essentially limited to showing how any possibilities that other animals or the land *might* have are being systematically closed off. To discover what possibilities they *do* have we must try to bring them out. We must actually try to make music with whales. Or we must break up the concrete and wait a few hundred years to see what happens. We must experiment in a dozen ways at once.

Self-validating reduction has a dialectical opposite: we might call it *self-validating invitation*, or maybe *self-fulfilling inclusion*. To trust someone who is unsure of her own trustworthiness is a way to make her feel more trustworthy, and hence makes it possible for her to become more trustworthy. We have to *offer* trust: that is the "invitation." We invite others to deserve it. Parents' love creates a kind of safety and support that makes the blossoming of a child possible, just as the lack of that love becomes its own self-fulfilling disaster. When adults fall in love, each responds, in part, to a vision of the loved one's possibilities, possibilities that (perhaps) no one else could see who was not a lover: and it also helps to bring those possibilities into actuality. That is why what we do with love is to "fall" into it: it is an open-ended and unpredictable cycle.

In just the same way, then, Nollman's monkeys, tranquilized and radio-tagged and reduced to shadowy movements on observers' graphs on the "objective" view, became companions and co-musicians when Nollman invited them to join him playing the flute beneath their trees. Nollman, though, had to go out on that limb first. Whole pods of gray whales have learned from a single whale to like human petting: these are the same whales formerly known as "devilfish," after their habit of attacking whaleboats. Offer hostility and create it in turn. Offer interaction, and wild possibilities open up. To create such spaces, to conceive ourselves not only as respectful co-inhabitants or good biotic citizens, but as potential co-constitutors and co-creators of this world: that is the real work in these times of uncertainty and origination.

Notes

1. Thomas Schelling, "Thermostats, Lemons, and Other Families of Models," in *Micromotives and Macrobehavior* (New York: W. W. Norton and Company, 1978), p. 115.

2. Marilyn Frye, "Male Chauvinism—A Conceptual Analysis," in Mary Vetterling-Braggin, ed., *Sexist Language: A Modern Philosophical Analysis* (Totowa, NJ: Littlefield, Adams, 1981), p. 17–18.

3. Frederick Douglass, "The Claims of the Negro Ethnologically Considered," in *The Frederick Douglass Papers*, Series One, vol. 2 (New Haven: Yale University Press, 1982), p. 507. There are all too many examples. A North Carolina Native American historian once told me that the practice of scalping was probably introduced by Europeans, after they began to put bounties on Indian heads: the scalp was easier to take than the whole head. In time, however, the Indians started scalping too, and it came to figure in the horror stories about Indians that in turn were used to justify still more bounties, still more extermination. Similarly, white missionaries were horrified by the Indian practice of torturing their captives, and persuaded them to enslave their captives instead. Thus the Indians, at least in the Carolinas, got reputations as slave traders, which again was used against them to great effect. Readers may also remember the poignantly understated scene in the Hollywood movie *The Mission*, in which the Portuguese attempt to justify their enslavement of the Indians on the grounds that, among other things, the Indians kill some of their children, proving that they are no more than animals. Their Jesuit defender counters that the Indians only kill those children that they cannot carry when they have to flee. And the threats they have to flee are primarily the slave traders. In effect, then, the slave traders themselves have reduced the Indians to killing their own children and then use this very behavior as a justification for further enslavement.

4. According to Schelling ("Thermostats, Lemons . . . ," p. 116), the term *self-fulfilling prophecy* originally referred to this kind of cycle. The term has since broadened quite a bit.

5. Ibid., p. 92.

6. Just as self-validating reduction is only one kind of self-fulfilling prophecy, so self-fulfilling prophecy is one instance of a still wider phenomenon of unintended or unexpected collective consequences of individual actions. In this sense, self-validating reduction is a remote cousin to some better-understood game-theoretic phenomena in which certain results can emerge, in Martin Hollis's words, as "the unintended sum of intended consequences." The summative effects are not necessarily bad. Adam Smith's "Invisible Hand" is one example of a positive result: individual egoism is supposed to produce, collectively, the common good. The "Tragedy of the Commons" is an example of a negative result: here individual utility-maximization produces dramatically lower utilities for everyone. (See Martin Hollis, *The Cunning of Reason* [Cambridge: Cambridge University Press, 1987], chapter 4.) All of these cases, however, involve strategic thinking: individual and intentional planning for certain consequences. Self-validating reduction is not at all so strategic or even self-conscious. Closer cousins might be some of the other unexpected downward-spiralling social phenomena Schelling describes in "Thermostats, Lemons, and Other Families of Models." Although game-theoretic analysis is fascinating, it also exemplifies our tendency to focus on the kinds of processes most easily quantified and (perhaps) most commodity-centered and competitive, leaving the larger, vaguer,

and deeper processes still mostly in the dark. Self-validating reduction in the sense discussed here is still, as far as I know, mostly unexplored.

7. Bruno Bettleheim, *The Informed Heart* (New York: Free Press, 1960). Cf R. A. Pois, *National Socialism and the Religion of Nature* (New York: St Martin's Press, 1986), p. 132: "The National Socialists had succeeded in creating that which they knew existed all along. Through degradation, humiliation, torture and total dehumanization they had created the non-human, in fact non-natural Jewish enemy, seemingly incapable of feeling those normal, human emotions that were characteristic of those decent folk engaged in annihilating them."

8. Peter Singer, *Animal Liberation*, 2nd ed. (New York: Avon, 1991), chapter 3.

9. James Serpell, *In the Company of Animals* (Oxford: Basil Blackwell, 1986), pp. 9–10.

10. D. Wise and A. Jennings, "Dyschondroplasia in Domestic Poultry," *Veterinary Record* 91 (1972) 285–86, as cited in Singer, *Animal Liberation*, p. 104.

11. Bill McKibben, *The End of Nature* (New York: Random House, 1989), p. 165.

12. Singer, *Animal Liberation*, pp. 99, 104.

13. Jim Nollman, *Dolphin Dreamtime* (New York: Bantam Books, 1987), pp. 94–97.

14. Singer, *Animal Liberation*, pp. 67–68.

15. Farley Mowat, *Sea of Slaughter* (Boston: Atlantic Monthly Press, 1982), pp. 97–98.

16. Diane Ackerman, *The Moon by Whalelight* (New York: Random House, 1991), p. 117.

17. Charles Doria, "The Dolphin Rider," in Joan McIntyre, ed., *Mind in the Waters* (San Francisco: Sierra Club Books, 1974), p. 38.

18. Barry Lopez, *Of Wolves and Men* (New York: Scribner's, 1978), p. 81.

19. Exod. 34:13–14.

20. J. Donald Hughes, *Ecology in Ancient Civilizations* (Albuquerque: University of New Mexico Press, 1975), pp. 1–2, 61, 68–70, 75–76, 101, 116.

21. William Strauss, "If It's East of the Mississippi, It's Blanketed in Pollution's Haze," *New York Times* 16 July 1990, p. C4.

22. Jean Baudrillard, *Simulations* (New York: Semiotext[e], 1983).

23. Jack Turner, "The Abstract Wild," *Witness* 3, no. 4 (Winter 1989), p. 89.

24. Albert Borgmann, *Technology and the Character of Contemporary Life* (Chicago: University of Chicago Press, 1984), p. 56.

25. Lance Morrow, "Trashing Mount Sinai," *Time*, 19 March 1990, p. 92.

26. Paul Shepard, *Nature and Madness* (San Francisco: Sierra Club Books, 1982), p. 38.

27. Roderick Nash, *Wilderness and the American Mind*, 3rd ed.(New Haven: Yale University Press, 1982), p. 30.

28. Tom Birch, "The Incarceration of Wilderness," *Environmental Ethics* 12 (1990): 3–26.

29. Both points are important. On the one hand, ideas do have consequences. Disvaluation is half of the cycle of self-validating reduction, and its effect is genuine, real-world devaluation. On the other hand, consequences also have ideas, as it were. Devaluation naturally produces more disvaluation. This is the point argued in the text. There is no reason to think that social causation only runs in one direction. Recognizing the cycle of self-validating reduction suggests a more "ecological" model of social processes.

30. Although in note 6 above I claimed that game-theoretic analysis is only remotely applicable to the phenomenon of self-validating reduction, there is a fairly tight parallel here. In situations such as the Prisoner's Dilemma or the "Tragedy of the Commons," each move of each individual actor is entirely rational, at any rate in the economic sense, even though the net (and foreseeable) result is disaster for all. Each farmer who adds a cow, further overgrazing the commons, at least gains that cow's output, marginal though it may be. Farmers who refrain gain nothing and the marginal benefit goes to their competitors. Everyone's sense of urgency is compounded by some farmers' evident willingness to squeeze every last ounce of marginal benefit out of the commons while it lasts. This is why these situations pose such difficulties for ethical argument. So here: once the cycle of self-validating reduction is underway, each step has its rationale. Nature *de*valued to degree x justifies *dis*valuation to degree $x+1$; nature *dis*valued to degree $x+1$ justifies *de*valuation to degree $x+2$; and so on; and the sense that the game is lost may well be created and intensified by the evident direction in which the whole process is going.

Chapter 4

Environmental Ethics as Environmental Etiquette

Toward an Ethics-Based Epistemology in Environmental Philosophy

With Jim Cheney

I. Introduction

Environmental philosophers have long suspected that environmental ethics is much more than the mere extension of general ethical principles and methods to a new applied area. Accordingly, environmental philosophers have been especially intrigued by those ways in which environmental philosophy has progressively called into question substantive and methodological assumptions about ethics itself. That ethics is an affair solely of humans, or even just rational or sentient beings; that standard ethical theories can be stretched to retrofit all new ethical insights; that ethical theories, standard or not, are what we should want at all: each of these assumptions, and more, have been called into question.

It is our view, however, that environmental ethicists have not yet gotten to the bottom of things. We have not yet uncovered the most radical of challenges that environmental philosophy poses to traditional assumptions. Environmental philosophy is most radical, we think, because it calls into question basic assumptions concerning the relationship

"Environmental Ethics as Environmental Etiquette" appeared in *Environmental Ethics* 21 (1999), pp. 115–134. It was reprinted in *Environmental Ethics: Divergence and Convergence*, edited by Susan Armstrong and Richard Botzler (McGraw-Hill, 3rd ed., 2002). A related essay by Jim Cheney is his "The Journey Home," in my collection *An Invitation to Environmental Philosophy* (Oxford University Press, 1999). In my other writing the theme is most fully developed in "The Hidden Possibilities of Things" and "Second Comings," chapters 3 and 4 of my *Jobs for Philosophers* (Xlibris, 2004).

between epistemology and ethics and, hence, basic assumptions concerning ethics itself.

We do mean basic. For example: What if environmental philosophy finally must call into question the seemingly most obvious assumption of all, that the world consists of a collection of more or less given facts to which we must respond, responses that ethics then systematizes and unifies? What if the actual, necessary relation is the other way around? What if the world we inhabit arises most fundamentally out of our ethical practice, rather than vice versa?

II. Two Ethical Epistemologies

Consider, very briefly, four features of the traditional view of the place of epistemology in ethics, what we call an "epistemology-based ethics."[1]

(i) *Ethical action is a response to our knowledge of the world.* Knowledge comes first; then, and only then, practice. Ethical arguments presuppose or articulate some factual situation to which the question is what our appropriate response is to be. That natural ecosystems, for example, may show integrity, stability, or beauty, as a matter of fact, is supposed to be the basis upon which we can "consider" them ethically. That animals feel pain, or are self-conscious, or have expectations that can be violated, is supposed to be the basis upon which they might be attributed rights. Indeed, to speak of a "basis" in this way is only a way of underlining the necessity of some factual appeal, some empirical starting-point. Often an object's or system's alleged possession of "intrinsic value" is itself supposed to be a kind of fact to which ethical action responds. That even the "possession" of value itself is thereby treated as a kind of *fact* illustrates just how taken-for-granted the fact-based model of ethics currently is.

(ii) *The world is readily knowable*—at least to the extent required for ethical response. Ethicists are confident about what it is we need to know in order to determine our ethical responsibilities, and are confident that this knowledge is attainable. We can understand ecosystems; we can know, even with precision, exactly what animals do or do not feel; we can even know what things have a special property called "intrinsic value," even though we cannot begin to cash out that notion ontologically or any other way. Even in cases where the relevant understanding is acknowledged to be far from complete, it is thought that we have enough to go on for ethical decision-making—or else that the very incompleteness of our knowledge is itself a critical fact that determines ethical response. In any case, *we know what we need to know.*

(iii) *Ethics is inherently an incremental and extensionist business.* If ethics is a response to the world, and the world is readily known, then ethics is likely to have a well-established core. Change and expansion are supposed to take place slowly, at the margins, and by extension from the (assumed) well-understood central models. Peter Singer's "expanding circle," for example, is quite explicitly *not* taken to be in any serious flux near its center. The whole idea is that we work out from the "given," from the reliable and established, to the less certain and more speculative. At the margins, of course, we ought to expect some surprises, but the common and given background against which any surprise must emerge is the stable and well-understood familiar world.

Even new experiences at the margins are interpreted and assimilated on the familiar models. Animals have rights, or we have duties to them, or "welfare" must be construed more broadly, or "no compromise" is now a principle to be asserted in a new area, and so on. The basic *patterns* of ethical relationship seem to be taken as "given," even at the margins.

These three assumptions lead in turn to a specific vision of the tasks of ethics:

(iv) *The task of ethics is to sort the world ethically*—that is, to articulate the nature of things in ethical terms. This is why the "considerability" question surfaces so early in the development of environmental ethics. Ethics thinks of itself as addressing the criteria for *mattering* ethically, for "counting," and these criteria are supposed to be articulated in terms of the relevant features of the things that "count." Of course there is room for debate about just what features are relevant, but once again it is usually supposed that this is merely a problem of making careful distinctions. We are already supposed to understand the relevant criteria. People are in, bacteria and rocks are out, and animals might be in or not depending on how much like us, and unlike bacteria or rocks, they are.[2]

All manner of familiar consequences follow from this model. For example, the familiar kind of careful distinction-making and legalistic principle-articulation is already well in view after (iv). A philosophy of language emerges: descriptive rather than expressive and performative functions of language are crucial. An account of ethical failure also follows. It follows directly from (i) that the great pitfalls of ethics—the primary ways in which we fail to be ethical—are inadequacies of *belief,* or have to do with the conformity of action to belief. We may be ignorant of, or blind to, the facts. We may resist acknowledging the facts: we may even, like the vivisectionists, cut animals' vocal cords so we do not have to hear them scream. Or we may acknowledge the facts but fail to act on our knowledge (which is why weakness of will is a topic of such interest in contemporary ethics). Still we remain in the orbit of facts.

Alternative foundational assumptions might be offered, however, which differ from the traditional assumptions *on every point*: an ethics-based epistemology, rather than an epistemology-based ethics.

(i') *Ethical action is first and foremost an attempt to open up possibilities, to enrich the world.* It is not an attempt to respond to the world as *already* known. On the usual view, for example, we must first know what animals are capable of, then decide on that basis whether and how we are to consider them ethically. On the alternative view, we will have no idea what other animals are actually capable of—we will not readily understand them—until we *already* have approached them ethically: that is, until we have offered them the space and time, the occasion, and the acknowledgment necessary to enter into relationship. Ethics must come *first*.

Consider the phenomenon of love in this regard. On a traditional ethical epistemology, love is a difficult, embarrassing, marginal case: love is supposed to be blind, irrational, and "pathological." On an alternative ethical epistemology, however, love is paradigmatic. Love is in fact a way of knowing, but its dynamics are the reverse of the usual models. Love comes first, and opens up possibilities. Without love people may never open up enough to reveal all that they can be. In this sense lovers *do* see what others cannot see—but the *others* are the ones who are blind. And love in this sense is already an ethical relationship. It thus stands at the beginning, at the core, of ethics itself: a venture as well as an adventure: a risk, an attitude that may (*may*—for we cannot say for sure at the beginning) lead in time to more knowledge of someone or something, wholly wild possibilities.

(ii') *Hidden possibilities surround us at all times.* The world is *not* readily knowable. People who were previously dismissed as below notice, even if "respected" in the purely formal sense, might turn out to be quite fantastic companions, lovers, adversaries, or who knows what, if offered the "space," the invitation. Or perhaps they would choose to have nothing to do with us—a state of affairs from which we could also learn. We must *ask* them, however: we must venture something, expose ourselves too; and for any number of reasons the invitation may be declined.

The same goes for other animals and for the larger worlds beyond. There is a vast fund of experience in Midgelyean "mixed communities," for example, in which all manner of animals, from cats, dogs and horses to cormorants, whales, racoons, and bees have shown unexpected powers—while some of them too, no doubt, would rather have nothing to do with us. We are still only beginning to sense the communication going on all around us: whales singing to each other across whole oceans, elephants rumbling in infrasound across the savannahs, bees dancing their comrades to new pollens.[3] Even in the face of the staggering reduction of nature in modern times, wild possibilities abound. We have only begun to consider that all life on Earth might itself function in an integrated, maybe even organism-like way. Who knows what else we will yet discover? The world has barely unfolded for us.

(iii') *Ethics is pluralistic, dissonant, discontinuous*—not incremental and extensionist. If established knowledge and ethical relationships in no way exhaust the possibilities, then ethical *discovery* is always possible, including discoveries that may be unnerving and disruptive. We may discover that even values we thought long-established might have to be rethought and changed. Rather than emphasize the continuities (animal rights, for example, as an extension of human rights, from males to females to historically disadvantaged races and, finally, beyond the human species to, maybe, adult mammals) the alternative notices that each of these revisions also upends the central and supposedly "given" models as well. If barbarians or females or even animals can have rights, then the meaning of rights-holding and our understanding of rights-holders themselves changes. Dissonance abounds.

A sense of familiarity and settledness characterize the tradition. The alternative needs a more uncertain and disruptive metaphor. Maybe this: consider the experience of living in a foreign land. Here it is evident to us that a great deal is going on that is mysterious and perhaps must remain so. Melodies, smells, a certain tilt of the head, the line of the hills or the way the rains start in the afternoons: all of this is more intricate and complex than surface attention would suggest, even right next to us. In foreign lands, a certain bare courtesy is extended both ways, because both we and the natives know we are reaching across a distance. We need to be carefully attentive, always aware that there is much we do not understand, open to discovery and surprise.

This is not merely an analogy, though, but the actual state of things. We do live among different others, every day and all the time. Other humans, even those close to us, see the world their own way, have their own structures of meaning, different from our own. Even the most seemingly established relationships may have to be regularly re-established. And the analogy applies quite precisely to other animals. Recall Henry Beston's famous words:

> In a world older and more complete than ours, they move finished and complete, gifted with extensions of the senses

we have lost or never attained, living by voices we shall never hear. They are not brethren, they are not underlings; they are other nations, caught with ourselves in the net of life, fellow prisoners of the splendor and travail of time.[4]

Other nations: beings with their own structures of meaning, which we conceivably could join or at least move in concert with, but not structures we should expect to fit neatly or smoothly with our own. What is really asked of us is courtesy, openness to surprise.

Finally, the three assumptions just outlined lead in turn to a specific vision of the tasks of ethics:

(iv') *The task of ethics is to explore and enrich the world.* Hidden possibilities surround us: the task of ethics is to call them forth. Rather than sorting relatively fixed-natured things into relatively well-established categories of considerability, thus not just ruling some potential consideranda *in* but also—and quite crucially for the traditional conception of things—ruling a great many potential consideranda *out*, what is asked of us, so far as we can manage it, is an open-ended, nonexclusive consideration of everything. People, bacteria, rocks, animals, everything, so far as we can.

This is what Tom Birch calls *universal consideration*. Birch offers an elegant and (it seems to us) unanswerable argument for its necessity. Since the self-proclaimed concern of ethics is to discover what things in the world demand practical respect, then we must *for that reason alone*, he says, "consider" them in the most fundamental way: by paying close, careful, and persistent attention. So all things must be considerable in this basic and unavoidable sense. Indeed, rather than any new potential considerandum having to meet a burden of proof, universal consideration requires us to reverse the usual burden of proof as we approach others in the world. "Others are now taken as valuable, even though we may not yet know how or why, until they are proved otherwise."[5] And actually, even more deeply, universal consideration requires us not merely to extend this kind of benefit of the doubt but actively to take up the case, so to speak, for beings so far excluded or devalued. And so once again ethics is primary: ethics opens the way to knowledge, epistemology is value-driven, not vice versa.

All manner of consequences follow from this alternative model. Once again, for example, a philosophy of language emerges: Rather than descriptive accuracy, the alternative will draw upon the evocative, expressive, and performative aspects of language. This theme is taken up in the next section. The alternative also has direct implications for the great pitfalls of ethics—the ways in which we fail to be ethical. On our view, these are inadequacies of *etiquette*, failures of *courtesy*. Blind to the possibilities right next to us, we may never know what we are missing, and we may close them down or even destroy them as a result.[6]

III. Ceremonial Worlds

In this section we examine in more detail the relationship between etiquette and epistemology in an ethics- or etiquette-based epistemology. Although we believe that *all* epistemologies are at least implicitly value- or ethics-based, we focus here on examples drawn from Indigenous cultures, since the ethics-based nature of epistemology is most clearly exemplified in them.[7]

Referring to the work of the Canadian Inuit philosopher Gordon Christie, Leroy Meyer, and Tony Ramirez argue that "one ought not to put too much stock in the word 'philosophy' . . . [T]here are alternative ways of intelligently engaging the world. To construe one's thinking in terms of belief is characteristic of a particular kind of world view and it remains to be seen whether those who share an indigenous world view conceive of experience in such an overtly intellectualized manner."[8]

Walter Ong and others have linked the visual metaphor of knowing—as in the term "worldview," as used to refer to a people's fundamental *beliefs* about the world—with the advent of the written word. Whereas "sight presents surfaces," Ong says, "sound reveals interiors" and "signals the present use of power, since sound must be in active production in order to exist at all." In a sound-oriented culture, "the universe [is] something one respond[s] to, as to a voice, not something merely to be inspected."[9] Words on the page no longer reveal interiors, they no longer signal the present use of power. Words are now *objects*; they are inert, in themselves lifeless. They become signs, symbols of something else. Words come to refer primarily to beliefs, systems of thought. Sam Gill reports (as have many others) that nonliterate people are often highly critical of writing. He says of this, however, that he does

> not believe that it is actually writing that is at the core of their criticism. The concern is with certain dimensions of behavior and modes of thought that writing tends to facilitate and encourage. And these dimensions are linked to the critical, semantical, encoding aspects of language. . . . We interpret texts to discern systems of thought and belief, propositional

or historical contents, messages communicated. Put more
generally, we seek the information in the text. We tend to
emphasize code at the expense of behavior, message at the
expense of the performance and usage contexts.[10]

The written word conspires with the visual metaphor to turn the world
into a passive object for human knowledge and to focus our attention
on language as a sign system primarily designed to encode beliefs.

In a number of articles, Sam Gill has attempted to reinstate the
fundamental nature of the *performative* function of language, using
Navajo prayer as a case study. Invariably, when he asks Navajo elders
what prayers *mean*, they tell him "not what messages prayers carry, but
what prayers *do*." Further, "the person of knowledge in Navajo tradition holds that [theology, philosophy, and doctrine] are ordinarily to
be discouraged. Such concerns are commonly understood by Navajos
as evidence that one totally misunderstands the nature of Navajo religious traditions."[11]

Generalizing from his analysis of prayer acts to religious practice
generally, Gill asserts that "the importance of religion as it is practiced
by the great body of religious persons for whom religion is a way of life
[is] a way of creating, discovering, and communicating worlds of meaning
largely through ordinary and common actions and behavior."[12]

We would like to explore the possibility of generalizing even further, arguing that the performative dimension of language be understood
as fundamental—not just in obviously religious settings, but *generally*.
Perhaps then we can understand the full import of Myer and Ramirez's
assertion that there are alternative ways of intelligently engaging the
world, alternatives to construing one's thinking in terms of belief. We
do things with words. Foremost among these performative functions
is the creation of what we call the *ceremonial worlds* within which we
live. Other performative functions of language are possible only within
these ceremonial worlds—promise making, for instance, is possible only
within an accepted set of social conventions, as is the progress achieved
within science.[13]

Take, for example, Diamond Jenness's report of an unnamed
Carrier Indian of the Bulkley River who says: "The white man writes
everything down in a book so that it might not be forgotten; but our
ancestors married the animals, learned their ways, and passed on the
knowledge from one generation to another."[14] His ancestors passed
down the means of creating, or re-creating, the worlds, the ceremonial
worlds, within which they lived—the stories, the ceremonies, the rituals, the daily practices. They passed down modes of action, which when
written down come to be understood as information. Euro-Americans

want to know what beliefs are encoded in the utterances of Indigenous peoples, they want to treat these utterances as mirrors of Indigenous worlds. This, however, may be to ask the wrong question. In fact, these utterances function primarily to *produce* these worlds. Euro-Americans tend to be concerned with ontology, correct descriptions of Indigenous worlds. Many Indigenous people, on the other hand, are concerned with right relationship to those beings that populate their worlds, they are concerned with mindfulness, "respect." It is this suggestion that we wish to explore in greater depth here.

N. Scott Momaday, in justly famous words, says: "It seems to me that in a sense we are all made of words; that our most essential being consists in language. It is the element in which we think and dream and act, in which we live our daily lives. There is no way in which we can exist apart from the morality of a verbal dimension."[15] Momaday is speaking not of sets of *beliefs* by which people constitute themselves, but more fundamentally of performance, enactment, the bringing into being of one's identity by means of action and practice, primarily *verbal*. It is the difference, for example, between the sacred as *object* of knowledge or belief (and, derivatively, of acts of faith and adoration) and sacramental *practice*—a matter of comportment, which brings into being a world, a ceremonial world, around it.

Ceremonial worlds are not fantasy worlds. We do, of course, experience the world. Experience is taken up into ceremonial worlds. It is part of the self-correcting feedback loop that makes it possible for the day-to-day activities of food gathering, child rearing, shelter building, and so on to take place, to succeed, not only on the terms set by the world, but within the context of a richly textured ceremonial world. In such a world, as Paul Shepard has observed, "everyday life [is] inextricable from spiritual significance and encounter," "natural things are not only themselves but a speaking."[16]

If language is performative, and if we have our being and identity fundamentally within ceremonial worlds, then the coherence we should be listening for is not merely the logical coherence of one sentence with another, one belief with another, but something more like the harmonic coherence of one note with another. Practices, including linguistic practices, create ceremonial songs of the world, worlds of meaning, within ecological niches. Within these ceremonial songs of the world language is a mode of *interaction* with the world. As Henry Sharp has put it, "symbols, ideas, and language . . . are not passive ways of perceiving a determined positivist reality but a mode of interaction shared between [humans] and their environment."[17]

Sacramental *practice* is the key—not the *sacred* as understood by ontologists. Ceremonial practice defines the world in which we live and work. The ontology of one's world is a kind of residue from one's ethical practice and the modes of attaining knowledge associated with that practice. This residue is highly prized, and receives intense scrutiny, in Euro-American cultures, but etiquette is the fundamental dimension of our relationship to, and understanding of, the world. Ontology is a kind of picture, or metaphor, of ethical practice.

Moving away from epistemology-based ethics and toward an ethics-based epistemology, we move closer to an older sense of the word *knowledge*: knowledge as intimacy and reciprocity. Contrary to the emphasis some place on the *constructed* nature of the worlds we live in, reflected in the catchphrase "It's words all the way down," we suggest a very different emphasis: It's *world* all the way *up*—even into the language of the ceremonial worlds we have been discussing.

The poet Robert Bringhurst speaks of poetry as "knowing freed from the agenda of possession and control." He understands poetry as "knowing in the sense of stepping in tune with being, hearing and echoing the music and heartbeat of being."[18] A friend says of Indian paintbrush—a plant we know well from the American West—that it "speaks the soil." Its palette, she says, varies with the mineral composition of the soil.[19] Similarly, language is most fundamentally an expression of the world—it "speaks the world." Language is rooted in being, rooted in the world as are we who speak forth that world in our language. And our language is a mode of interaction with, and hence a mode of knowing, that world. Knowing can take shape as a form of domination and control. It can also take shape as a way of "stepping in tune with being."

Though the epistemologies of modernism have detached themselves from the world—treating the nonhuman world and even the human world as objects of domination and control—and though the postmodern view of language and self (the self as solipsistic maker of worlds of words) to a large extent reflects this detachment, we and our languages are fundamentally *of* the world. Before they convey information, before they are assertions with "truth values," our words are a welling up of the world. The more-than-human world[20] bursts forth in multiple songs of the world—human songs in a more-than-human world, songs rooted in, and expressive of, that world. They carry the power and energy of that world.

Ceremonial worlds, then, embody *ethics-based epistemologies.* This is why they have the potential to open up the hidden possibilities of the world, possibilities shut down by epistemologies driven by values of domination and control. Traditional epistemology-based ethics, as we have seen, tend to keep these hidden possibilities hidden, thereby effectively blocking any ethical relationship premised on them. In setting out criteria of moral considerability, contemporary epistemology-based environmental ethics is engaged (even if implicitly) at least as much in domination and control as it is in the liberation of heretofore ethically disenfranchised "citizens" of the land community.[21]

The centrality of the notion of "respect" for nature is pervasive in Indigenous cultures and underscores the rich possibilities inherent in opting for an ethic that opens up the hidden possibilities of the world. To Euro-American ears, "respect" may have overtones of hierarchically structured relationships, or it might have a Kantian flavor of obedience to moral law. But to Indigenous ears it points to an epistemological-ethical complex the central concept of which is *awareness* of all that is, an awareness that is simultaneously epistemological and ethical, as Carol Geddes explained in response to a question concerning the meaning of the Indigenous notion of respect: "I asked a similar question of someone who knows the Tlingit language very well. Apparently it does not have a very precise definition in translation—the way it is used in English. It is more like awareness. It is more like knowledge and that is a very important distinction, because it is not like a moral law, it is more like something that is just a part of your whole awareness."[22]

The pluralistic, dissonant, and discontinuous (vs. incremental and extensionist) nature of such an ethic is also richly exemplified by Indigenous cultures. Indigenous people not only acknowledge but *celebrate* the differences that exist among the various Indigenous peoples in truly remarkable ways, ways that have inclined us to prefer the terms *ceremonial worlds* and *songs of the world* to *worldviews*, which suggests the idea of a set of *beliefs* about how the world actually *is*. Belief figures in Indigenous worlds rather more obliquely than is suggested by the term *worldview*. In Indigenous worlds epistemology is, once again, *ethics-based*, and, given the notion of "respect" that underlies Indigenous ceremonial worlds, a richly pluralistic set of worlds unfolds.

IV. Reduction and Invitation

In sections IV and V we pick out two aspects of our reconceived ethical epistemology for particular emphasis: invitation in this section, and narrative in the next. Our aim in doing so is twofold. First, both themes illustrate and deepen the practical turn that the alternative ethical epistemology requires. Practice is no longer some application of ethical knowledge: it is now *constitutive of ethics itself*, our very mode of access to the world's possibilities. Second, conversely, the alternative epistemology also helps to ground these themes and practices themselves. These are not merely specific topics, disjunct from each other, but connected and central to the field as we reconceive it. These themes both exemplify an ethics-based epistemology and are highlighted and required by it.

"Etiquette" is a genuine means of *discovery*. As we said above, we oppose the usual view that puts knowledge of animals, for instance, before any possible (serious, intellectually respectable) ethical response to them. On our view, we can have no idea of what other animals are actually capable *until* we approach them ethically. Now we need to spell out this reversal more carefully.

Begin here: Certain kinds of self-fulfilling prophecies turn out to be crucial in ethics. There is, in particular, a kind of self-fulfilling prophecy in which one of the main effects of the "prophecy" is to reduce someone or something in the world—to make that person or thing less than they or it are or could be, to diminish some part of the world's richness and depth and promise—and in which this reduction in turn feeds back not only to justify the original prophecy but also to perpetuate it. This process is therefore *self-validating* reduction. There are all too many examples. Animals reduced to pitiful or hostile vestiges of their former selves, whose incapacities and hostility are then taken to justify exploitation or further violence. The land itself, scourged, deliberately desacralized (Yahweh even commands the Israelites to destroy the ancient world's sacred groves), subdivided, ravaged, then of course has very little of the stability, integrity, or beauty that might give it any kind of noninstrumental value. Cut down the sacred groves and you succeed in driving the sacred out of this world.[23]

To break this cycle of "reduction" it is necessary to invoke a parallel cycle of "invitation": indeed, quite precisely, self-validating invitation. Here the kind of practice asked of us is to venture something, to offer an invitation to, or to open a possibility toward, another being or some part of the world, and see what comes of it. We are called, in fact, to a kind of etiquette once again, but here in an experimental key: the task is to create the space within which a response can emerge or an exchange co-evolve.

Trust, for example, is crucial. Think for example of how we approach children, or students: already offering trust and love. This is what enables them to grow into it. We could even define a good teacher as someone who offers that kind of respect "up front," and for all of his or her charges (hence it is also "universal," returning to Birch's notion of universal consideration).

Here, then, the reversal from an epistemology-based ethics to an ethics-based epistemology becomes most evident. "Invitation" in this sense is not an assessment of something's value based on an inventory—even the most open-minded or objective inventory—of the thing's present characteristics. The point, once again, is that those present characteristics do not exhaust the thing's possibilities. Knowledge does not and cannot come first; first must come the invitation. Consequently, invitation cannot represent some formal kind of respect, but rather an experimental, open-ended and sometimes even personally risky kind of offering.

Birch's insistence that universal consideration "reverse the usual burden of proof" prefigures this same logic. We suggest that this reversal is not merely a matter of epistemological caution. It is a matter of setting the dynamics of relationship going in a different direction. For the very necessity to "prove oneself" may prove debilitating, may make its own satisfaction impossible. Precisely that demand already represents a way of closing ourselves off from the beings in question. Human beings trip over their own feet when treated with such distance and skepticism, when put into question in this way, and there is no reason to expect other animals to do any better, especially when many animals are exquisitely more sensitive to the affective environment than we are. Conversely, though it may seem paradoxical, removing the "burden" of proof may be precisely what is necessary if it is to be met. Only in this way are we likely to discover what kind of relationship actually is possible. To "invite," then, is not merely to make a space for something, to let it in: it is, literally, bringing new possibilities to *life*. Without it, without venturing real-world invitations, we cannot begin to know what the real possibilities are.

There are many styles of invitation. Sometimes what we need most of all to do is to give a child or animal or plant or river *time*: time to grow to its natural lifespan, at its own tempo. "Invitation" in the case of nonsentient beings—rocks, for example—may have to move at their tempo: millions of years, perhaps. Or perhaps not: Indigenous traditions generally consider rocks rather tricky beings. Places, buildings, communities can be more or less inviting: we need to *plan* for what Mary Midgley calls the "mixed community." Considering—inviting—other animals in this sense, for example, partly means designing places and media where we can meet each other halfway. Sometimes it is as simple as designing places that they and we can safely share.

The theme of environmental etiquette is actually a major subtheme of environmental writing already. An ethics-based epistemology brings this strand into focus. Grizzly tracker Doug Peacock insists on what he calls "interspecific tact." Wendell Berry speaks of an "etiquette" of nature. Calvin Martin, citing a global range of native practices, speaks of "courtesy." Gary Snyder writes of "grace." Birch writes of "generosity of spirit" along with "considerateness." All of these terms have their home in a discourse of manners and personal bearing. So to enter the realm of "invitation" calls us to a kind of deftness, understatement, circumspection: it points back toward something very close to us, bound up with who we are and how we immediately bear ourselves toward others and in the world.

Animal trainer and writer Vicki Hearne visits an animal training facility to observe Washoe, one of the chimpanzees trained to use American Sign Language. In a remarkable passage, she describes how she ends up observing the people instead.

> There were roughly three categories of people going in and out of the main compound. There was the group that included trainers, handlers, and caretakers, there were Hollywood types of one sort and another and there were academics who were there mostly because of the presence of the signing chimpanzees. I realized that I was able, without consciously thinking about it, accurately and from several hundred yards away to identify which group anyone who came in belonged to. . . .
>
> The handlers, I noticed, walked in with a soft, acute, 380-degree awareness: they were receptively establishing . . . acknowledgment of and relationships with all of the several hundred pumas, wolves, chimps, spider monkeys and Galapagos tortoises. Their ways of moving fit into the spaces shaped by the animals' awareness.

And surely, we want to add, for the very same reason, the handlers' behavior opened up the possibility of response. These were the people, after all, who drew out Washoe's language abilities, not the academics.

> The Hollywood types moved . . . with vast indifference to where they were and might as well have been on an interior set with flats painted with pictures of tortoises or on the stage of a Las Vegas nightclub. They were psychically intrusive, and I remembered Dick Koehler [an animal trainer and writer] saying that you could count on your thumbs the number of actors, directors and so on who could actually respond meaningfully to what an animal is doing.
>
> The academics didn't strut in quite that way, but they nonetheless psychically intrusive and failed to radiate the intelligence the handlers did. . . . They had too many questions, too many hidden assumptions about their roles as observer.

> I am talking about nice, smart people, but good handlers
> don't "observe" animals in this way, . . . with that stare that
> makes almost all animals a bit uneasy.[24]

This is very precisely put, and goes to the heart of the re-vision we
have proposed in these pages. Our task is not to "observe" at all—that
again is a legacy of the vision of ethics as belief-centered—but rather
to *participate*. And the first condition of participation is acknowledgment, actually sharing a world with other creatures. About some people
who do well with animals or children, where honesty is everything, we
sometimes say that they "have a way" with animals or children: as if
it were some magical trait that one either is blessed with or not. This
characterization misses the point. It is no magic, only etiquette, starting
with that profound kind of participation-as-acknowledgment.

Part of the upshot, then, is a shift entirely out of the preoccupa-
tions of contemporary environmental-ethical debate. Right now most
of the combatants are confident that we are hot on the trail of formal
principles and even a theory of animal rights or environmental ethics. Yet
it may after all be our *comportment* that is the single most crucial thing.
Self-validating invitation is a process: it takes time. And it is certainly not
the same as "just being nice." Again, it is actual, practical etiquette. When
an animal looks at you, return the look. Speak back; use real names; touch.
These actions are basic, fundamentally a matter of instinctive responses,
in the body, below or beyond the level where conscious resolution can
make a difference—except slowly and painfully too, over time. Certainly,
self-conscious "niceness" is the *last* thing we need: better to simply be
oblivious. Consider what things are like for the animal: what "communication" for example would really be for a herring gull or a dolphin.
Consider Jim Nollman jamming with orcas, using musical media which
all cetaceans seem to prefer, paddling out to them in his floating rhythm
section, thus in a way that allows them to decline encounter entirely or
to break it off whenever they wish.[25] Could *this* be, just possibly, the
environmental-philosophical challenge of the future?

V. Songs of the Earth

When Indigenous peoples are presented with what Euro-Americans would
call *beliefs* or *worldviews* different from their own, they tend to respond
not with an inquiry into which are *true* but by saying that "they tell
different stories than we do."[26] In this section we focus on the *narrative* component of Indigenous ceremonial worlds.

As Carol Geddes says, in explaining the difference between Western epistemology-based ethics grounded in scientific knowledge of the nonhuman world and Indigenous thought on right relationship with the nonhuman world:

> We would never have a subject called environmental ethics; it is simply part of the story. . . . Too many people say, well let's take lessons from First Nations people, let us find out some of their rules, and let us try and adopt some of those rules. . . . But it is not something that you can understand through rules. It has got to be through the kind of consciousness that growing up understanding the narratives can bring to you. That is where it is very, very difficult, because people have become so far removed from understanding these kinds of things in a narrative kind of way.[27]

In Indigenous stories, knowledge follows upon correct behavior, proper etiquette; they clearly illustrate an ethics-based epistemology. And stories are *inviting*. They *invite* the telling of other stories, other songs of the world. They invite others into the stories—human and nonhuman, the whole land community.

Theory is not inconsistent with storied understanding of self, community, and world. Indeed, as philosophers and sociologists of science have amply demonstrated, theories are fully intelligible only when embedded in stories—at the very least, in stories that exemplify in actual cases the application of scientific concepts, laws, and theories (what Thomas Kuhn calls "paradigm applications"), but also, and more importantly for our purposes, in the wider cultural stories that define us as individuals and define the cultures within which we live and come to understand ourselves. The storied nature of Indigenous knowledge shows clearly that Indigenous knowledge is grounded in ethical practice, that Indigenous epistemology is ethics-based. Stories provide a more nuanced, "ecological" understanding of our place in the world—including our *ethical* place. Stories are the real homes of so-called thick moral concepts, concepts in which evaluation and description are so intertwined as to be conceptually inseparable. And stories *exemplify* what theory cannot—namely, as Lee Hester says, that in addition to the "true" statements that can be made about things, things have their *own* truth.[28] To say that everything has its *own* truth (if we understand Hester correctly) is not so much a theoretical claim about the world as it is an expression of the thought that unless we extend a very basic courtesy to things in our attempts to understand them, we cannot arrive at an understanding of them *or* ourselves that makes *sense*, that makes sense of our lives, our cultures, our relationship to all that is.

As environmental ethicists, then, we might begin to explicitly discover and acknowledge the stories within which we think about environmental ethics. Although we know that theories are deeply shaped by personal and cultural values and that these values are deeply shaped by stories—that is, they are carried and propagated by the stories that define us—this understanding is not often reflected in practice; nor is it reflected in our meta-level analyses of practice. Articles in environmental ethics, including this one,[29] do not first invoke worlds within which discussion might meaningfully proceed. The implicit assumption is that we can profitably discuss these matters without defining and locating the ceremonial worlds and stories within which our discussions proceed. We speak as though *from* no world at all; and we presumptuously speak *for* all worlds.

An elder telling Papago origin stories at a meeting about educational programs for Indigenous people constructs a world in which discussion can meaningfully proceed.[30] Yukeoma begins his argument for why Hopi children shouldn't attend white schools by "speaking within the framework of the Hopi origin saga and its prophecies."[31] Most of our own culture's stories, however, touch on our biological and ecological existence only incidentally. Still, our existence is deeply ecological, and our cultural identities should reflect this, as do those of Indigenous peoples. "The mythtellers speak of the powers *in relation to* each other, and with an eye to the whole ecology, not separable functions of it."[32]

Jeannette Armstrong adds an ecological dimension to Momaday's thought that "we are all made of words": "The Okanagan word for 'our place on the land' and 'our language' is the same. The Okanagan language is thought of as the 'language of the land.' This means that the land has taught us our language. The way we survive is to speak the language that the land offered us as its teachings. . . . We also refer to the land and our bodies with the same root syllable. . . . We are our land/place."[33]

We find a Euro-American echo of this connection between language, land, and self in Conrad Aiken's words: "The landscape and the language are the same./And we ourselves are language and are land."[34] The landscapes that shape Euro-American identities are mostly human landscapes, however, landscapes of human culture and humanly transformed nature—broken landscapes that mirror our own brokenness. This has not always been so and is even now not so for perhaps most Indigenous peoples. The *deepest* sources of personal and cultural identity are the ecological and geological landscapes that shape and sustain us.

This, and our present loss, are given voice in what are surely Momaday's most memorable words:

> East of my grandmother's house the sun rises out of the plain. Once in his life a man ought to concentrate his mind upon the remembered earth, I believe. He ought to give himself up to a particular landscape in his experience, to look at it from as many angles as he can, to wonder about it, to dwell upon it. He ought to imagine that he touches it with his hands at every season and listens to the sounds that are made upon it. He ought to imagine the creatures there and all the faintest motions of the wind. He ought to recollect the glare of noon and all the colors of the dawn and dusk.[35]

These unbroken landscapes are characterized by their integrity. As Barry Lopez has put it, the "landscape is organized according to principles or laws or tendencies beyond human control. It is understood to contain an integrity that is beyond human analysis and unimpeachable."[36] It is this integrity, beyond human analysis and unimpeachable, that marks the land as sacred for most Indigenous peoples. The "sacred" (for example, the Lakota *wakan tanka*, "great mysterious") is the more-than-human quality of *this* world, not a being transcendent to the world. A Lakota asked older Lakota about the meaning and origin of the term *wakan tanka* and received this story as his answer:

> Way back many years ago, two men went walking. It was on the prairies. As they walked, they decided, "Let's go up the hill way towards the west; let's see what's over the hill."
>
>   So they walked and they came to the top of this hill and they looked west and it was the same. Same thing as they saw before; there was nothing. They just kept going like that, all day and it was the same. They came to a big hill and there was another big hill further back. Finally they stopped and they said, "You know, this is Wakan Tanka."[37]

In *this* sense of *sacred*,[38] it is possible that even evolutionary biology and ecology may provide us with some compelling myths of origin, for they portray the world as more-than-human in a way that may evoke an inclusive sense of kinship with the world around us. Nature's complexity, its generosity, and its communicative ability make it possible for us to once again experience the deep unity of the sacred and the natural. The particular virtues of specifically human being are embedded in natural mystery and nourished by a broader, deeper, more powerful and enduring earth matrix.

But these biological stories are quite abstract. They do not speak to us of the particularities of our homes, our places on earth. Within Indigenous cultures, myths of origin and other stories are creations and renewals of ceremonial worlds that tie cultural identity, even survival itself, to specific landscapes. Simon Ortiz, in "Survival This Way," from *A Good Journey*, writes:

> Survival, I know how this way.
> This way, I know.
> It rains.
> Mountains and canyons and plants
> grow.
> We traveled this way,
> gauged our distance by stories
> and loved our children.
> We taught them
> to love their births.
> We told ourselves over and over
> again,
> "We shall survive this way."

Another of Ortiz's poems concludes: "My son touches the root carefully,/aware of its ancient quality./He lays his soft, small fingers on it/and looks at me for information./I tell him: wood, an old root,/and around it, the earth, ourselves."[39]

Euro-Americans, too, have stories that define us in relationship to the land. One such tale is Aldo Leopold's "Marshland Elegy," in his *A Sand County Almanac*, which ends:

> And so they live and have their being—these cranes—not in the constricted present, but in the wider reaches of evolutionary time. Their annual return is the ticking of the geologic clock. Upon the place of their return they confer a peculiar distinction. Amid the endless mediocrity of the commonplace, a crane marsh holds a paleontological patent of nobility, won in the march of eons. . . . The sadness discernible in some marshes arises, perhaps, from their once having harbored cranes. Now they stand humbled, adrift in history.[40]

"Marshland Elegy" helps define many who live in the upper Midwest in relationship to the geologic and ecosystemic legacy of the last Wisconsin Ice, as a prairie/wetland people. The elegy also haunts us—it is a story of loss. This fits our cultural temper. It is a fair question whether our religions of loss and redemption are in some way tied to the mutual estrangement of the natural, the personal, and the sacred in Western culture.

The search for roots can take other shapes than that of a search for redemption in the mode of a search for the "Truth" of one's origin and identity. As Lee Hester recounts,[41] the Choctaw people migrated long ago to Mississippi carrying the bones of their ancestors with them. When they reached Mississippi they are said to have built the mound of *Nanih Waiyah* to house these bones. Yet, *Nanih Waiyah* is also said to be the great "Productive Mound" from which all people emerged. From the point of view of the "One (literal) Truth" this seems contradictory—the *new* burial mound could *not* be the Choctaw place of *origin*, emergence. From the point of view of Choctaw *practice*, however, a different meaning of emergence and origins arises.

VI. Conclusion

The following remarks by the anthropologist Henry Sharp sum up some of the salient features of the ethics-based epistemology that we have elaborated in this paper, as well as some of the dangers inherent in an epistemology-based ethics:

> We are now conditioned to accept that the symbols, ideas, and language of alien cultures are ways of knowing the environment within which they dwell, but we have conveniently managed to subordinate the significance of that understanding to our quest for objectivity. These things are not passive ways of perceiving a determined positivist reality but a mode of interaction shared between the *dene* and their environment. All animate life interacts and, to a greater or lesser degree, affects the life and behavior of all other animate forms. In their deliberate and splendid isolation, the Chipewyan interact with all life in accordance with their understanding, and the animate universe responds.
>
> White Canada does not come silently and openly into the bush in search of understanding or communion, it sojourns briefly in the full glory of its colonial power to

exploit and regulate all animate being and foremost of all, the *dene*. It comes asserting a clashing causal certainty in the fundamentalist exercise of the power of its belief. It talks too loudly, its posture is wrong, its movement harsh and graceless; it does not know what to see and it hears nothing. Its presence brings a stunning confusion heard deafeningly in a growing circle of silence created by a confused and disordered animate universe.[42]

Swaggering, talking too loud, not knowing how to listen: this very (often innocent) clumsiness we now reconceive as *the* fundamental ethical failure: failure to acknowledge and understand ourselves as living in a larger animate universe; and failure too—crucially—to draw out, to coparticipate with, that very universe. Instead, we drive it into silence, and then take that silence to confirm our own centrality, as if we really were the only ones with anything to say.

In contrast to this, Sharp portrays a people for whom symbols, ideas, and language constitute an ethical world in which revelatory interaction with the nonhuman world is made possible, a ceremonial world in which the nonhuman world *responds* and is *known*, a world in which this etiquette and knowledge constitute an ongoing and fluid relationship. *Etiquette is a condition of knowing the world itself.*

Notes

1. It is almost impossible to give citations for this model in general, since it is the common assumption of nearly all contemporary philosophical work recognized as ethics, and consequently is almost never explicitly articulated. It is both immediately familiar and never spelled out.

2. See Thomas H. Birch, "Moral Considerability and Universal Consideration," *Environmental Ethics* 15 (1993): 313–32.

3. See Anthony Weston, *Back to Earth: Tomorrow's Environmentalism* (Philadelphia: Temple University Press, 1994), chapters 2 and 3.

4. Henry Beston, *The Outermost House* (New York: Viking, 1976), p. 25.

5. Birch, "Moral Considerability," p. 328.

6. This discussion, of course, is only the briefest sketch, and leaves many questions unaddressed. Could ethics-based epistemology and epistemology-based ethics each be appropriate at different times or in different spheres, for example? (Maybe.) Is "care" ethics closer to an ethics-based epistemology than traditional ethics? (Again, maybe: this strand does emerge in some care ethicists, although there is a strong strand of epistemology-based care ethics as well.) These are questions for another place.

7. The Indigenous ideas on which we draw are filtered—indeed, double-filtered in cases where we work from secondary sources—through the conceptual lens of the Western-defined problematics in environmental ethics that we address in this paper. We do not claim to understand Indigenous thought as that thought lives in Indigenous worlds. The *only* real authorities on Indigenous thought are Indigenous peoples themselves. We only claim that this thought *as we understand it* sheds light on current problems in environmental ethics.

8. Leroy N. Meyer and Tony Ramirez, " 'Wakinyan Hotan' ('The Thunderbeings Call Out'): The Inscrutability of Lakota/Dakota Metaphysics," in Sylvia O'Meara and Douglas A. West, editors, *From Our Eyes: Learning from Indigenous People* (Toronto: Garamond Press, 1996), p. 104.

9. Walter J. Ong, S. J., "World as View and World as Event," *American Anthropologist* 71 (1969), pp. 63–67.

10. Sam Gill, "Holy Book in Nonliterate Traditions: Toward the Reinvention of Religion," in Sam Gill, *Native American Religious Action: A Performance Approach to Religion* (Columbia: University of South Carolina Press, 1987), pp. 139–40.

11. Sam Gill, "One, Two, Three: The Interpretation of Religious Action," in Gill, *Native American Religious Action*, pp. 162–63, 151.

12. Gill, ibid., p. 162.

13. These examples make it clear, we hope, that the term *ceremonial worlds* is not intended to refer to ceremonies such as baptisms and sun dances that occur within cultures.

14. Diamond Jenness, "The Carrier Indians of the Bulkley River," *Bureau of American Ethnology Bulletin*, no. 133 (1943), p. 540.

15. N. Scott Momaday, "The Man Made of Words," in Sam Gill, *Native American Traditions: Sources and Interpretations* (Belmont, CA: Wadsworth Publishing Company, 1983), p. 44.

16. Paul Shepard, *Nature and Madness* (San Francisco: Sierra Club Books, 1982), pp. 6 and 9.

17. Henry S. Sharp, *The Transformation of Bigfoot: Maleness, Power, and Belief among the Chipewyan* (Washington DC: Smithsonian Institution Press, 1988), p. 144.

18. Robert Bringhurst, "Everywhere Being Is Dancing, Knowing Is Known," *Chicago Review* 39 (1993), p. 138.

19. Irene Klaver, in conversation.

20. This term is from David Abram, *The Spell of the Sensuous: Perception and Language in a More-Than-Human World* (New York: Pantheon Books, 1996). As used here, it has primary reference to the wider biological dimensions in which we are embedded. See note 38.

21. This point is well argued in Birch, "Moral Considerability."

22. Carol Geddes, panel discussion by Yukon First Nations people on the topic "What is a good way to teach children and young adults to respect the land?" transcript in Bob Jickling, editor, *Environment, Ethics, and Education: A Colloquium* (Whitehorse, YT: Yukon College, 1996), p. 46.

23. See Anthony Weston, "Self-Validating Reduction: Toward a Theory of the Devaluation of Nature," *Environmental Ethics* 18 (1996): 115–32. [Chapter 3 of this book.]

24. Vicki Hearne, *Adam's Task* (New York: Knopf, 1986), pp. 229–30.

25. Jim Nollman, *Dolphin Dreamtime* (New York: Bantam Books, 1987).

26. Conversations with those involved in the Native Philosophy Project in Thunder Bay bear this out. See also Geddes, panel discussion, in Jickling, *Environment, Ethics, and Education*, pp. 32–33.

27. Ibid.

28. In conversation at the Native Philosophy Project.

29. In admitting this, we acknowledge that we speak of Indigenous worlds from the quite different world of academic philosophy. One reviewer worried quite rightly about what he called "performative contradiction" in this regard. Fair enough. We are indeed trying to cross a formidable boundary here, to speak of things in an academic voice that truly calls for the voice of ceremony and song, a personal stance more than an intellectual attitude. We accept the awkwardness and clumsiness (indigenous people might see it as irony) of the attempt. Better this than the only alternative (at present): silence. May those who come later find the way easier.

30. Sam Gill, "The Trees Stood Deep Rooted," in *Native American Religious Action*, p. 17.

31. Peter Nabokov, "Present Memories, Past History," in Calvin Martin, ed., *The American Indian and the Problem of History* (New York: Oxford University Press, 1987), p. 147.

32. Sean Kane, *Wisdom of the Mythtellers* (Peterborough, Ontario: Broadview Press, 1994), p. 36.

33. Jeannette Armstrong (Okanagan), "Keepers of the Earth," in *Ecopsychology: Restoring the Earth, Healing the Mind*, ed. Theodore Roszak et al. (San Francisco: Sierra Club Books, 1995), p. 323.

34. Conrad Aiken, quoted in Edith Cobb, *The Ecology of Imagination in Childhood* (New York: Columbia University Press, 1977), p. 67.

35. N. Scott Momaday, *The Way to Rainy Mountain* (New York: Ballantine Books, 1970), p. 113.

36. Barry Lopez, "Landscape and Narrative," in *Crossing Open Ground* (New York: Random House, 1988), p. 66.

37. Elaine Jahner, "The Spiritual Landscape," in D. M. Dooling and Paul Jordan-Smith, editors, *I Become Part of It: Sacred Dimensions in Native American Life* (San Francisco: HarperCollins, 1992), p. 193.

38. This is a sense of the sacred that resonates well with Rolston's view that "there comes a point in environmental ethics when we ask about our *sources*, not just our *resources*. The natural environment is discovered to be the womb in which we are generated and which we really never leave. That is the original meaning of *nature*, from the Latin *natans*, giving birth, Mother Earth." Holmes Rolston III, *Environmental Ethics: Duties to and Values in the*

Natural World (Philadelphia: Temple University Press, 1988), pp. 197–98. See also Jim Cheney, "Naturalizing the Problem of Evil," *Environmental Ethics* 19 (1997): 299–313.

39. Simon Ortiz, *A Good Journey*, collected in *Woven Stone* (Tucson: The University of Arizona Press, 1992), pp. 167–68 and 202.

40. Aldo Leopold, *A Sand County Almanac* (New York: Ballantine Books, 1970), pp. 101–03.

41. In correspondence.

42. Sharp, *Transformation of Bigfoot*, pp. 144–45.

Addendum, 2007:

Our mutual friend Tom Birch spent the better part of a decade's worth of high-country philosophical companionship inveighing, alas in vain, against our reconception of ethics in the direction of etiquette. It is not merely that for him the term *etiquette* has an ineradicable association with a dreary insistence on formal manners. It is also that the flowing, dependent, and fragile character of ethics so conceived does not have a deontological enough flavor to do what he thinks needs to be done. How mightily we have striven around the campfire to bring him around! Despite few people being more adept at actual wilderness etiquette, though, Birch—unaccountably—resists. Still, you will find outlines of his views in the present paper and also in "Multicentrism: A Manifesto" (chapter 6 of this book), where we/I argue that his enormously suggestive "universal consideration" approach is at the very least highly congruent with the approach sketched here. We take up his work directly in a paired set of pieces in response to his original article on that theme: Jim Cheney's "Universal Consideration: A Epistemological Map of the Terrain" and my "Universal Consideration as an Originary Practice," both in *Environmental Ethics* 20 (1998).

Chapter 5

Multicentrism

A Manifesto

I. A Question of Geometry

Environmental ethics is often framed in geometrical terms. We are invited to ask how big the circle of moral consideration can or should get and where to draw the line between what counts and what doesn't. Historically, according to this view, ethics began by stretching the circle of the self first to include some other humans (family, community, etc.) and then, eventually, to a "universal" view on which all humans count. The familiar extensionist argument insists that we cannot justly draw the line at the boundary of the human species either. Why should the species border be any more impenetrable, truly any more natural, than the boundaries of human clan or nation? Other animals present themselves—first only some, then arguably all. The "expanding circle," as Peter Singer famously called it,[1] keeps pushing outward: to all living things next, including plants and trees, which may not be conscious subjects but are surely self-organized and responsive systems. Then to the land—the community of life. Farther still and we have to consider the rivers, mountains, the air as well, and perhaps even the Earth as a whole.

"Multicentrism: A Manifesto" appeared in *Environmental Ethics* 26 (2004), pp. 25–40. My aim was to draw together a great deal of work, both in environmental ethics proper and in many related fields, which is already multicentric in spirit. Indeed I began work on the paper with a vision of a multiauthored outcome that might be published pseudonymously: an explicit, alternative framework for environmental ethics. A variety of factors finally led to the present version, authored by me though still in extensive back-and-forth with some of the central figures involved, especially Val Plumwood, who engaged generously and unflaggingly with the project and who I repaid by continuing to differ with her about the central concept itself. In spirit, though, I still think of this paper as a joint product, and have found that it resonates with many people who approach environmental philosophy in many different ways—much like the "Deep Ecology Platform," to which it is, in a sense, both a complement and an alternative.

This familiar geometry I call "con-centric." Each new circle of moral consideration is supposed to enclose the previous circles neatly, evenly, and totally, all the way back to the single original center, just like the concentric ripples from a single stone dropped into a still pond.

Concentrism is a natural and indeed generous way of framing environmental ethics. Yet it cannot be said to be the only possible approach. Even in purely geometrical terms, there is an obvious alternative: a *multi-centered* vision according to which more-than-human others enter the moral realm on their own terms, rather than by expansion from a single center—a vision according to which there are *diverse* centers, shifting and overlapping but still each with its own irreducible and distinctive starting-point. For a multicentered ethic, then, the growth of moral sensitivity and consideration does not proceed through an expanding series of concentric realms, each neatly assimilating or incorporating the previous stage within a larger and more inclusive whole. No: instead we discover a world of separate though mutually implicated centers. Moral growth consists in experiencing more and more deeply the texture of multiplicity in the world, not in tracing the wider and wider circles set off from one single center.

Such a multicentric vision reflects our experience of the *difference* of more-than-human others, without on the other hand wholly denying commonality either. Real experience is just not so unicentric—not out here with the bugs and the lightning, the mountains and the stars, and maybe not even with each other. Moreover, even the barest sketch of a multicentered vision quickly reminds us of many themes that have occupied certain rich lines of alternative environmental philosophizing for years: of feminist and phenomenological critiques of the sameness-versus-difference construction of so many "Others," both human and other-than-human; of the possibility of a relational and dialogical environmental ethic intimated both by these postmodern kinds of philosophizing as well as by certain premodern or indigenous thought-lines; and of certain other suggestive but as yet unassimilated concepts in the field, such as "universal consideration," "environmental etiquette," and the first sketches of a possible "communicative ethics for the biosphere."

Many hands already do this work. My aim is not to add another specific piece to it here. I am concerned instead with its overall visibility as a shared program fundamentally alternative to the prevailing paradigm. Of necessity it does not fit the prevailing model of what a theory in environmental ethics must look like. All the same, this work, considered together, has a coherent and compelling direction of its own. Something bigger and more dramatic is afoot than a mere set of offbeat complaints. This essay proposes that the theme of a multicentered ethic represents a new paradigm or unifying "platform" in environmental philosophy, and offers a provisional sketch to that end.

II. Concentrism Challenged

On the concentric vision, each previous circle, each previous set of moral consideranda and each previous moral stage, is wholly nested within the next. We are invited to see the claims of the self in the context of, and as an instance of, the claims of humans as such. We are invited to see the claims of humans in the context of, and as an instance of, the claims of animals as such; and so on. This has long been a source both of deep-rooted objections—distinctiveness is lost, say the critics, "there is nothing special about X (me, humans, animals, etc.) anymore"—but also, for the same reason, is a point of pride for many environmental philosophers. This is supposed to be our latter-day universalism, the cutting edge of ethics. Everything is to be valued under the aspect of wider and wider categories: sentience, or life, or creative dynamism, or, in the end, sheer being.[2]

The suggestion is that what we have in common, even with tigers and trees and probably even with rocks and bacteria, is more important than that which divides us. We are supposed to come to "identify" with the entire world.[3] And there are surely commonalities to be found, identifications that apart from this procedure we would no doubt overlook. The implicit monism, though—arranging our argument so that the commonalities and identifications alone ground the ethic—is more troubling.

For one thing—the simplest point—an approach based purely on commonality necessarily slights difference. Specific modes of life or styles of consciousness, or ultimately even the fact of life or consciousness itself, may no longer count at all. As the circle becomes wider and wider, commonalities become thinner and thinner.[4] The search for a single, inclusive criterion of moral standing ultimately washes out nearly everything.

Arguably, though, the underlying dynamic of this argument is more unsettling still. Despite its veneer of egalitarianism, concentrism is profoundly human-centered underneath. Since "the expanding circle" expands by finding commonalities with what lies within the already-accepted circle, the self and its essential character—and, a little farther out, the *human* and *its* essential character—still sit as ultimate arbiter. The suffering of others, human or nonhuman, for example, comes to count in the utilitarian argument because I can connect it to my own, because I recognize that suffering is bad for me and therefore, unable to draw any morally relevant distinction between me and a wider range of others, I must conclude that it is equally bad for them. All commonality refers back to the already-given center, and in fact it is guaranteed that whatever commonality drives any given "expanded" ethics, I have got to have it—indeed par excellence.

In short, a kind of ego-centric and species-centric model, so familiar from the ethical tradition generally, has not been deeply challenged but in fact is almost unconsciously imported into the ethics of "the expanding circle." As Val Plumwood concludes, Singerian moral extensionism "does not really dispel speciesism; it only extends and disguises it."[5] Man (often literally) is still the measure of all things. Sometimes it barely even dispels egoism, as when a wide range of otherwise quite different philosophers struggle mightily to bring all of nature *inside the self*, of all places, so as to engage self-protectiveness and self-interest in the service of environmental values.[6] You understand the motive, but when John Seed for example suggests that the natural outcome of "expanding identifications" is the recognition that "I am the rainforest," you have to seriously wonder what is becoming of the rainforest. A truly radical environmental ethic may have further to go than we thought—and perhaps in less familiar and less comfortable directions as well.

III. Multicentrism

Many alternative lines of thinking now converge on a view that calls all the existing concentrisms into question—an alternative, systematic, multicentric project.

Decentering the Human

Multicentrism begins by insisting that neither one's own self nor the human/species self is the only model of being or presence or the only possible touchstone for moral consideration. Others have their own stories, not to be "measured by man." Only understanding our place in this way is it possible for us to honor our distinctiveness as essential to our particular mode of being and (in part) to what we take to be our consequent moral standing, yet not impose ourselves as models for everyone and everything else's being and moral standing.

Philosophers may hear this as nothing more than the typical rejection of anthropocentrism. The typical follow-on assumption, however, is that anthropocentrism must be replaced with some other, bigger centrism. *Multi*centrists strive for *de*centering instead: we reject *any* monocentrism.

The conceptual apparatus for this decentering emerges from a number of related critical fields: in feminist and postcolonial work, for instance, where the aim is to decenter the "male subject" (androcentrism) or the colonizers' identities (Eurocentrism), respectively. A recent anthology linking both of these areas is even titled *Decentering the Center*.[7] Ecofeminists draw out the parallels between the construction of oppressive Self-Other dichotomies in human spheres such as these and similarly oppressive dichotomies beyond the human sphere ("[hu]man versus animal," for instance, and "[hu]man versus nature").[8]

In all of these cases the danger is what Plumwood labels "hegemonic" centrism: establishing one's own (or one's group's) centrality by systematically reconstructing all otherness either as some version of the One Center's dynamic, and/or by marginalizing and radically devaluing it in relation to that Center, reducing it to orbit and periphery.[9] Indeed the hegemonic type of centrism is so pervasive, and perhaps seems so natural, that we may become uneasy with characterizing a (hopefully) nonhegemonic alternative as any form of centrism whatsoever—although words like "polycentric" and "multipolar" are in the air too. Still, at least, *de*centering is the necessary starting-point. We must resist the dynamic of assimilation and marginalization that ecofeminists identify so clearly, and thus recognize a world of multiple voices and beings that do *not* reduce to a single type and do *not* naturally fall into the orbit of one single sort of being's center.

A Diversity of Centers: or, the Multiverse

Drop a single pebble in a pond and you create a concentric set of ripples. Toss in a handful of pebbles and ripples set off from a dozen points at once, each its own "center," each soon intersecting and intermingling with others without losing its distinctness, its own place of origin and its own way of "making waves." This, multicentrism insists, is what the world is actually like. A *de*centered world is not (need not be) an *a*-centered world. Instead we envision a *many*-centered world, a diversity of centers, a world of thick and polynodal texture. Each of a thousand human and more-than-human presences organizes a certain part of the world around itself, forms a distinctive local pattern, a certain organic completeness and cohesion. David Abram proposes as an illustration Van Gogh's painting *Starry Night*: each star is its own vortex or spiral of energy, not somehow drawing all the rest into its orbit, but surely and visibly a presence in its own right.[10]

The very first example of an "I/Thou" relation that Martin Buber offers in his book of the same title involves a tree. We can experience a tree as a "picture," Buber says, or as an invitation to botanizing or chemistry or in many other ways. We can also "be drawn into a relation" with "the tree itself," he says, as it stands "in conversation with the elements and with the stars" as well as with ourselves.[11] Here we enter a world of *difference* that is nonetheless not *alien*—of separate identities that somewhat intermingle. Always there are other stories being unfolded; always other "force-fields" (Neil Evernden's term[12]) within which we move.

Intentional consciousness is one kind of "centering," then, but not the only one.[13] Around us are not merely a multitude of humans or of conscious centers, and not merely a multitude of other midsize and discrete force fields like rocks and trees, but a multitude of other *kinds* of force fields—rhizomes, tectonic plates, bacteria, nebulae—at many different levels of organization too, from species and ecosystems to individual cells. Indeed, in place of the notion of "universe" itself, it is high time to speak instead, following William James, of the "Multiverse."[14] To speak of multicenteredness, then, is to invoke a world thick with many sorts of presence, in which we move amid and within other or larger force fields or centers of gravity.[15] I believe that this is the root intuition for which environmental ethics from the start has tried to speak—only in a monocentric language unsuited to a world brimming not just with life but with shifting and self-organizing energies of many different kinds.

The Multiverse Calls Forth an Etiquette

In a diverse world of unsuspected depths, we are called to a kind of attentiveness much wider and much less pre-structured than the existing monocentrisms suggest.

Tom Birch lays out certain essential arguments for what he calls "universal consideration." Nothing, says Birch, is to be pushed aside without a thought—not, however, because we have or can find some universal criterion of moral standing, but because the very process of paying attention, even to devise or apply such a criterion, already has to be universal, already has to take in everything. What is required, in short, is moral consideration in what Birch calls "the root sense": the process of actually, carefully, considering all things. *All* things. Moral consideration is a process, open-ended toward the other creatures, toward whatever lies on the other end. In fact, universal consideration requires us to reverse the usual burden of proof as we approach others in the world. "Others are now taken as valuable, even though we may not yet know how or why, until they are proved otherwise."[16]

The practice of universal consideration, moreover, requires a new kind of comportment. An open-ended world of multiple, diverse and always somewhat opaque centers requires us to move with caution, attentiveness, circumspection. Ethics is no longer constituted by a merely abstract respect, but demands something far more embodied: a willingness and ability to make the space, not just conceptually, but in one's own person and in the design and structure of personal and human spaces, for the emergence of more-than-human others into relationship. Here multicentrism embraces a leading theme in the larger environmental literature that so far has only barely percolated into philosophical ethics: what Gary Snyder, echoed by many others, calls "etiquettes of freedom and of grace."[17]

This is not a merely one-way practice. Many postmodernisms converge with the claim that the world we think we know is profoundly shaped by our approach to it, by our established ethics and ways of knowing. The attitudes and comportment with which we approach other centers partly determine the ways in which they respond or show up. Thus, as Jim Cheney and I have argued, we can no longer think of ourselves as merely responding to a world considered to be given and fixed.[18] If our very mode of approach shapes that world in turn, then ethics itself must be a form of invitation or welcoming, sometimes of ritual invocation and sometimes of literally creating the settings in which new possibilities might emerge. On the usual view of other animals, for instance, we must first know what animals are capable of and then decide on that basis whether and how we are to consider them ethically. On a more open-ended view, we will have only inadequate ideas of what other animals are actually capable until we *already* have approached them ethically: that is, until we have offered them the space and time and occasion to enter into relationship. Ethics both implies and is implied by etiquette, in this sense, itself.

Ethics as a Constituted Process

If there is but one circle of moral consideration with ourselves at the center, it is natural to suppose that we can and must make moral decisions by our own lights. One kind of consideration remains, though perhaps operating over a wider sphere. Monocentrism thus extends and disguises a monological ethic as well. Unicentrism extends and disguises uni*lateralism*.

Multicentrism undercuts the very possibility of this sort of unilateralism. *We cannot practice ethics on our own.* Once other centers are acknowledged, always somewhat opaque to us as we are to them, there is no alternative but to work things out together, as far as is possible, when all are affected by the decisions taken. The key to ethical life in the multiverse becomes what Paul Shepard calls "the elaboration of covenants and negotiations with the Other."[19]

Such an alternative vision of ethics is evolving as a wide range of thinkers challenge the traditional conception of ethics as a principle-based decision-making method for resolving ethical quandaries. Many feminists argue for a concept of ethics as, in Margaret Walker's lovely words, "a collection of perceptive, imaginative, appreciative, and expressive skills and capacities which put us and keep us in contact with the realities of ourselves and specific others."[20] A number of philosophers and other writers are patiently exploring the theme of dialogue beyond—sometimes way beyond—the human sphere.[21] Carolyn Merchant elaborates a "partnership ethics" in which "both humans and nature are active agents."[22] In the work of musicians such as Jim Nollman we catch glimpses of unimagined possibilities of cross-species connection.[23] From another angle, communicative ethicists have worked out a model that locates key ethical features—impartiality, mutual recognition, freedom from deception and self-deception—not in specific principles or outcomes but rather in the procedures by which such decisions are made, and recent writers such as John Dryzek and again Val Plumwood are bringing that tradition into environmental thinking to sketch what Dryzek calls a "communicative ethics for the biosphere."[24]

I say more of this below. The point for now is just that, however difficult or unfamiliar, this is multicentrism's mandate, and in fact a great deal of ongoing work is already in this key. Ethics is an ongoing process, co-constituted far beyond the human sphere, and recognizing, sustaining, and enriching that process is itself ethics' deepest requirement.

IV. Questions and Contrasts

Plumwood challenges the use of any kind of "centrism" label for a positive alternative. In several detailed works she lays out a systematic theory of centrism as such, including egocentrism, androcentrism, and Eurocentrism as well as anthropocentrism and the transhuman centrisms. In each case, one center claims priority and superiority, devaluing and consequently opening the way for exploitation of all other poles, reducing them to feeble, inferior, and deficient reflections of itself.[25] This, again, she calls "hegemonic" centrism. And here is the rub: *any* centrism, in Plumwood's view, is at least implicitly hegemonic. At the very least, using the term in the way I propose may confuse and dilute the critique of hegemonic centrism. Moreover, the multiplication of centers by itself does not guarantee that the multiple centers will not themselves be hegemonic, as colonialism's record suggests.[26]

Plumwood's preferred responses are "counter-hegemonic" or "counter-centric" strategies: foregrounding interdependence rather than independence, for instance; emphasizing within-group differences and cross-group commonalities rather than vice versa; affirming rather than devaluing the distinctive characteristics of nonhuman others.[27] The aim, she says, is to "attain solidarity with others in their difference," rather than either incorporating and ultimately subsuming difference ("I am the rain forest") or making difference radical and absolute.[28] Solidarity's demands are thoroughly practical and political, adapted to the demands of particular struggles and our own culture's peculiar burdens and pitfalls.

It is absolutely true that we do not want to find ourselves rejecting the familiar hegemonic centrisms only to erect a new one of exactly the same type. Despite the stereotypes, few feminists want to simply replace patriarchy with matriarchy. Few Afrocentrists want to devalue everything European in favor of a new African hegemony. On the other hand, many (not all) philosophers and activists working in these areas continue to speak of their projects as "centric." Indeed the project of creating a new *kind* of centrism seems to them essential. What they offer is not really a rejection of centrism as such but rather a new understanding of centeredness, a new understanding of power, opening the possibility of a genuine kind of centrism free from the hegemony, so to say, of hegemonic centrism itself. In this sense we call a person "centered" when they have a focus, an equilibrium, some balanced sense of self to fall back on. It does not preclude other, similar or not so similar "centers." Plumwood herself speaks eloquently of defending nonhuman earth others as "independent centers with potential needs, excellences, and claims to flourish of their own."[29] Leading African philosophers and activists write of Afrocentrism as making Africa "subject, not object"—not, however, to exclude other "subjects"—and of "placing Africans at the center of knowledge about themselves."[30]

The critical words here are *empowerment, self-definition, inclusion*— and, once again, *center*. These thinkers are not looking for an a-centered world but rather a *poly*centric world, centered many times over, only without a *dominant* center. Plumwood is surely right that any center, defined too readily by simplistic self-conceptions and the exclusion of others, slides toward a kind of self-aggrandizement. Contemporary international politics offers all the example one needs. On the other hand, on a genuine pluralistic vision, what is excluded is not devalued but is instead *re*valued in terms of its own dynamic self-centering, and the exclusions are never total. Separate centers may be both sharply different in some ways, even totally different in some ways, and similar in others. There can be both overlap and heterogeneity. Plumwood is right that these points must be continually insisted upon—but that is true regardless of what terms we adopt.[31]

Consider several other brief contrasts. Multicentrism obviously can be called *pluralistic*, but it has only an oblique connection with the "pluralism debate" that has unfolded over the past decade or so in environmental ethics. The advocates of this sort of pluralism have typically defended the usefulness of multiple ethical theories rather than just one. J. Douglas Rabb speaks of "polycentrism," for instance, but his multiple "centers" turn out to be different ethical theories.[32] Correspondingly pluralism's critics have mostly contested just this point.[33]

Multicentrism, by contrast, implies a much more radical and polymorphous pluralism. Multiplicity and variety, as on James's view, are fundamental to the world itself: to things themselves, in short, not just to values. Rather than the usual sorts of moral theories, then, multicentrists are more apt to seek diverse articulations or manifestations of values that do not claim universality, and conceive the reconciliation of apparently competing values as a form of integrative practice and on-the-ground (there's "grounding" for you!) negotiation, rather than somehow necessarily a theoretical activity.[34] Theories, whether one or many, may not be necessary at all.

Multicentrism might seem to imply a form of environmental "holism" or "biospheric egalitarianism." Contra holism, though, multicentrism does not assert a single ecological "whole" that is somehow the single, prior ethical center. The multiverse is more mixed and complexly textured, including both ecological "wholes" and individuals of various sorts and levels—species, organisms, biotic communities—all in flux and flow, and none always or necessarily prior. Again, the real work of decision-making is more like a balancing act. "Biospheric egalitarianism" is a little closer, maybe, but it is too formal, abstract, unworkable, and above all unilateral: it seems to suggest that once rights or values are appropriately ("equally"?) distributed, human decision-makers can figure out what to do without the need to consult or negotiate. Multicentrism, once again, proposes a different *kind* of decision-procedure: a procedural model based on open-ended dialogue and negotiation.

Multicentrism also suggests an unexpected critical angle on familiar mega-centrisms such as biocentrism and ecocentrism. It begins to seem that these views are emboldened to call themselves centrisms in the first place only because they are—implicitly—wholly oppositionally defined.

The aim is to center on something bigger than humanity. Both of these views, though, to put it crudely, are *too big* for "centers" in the sense being advanced here. They are not nodes of a matrix but the matrix itself.[35] It is certainly not clear how we can "center" on the Earth as such: this is more like *a*-centrism than any actual centrism whatsoever.[36] I suspect, then, that such mega-centrisms really represent only a form of resistance or refusal of the usual anthropocentrism. To "go beyond" anthropocentrism, on a multicentric view, what we must really challenge is not the "anthropo-" part but the implicit (con)*centrism*.

V. Multicentrism in Practice

Multicentrism asks us to "take care" with respect to *everything*, and the sort of mindfulness thus implied can only be called polymorphous too. That animals must suffer if we eat meat is certainly a point in favor of vegetarianism, for instance, but then again, the whole universe "suffers," in a certain sense, no matter what we eat. There are wide-ranging effects both subtle and not so subtle. So we must be self-conscious and careful in any case, taking care to walk as lightly as we can. There may be quite different and even unexpected practical implications in different places and times. We are also called to "take care" in the spiritual sense of thankfulness and awareness of communion: care, for example, not to waste food, to share it generously, and to prepare it with an eye to retaining its particular gifts. A further step would be to begin to recover native people's practices of negotiating food with the beings we might consume (and, reciprocally, with those who might consume *us*[37]).

These are not the kinds of implications one probably expects for what is after all, in part, a practical ethic. That such an ethic must wholly concern itself with decision-making methods, however, is not the only possible practicality one might ask of it. We might do better to see certain quintessentially ethical features precisely in multicentrism's "universal carefulness"—a kind of honor, for example, and an overriding commitment to attentiveness. Its practicality is of a different kind: fully engaging a complex practical question, for instance, even if the consequence is to leave us more tentative, rather than insisting on a more or less final, arguable, conclusive answer.

To conceive ethics along the lines of *etiquette*—opening of the "space" for interaction, for the re-emergence of a larger world—also calls for a kind of particular, embodied exploration. Anthropologist Henry Sharp writes that for the Chipewyan Indians, "all animate life interacts and ... affects the life and behavior of all other animate forms." His exact and telling words bear repeating:

> [T]he Chipewyan interact with all life in accordance with their understanding, and the animate universe responds. White Canada does not come silently and openly into the bush in search of understanding or communion, it sojourns briefly in the full glory of its colonial power to exploit and regulate all animate being. . . . It comes asserting a clashing causal certainty in the fundamentalist exercise of the power of its belief. It talks too loudly, its posture is wrong, its movement harsh and graceless; it does not know what to see and it hears nothing. Its presence brings a stunning confusion heard deafeningly in a growing circle of silence created by a confused and disordered animate universe.[38]

Graceless movement, a jarring presence, even just talking too loud: this innocent clumsiness reflects a failure to carry in our very bodies an understanding of ourselves as living in a larger animate universe; and failure too, crucially, to draw out, to coparticipate with, that universe. "Environmental etiquette," then, has none of the trivial connotations of mere manners. It calls for a visibly enacted openness to the world. It also goes far beyond individual comportment. We need to design neighborhoods specifically for darkness and quiet, building a world that invites animal dwelling and migration. We might time new holidays to animal migrations or the Aurorae Borealis, turn out all the lights on the solstices and equinoxes and nights of meteor showers or comets, teach gardening and bird identification in the schools, go on walkabouts for class trips.[39]

Multicentrism's most striking implication is its move toward a "communicative ethics" that ranges far beyond the human sphere. Imperative is to move from the familiar one-species monologue to a truly multipolar dialogue. The root intuition is profoundly simple, though enormously difficult for us late moderns: it is to recognize the larger world itself as a communicative realm. "All animate life interacts." As Abram reminds us:

> For the largest part of our species existence, humans have negotiated relationships with every aspect of the sensuous surroundings. . . . All could speak, articulating in gesture and whistle and sigh a shifting web of meanings that we felt on

our skin or inhaled through our nostrils or focused with our
listening ears, and to which we replied—whether with sounds,
or through movements, or minute shifts of mood. . . . Every
sound was a voice, every scrape or blunder was a meeting—with Thunder, with Oak, with Dragonfly. . . .[40]

"We are never alone," native peoples say—not even in seemingly
most wild or "empty" of places. We live and move, always, among
other "centers." As Abram makes clear, this is at once a basic experience and the upshot of the latest science. The last decades have seen a
proliferation of research and narrative writing on animal cognition and
the subtle flows of communication involving everything from cetaceans
and insects to the Earth itself.[41]

In many specific ways, often below the cultural radar, a kind of
more-than-human reciprocity and mutual accommodation is in play
already. Sometimes it is even in plain-as-day words:

In the 1950s, Western anthropologists visiting the [Kalahari
Desert] noted the eyes of many lions glowing just beyond
the [Bushmen's] cooking fire; the animals would cease their
roaring when a hunter sauntered off to the edge of camp and
asked them to keep the noise down so the children could
sleep. Human and lion shared a watering hole, one using it
by day and the other by night.[42]

Parks throughout the United States and Canada now routinely
instruct backcountry visitors in the appropriate etiquette for encounters
with bears (Speak firmly but not threateningly; Back away but do not
turn or run; Do not stare. . . .). Many writers highlight ways in which
wild animal populations systematically negotiate boundaries and other
practices with adjacent human communities. Abram writes of the little
rice offerings by means of which ants (yes, ants!) and people in Bali
arrange the borders of their respective living spaces.[43] Arne Naess and
Val Plumwood write of the almost-formal mutual accommodation of
farmers and bears in Scandanavia, dingos and humans in Australia.[44]
Vine Deloria reminds us that native peoples attend to a whole range of
interspecies communications—encounters, dreams, visions—and tell stories
of animals *becoming* humans, and vice versa, creating the covenants that
later generations (of both) can enter.[45] Entire new schools of architecture
and city design are based on what Ian McHarg famously called "design
with nature"—very much with the emphasis on the word "with."[46]

When we begin to make a systematic practice of multicentric "negotiation" in this sense, further unexpected possibilities open up.[47] Think of negotiation in much longer time-frames, too—stretching over centuries, perhaps—and we can imagine a kind of dialogue in which we put questions to nature, in the form perhaps of a variety of small and slow experiments, carefully attended to, in which alternative forms of suburban development or farming or even genetic engineering are tried out. Nature responds: the land languishes or flourishes, we and the ants or the lions live together in peace—or not. And there are other forms of direct presence as well. Rivers and mountains are not going to enter Congress themselves, for example, but why not expect Congress to meet on *their* terms—for example, in the Grand Canyon or in the Great Smoky Mountains? Would the votes on Alaskan oil drilling look the same if they were held in the Arctic National Wildlife Refuge?

Christopher Stone points out that the law has long admitted nonhuman participants—ships, bridges, colleges, municipalities, corporations—who take part in litigation and negotiation through their representatives.[48] So do individual humans who are unable to participate in their own voices; so may future human generations as well. At the very least, then, other "centers" should, and can, have similar representation. Again, as Vine Deloria reminds us, such a practice is already ancient in the councils of native peoples.[49] Gary Snyder points out that it is part of the practice of the commons as well.[50] Now we might imagine a new kind of priesthood of cross-species emissaries, an extension of John Seed and Joanna Macy's ritual of the Council of All Beings, or of the "ecosteries"—ecological monastaries—under development by Alan Drengson and others, where people can devote their lives to achieving an attunement with nature, making them natural representatives of the more-than-human in the most practical of decisions.[51]

Ethics so reconstructed will not necessarily produce the quickest and most efficient decisions. This is true of any ethic that values process: the very constitution of relationship *in* process is part of the point. We might even learn to mistrust the quick and efficient: perhaps it is part of the real function of ethics to slow things down. Still, there may also be times when certain questions and challenges cannot wait. For such times we need a provisional, temporary, even "emergency" multicentric ethic: Go light, Treasure what is left, Rebuild where we can, Minimize big risks. As Plumwood notes, this is what good ecological activism already is geared to to accomplish. It is a basic kind of environmental ethic that backgrounds anything deeper. What multicentrism adds is the wider and wilder vision: a sustainable, participatory, multivocal philosophical practice—a way back into the Multiverse.

Notes

1. Peter Singer, *The Expanding Circle* (New York: Farrar, Straus, and Giroux, 1981).

2. Singer's *Animal Liberation* (New York: Random House, 1990) and Tom Regan's *The Case for Animal Rights* (Berkeley: University of California, 1983) make the case for animals; Paul Taylor's *Respect for Life* (Princeton: Princeton University Press, 1986) and Albert Schweitzer, *Out of My Life and Thought* (Baltimore: Johns Hopkins, 1998) make the case for the considerability of all life; Aldo Leopold's *Sand County Almanac* (New York: Oxford University Press, 1949) is often read as a form of "ecocentrism." Thomas Berry and Brian Swimme, in *The Universe Story* (New York: Harper, 1994), celebrate the being of absolutely everything.

3. On "identification" the classic source is Arne Naess, in "The Shallow and the Deep, Long-range Ecology Movement: A Summary," *Inquiry* 16 (1973): 95–100, and " 'Man Apart' and Deep Ecology," *Environmental Ethics* 12 (1990): 185–92.

4. This way of putting it I owe to a reviewer for *Environmental Ethics*. In regard to human affairs the concern that universality has its costs, especially to the culturally particular, has been voiced by critics from Marx in "On the Jewish Question" to contemporary communitarians.

5. Val Plumwood, *Environmental Culture: The Ecological Crisis of Reason* (London: Routledge, 2002), p. 148.

6. Naess's appeal to "expanded identification with the non-human world" as the ground for environmental ethics is explicitly linked to "self-realization." Australian eco-activist John Seed famously insists that in acting to save the rain forest I am essentially acting to save myself, because what environmental philosophy must teach, in the end, is that "I am the rain forest" (John Seed, Joanna Macy, Pat Fleming, and Arne Naess, *Thinking Like a Mountain: Towards a Council of All Beings* [Gabiola Island, B.C.: New Society Publishers, 1988]). J. Baird Callicott offers a metaphysical analogue to this argument in "Intrinsic Value, Quantum Theory, and Environmental Ethics," *Environmental Ethics* 7 (1985): 257–75.

7. Edited by Uma Narayan and Sandra Harding (Bloomington: Indiana University Press, 2000). For other representative anthologies, see Nancy Duncan, ed., *Bodyspace: Destabilizing Geographies of Gender and Sexuality* (London: Routledge, 1996) and Chandra Talpade Mohanty, Ann Russo, and Lourdes Torres, eds., *Third World Women and the Politics of Feminism* (Bloomington: Indiana University, 1993).

8. See Plumwood's *Feminism and the Mastery of Nature* (London: Routledge, 1993) and *Environmental Culture* as well as a wide range of other books such as Karen Warren's *Ecofeminist Philosophy* (Lanham, MD: Rowman and Littlefield, 2000) and Susan Griffin's classic *Women and Nature* (New York: Harper and Row, 1978).

9. *Environmental Culture*, chapter 5. I return to this theme in section IV below.

10. In discussion, Spring 2002. Abram also suggested the lovely term *polynodal*.

11. *I and Thou* (W. Kaufmann trans., New York: Scribner's, 1970), pp. 57–59.

12. In *The Natural Alien* (Toronto: University of Toronto Press, 1985), pp. 40–41 and 98–99.

13. "Does the tree then have consciousness, similar to our own? I have no experience of that. . . . What I encounter is neither the soul of a tree nor a dryad, but the tree itself." (*I and Thou*, pp. 58–59)

14. *Essays in Radical Empiricism and A Pluralistic Universe* (New York: Dutton, 1971), p. 275. "Things are 'with' one another in many ways, but nothing includes everything or dominates over everything. . . . The pluralistic world is . . . more like a federal republic than like an empire or a kingdom. However much may be collected, however much may report itself as present at any effective center of consciousness or action, something else is self-governed and absent and unreduced to unity." (p. 274).

15. They move within us too, for the self is a kind of multicentric "federal republic" as well. It is multicentrism all the way down. I am indebted to Bob Jickling for this point.

16. Tom Birch, "Moral Considerability and Universal Consideration," *Environmental Ethics* 15 (1993): 313–32.

17. Gary Snyder, *The Practice of the Wild* (San Francisco: North Point Press, 1990), pp. 3–24. Grizzly tracker Doug Peacock insists on "interspecific tact," Wendell Berry speaks of an "etiquette" toward nature, Calvin Martin of "courtesy" between very different beings. I develop this theme in chapter 7 ("Transhuman Etiquettes") in my *Back to Earth* (Philadelphia: Temple University Press, 1994).

18. Jim Cheney and Anthony Weston, "Environmental Ethics as Environmental Etiquette: Toward an Ethics-Based Epistemology in Environmental Philosophy," *Environmental Ethics* 21 (1999): 115–34 (chapter 4 of this book).

19. *Nature and Madness* (San Francisco: Sierra Club Books, 1982), p. 38. Vine Deloria uses similar terms in his *Spirit and Reason* (Golden, CO: Fulcrum Publishing, 1999), pp. 51–52.

20. "Moral Understandings: Alternative 'Epistemology' for a Feminist Ethics," *Hypatia* 4 (1989), p. 21. A classic source for revisioning ethics in this key is Eva Kittay and Diana Meyers's collection *Women and Moral Theory* (Totowa, NJ: Rowman and Littlefield, 1987).

21. See Christopher Manes, "Nature and Silence," *Environmental Ethics* 14 (1992): 339–50; Christopher Preston, "Conversing with Nature in a Postmodern Epistemological Framework," *Environmental Ethics* 22 (2000): 227–40; and Scott Friskics, "Dialogical Relations with Nature," *Environmental Ethics* 23 (2001): 391–410.

22. In *Reinventing Eden* (London: Routledge, 2003), chapter 11. The citation is from p. 228.

23. Jim Nollman's *Dolphin Dreamtime* (New York: Bantam, 1987) is subtitled "The Art and Science of Interspecies Communication." Rich and

wide-angled treatments are David Abram, *The Spell of the Sensuous* (New York: Pantheon, 1996) and Derrick Jensen, *A Language Older Than Words* (New York: Context Books, 2000).

24. Dryzek, "Green Reason: Communicative Ethics for the Biosphere," *Environmental Ethics* 12 (1990): 195–210; Val Plumwood, *Environmental Culture*, chapters 5 and 8.

25. The "otherized" group, as she calls it, is first marked out as radically separate (women from men; colonized from colonizer; animals from humans). Differences within the otherized group are then denied and submerged (all women are radically distinguished from all men; all animals from all humans . . .). Mutual dependence is denied and the Other is construed as inessential or defective, and made invisible. Finally, the Other is viewed as valuable only as means to the One's ends (nature for human ends, etc.). *Environmental Culture*, chapter 5.

26. Plumwood has urged this concern on me as part of an extensive and energetic correspondence since I began this project several years ago. I am grateful for her persistence and insight, which have immeasurably improved my thinking on this and many other points. I regret that it is not quite improved enough for her on this one.

27. *Environmental Culture*, chapter 8.

28. "The choice these two frameworks offer us, of valuing nature either as Same or as Different, is ultimately an anthropocentric one, since to base value exclusively on either sameness or difference from the human implicitly construes the human as the center and pivot of value," ibid., p. 201.

29. Ibid., p. 167.

30. Molefi Asante, *The Afrocentric Idea* (Philadelphia: Temple University Press, 1987), p. 3, and C. Tsehloane Keto, *Vision and Time: Historical Perspective of an Africa-Centered Paradigm* (Lanham, MD: University Press of America, 2001), "Vulindlela" (Preface). The term *polycentric* is adopted by Samir Amin, in *Delinking* (London: Zed Books, 1990). He defines it as "subjecting the mutual relations between the various nations and regions of the planet to the varying imperatives of their own internal development and not the reverse" (p. xii). Keto explicitly speaks of a "multicentered scholarship" and of a "nonhegemonic African-centered analysis"—as well as a nonhegemonic Europe-centered analysis (*Vision and Time*, pp. xii and 25). Though he carefully distinguishes an "Africa-centered paradigm" from "Afrocentrism," this, he says, is a reaction to certain unscholarly excesses by some writers who use the latter label, not a conceptual difficulty with "centrism" itself (p. xvii).

31. Still, in the end, why not some other descriptive and less risky label? Apart from the difficulty of actually coming up with a decent alternative label (OK, *you* try it), the fact remains that the debate between "centrisms" still claims the spotlight in the teaching anthologies and in the journals. The rest of us, then—the many and varied alternative voices I have tried to draw into this essay—must enter the lists in a way that is as obviously and constructively as possible engaged with the dominant range of views. In my judgment this requires advancing a view under the heading of "centrism" itself. No list of centrisms, I would hope, can now be considered complete without *multi*centrism—but

the very concept is also a kind of Trojan horse, for multicentrism offers an alternative to the entire centric project as so far understood. In time it may be better to go back to James and label the new view something more like "multiversalism," or adopt Irene Klaver's punnish suggestion and call ourselves "*ex*centric." But only in time.

Addendum, 2007:

After this paper was published I received a spirited e-mail from Ralph Acampora of Hofstra University, in which he took on the challenge of finding a decent alternative label for the sort of view proposed here. He offered the phrase "manifestival of beings" for that purpose, and explains:

> I think it aptly connotes the dynamics of both revelation and celebration that you marshal; moreover, there's a nice doubling on the "man-" of "many" (as in "manifold") and of the hand (as in "manufacture")—which plays up at once the themes of both diversity and embodied engagement. "Manifestivism" is probably too obscure a label for a method or a movement, but "manifestival" might work as the object of our endeavors. Let the relevant manifestivities begin!

32. J. Douglas Rabb, "From Triangles to Tripods: Polycentrism in Environmental Ethics," *Environmental Ethics* 14 (1992): 177–83, and Peter Wenz, "Minimal, Moderate, and Extreme Moral Pluralism," *Environmental Ethics* 15 (1993): 61–74.

33. J. B. Callicott, "The Case Against Moral Pluralism," *Environmental Ethics* 12 (1990), esp. p. 104.

34. See my "On Callicott's Case against Pluralism," *Environmental Ethics* 13:3 (1991), and "What Are We Arguing About?" Symposium presentation on "Monism v. Pluralism in Environmental Ethics," APA Central Division meeting, Chicago, 1993.

35. David Abram made this point in discussion, Spring 2002.

36. Except from a galactic point of view, which someday may be important.

37. See Plumwood's *Environmental Culture*, pp. 225–27. Once again she is way out in front.

38. Henry S. Sharp, *The Transformation of Bigfoot: Maleness, Power, and Belief Among the Chipewyan* (Washington, DC: Smithsonian Institution Press, 1988), pp. 144–45. I am indebted to Jim Cheney for this citation.

39. Along with our joint paper cited above (n. 18), commentaries by Jim Cheney and myself on Birch's concept of universal consideration expand this theme ("Universal Consideration: A Epistemological Map of the Terrain" [Cheney] and "Universal Consideration as an Originary Practice" [Weston] both appear in *Environmental Ethics* 20 [1998]). The celebratory note is especially important: think of the appeal of what we could call "celebratory environmentalism" as

opposed to "environmentalism of threats." There are implications for teaching as well: See my essay "What If Teaching Went Wild?" in Scott Fletcher, ed., *Philosophy of Education 2002* (Urbana, Illinois: Philosophy of Education Society, 2003): 40–52 (chapter 7 of this book).

40. Abram, *The Spell of the Sensuous*, p. ix.

41. See my *Back to Earth*, chapters 2–4.

42. Jim Nollman, in *Utne Reader*, March/April 98, p. 100. There is more to this story, though: "When ranching was introduced [, . . .] cattle began to share the watering hole without regard to schedules. At first lions kept their distance, as if cattle were an extension of the human family. But eventually they attacked. Ranchers reciprocated by shooting the lions, and within a few years lions had killed several Bushmen." Notice that this is still a communicative form—just a different and more lethal one.

43. *The Spell of the Sensuous*, p. 11ff.

44. Arne Naess, "Self-realization in Mixed Communities of Humans, Bears, Sheep and Wolves," *Inquiry* 22 (1979): 231–41; Val Plumwood, "The Fraser Island Dingo Cull and the Ethics of Negotiation," paper presented at Environment Day Symposium, Social and Political Theory Program, Australian National University, June 2001. See also Bob Jickling and Paul Paquet, "Wolves, Ethics, and Epistemology," paper presented at "Culling Mammals," a symposium organized by the Mammal Society and the International Fund for Animal Welfare, London, November 2000.

45. *Spirit and Reason*, chapters 4, 5, and 10; see also Gary Snyder's lovely essay "The Woman Who Married a Bear," in *The Practice of the Wild*, pp. 155–74. "Covenant" is a precise word, too (remember it is also Shepard's). The mutual obligations and expectations that arise from such species-border-crossings are not entirely voluntary, can be renewed or broken, but are not constantly created anew (a point emphasized by Jim Cheney).

46. Ian McHarg, *Design with Nature* (Garden City, NY: Doubleday, 1969). See also Merchant, *Reinventing Eden*, pp. 236–39.

47. See my essay "Self-Validating Reduction: Toward a Theory of Environmental Devaluation," *Environmental Ethics* 18 (1996): 115–32 (chapter 3 of this book).

48. Christopher Stone, *Should Trees Have Standing?* (Los Altos, CA: William Kaufmann, 1974).

49. Deloria, *Spirit and Reason*. A lovely teaching tale is Paula Underwood, "Who Speaks for Wolf?" in *Three Native American Learning Stories* (San Anselmo, CA: Tribe of Two Press, The LearningWay Company, 2002).

50. See Snyder, *The Practice of the Wild*, pp. 25–47.

51. Seed, et al., *Thinking Like a Mountain*. See also the "Workshop Manual" at <www.rainforestinfo.org.au/deep-eco/cabcont.htm>. The Web site for the Ecostery Foundation of North America is <www.ecostery.org>.

Chapter 6

De-Anthropocentrizing the World

Environmental Ethics as a Design Challenge

Nobody can save the world,
but any of us can help set in motion a self-saving world.

—Stewart Brand

In the face of environmental crisis we are prone to say that everything must be rethought: what we eat, how well we insulate the attic, how we drive and with how many people. And of course, we add, our very thinking itself must be rethought as well. Luckily a philosophical kind of environmental professional now stands at our service too. If it is the job of automakers to retool our cars, it is the job of these philosophers to retool our philosophies, our root understandings of ourselves in the world. Thus we are offered a philosophical analysis—and often a parallel theological and/or literary analysis—of the current crisis. We have been under the influence of too narrow a view of things, we are told—too human-centered or "anthropocentric" a vision of how the world goes and what matters in it. A philosophical response naturally follows: we

---

This essay originally appeared in my book *Jobs for Philosophers*, which I self-published through Xlibris Corporation in 2004 as a kind of edgy circular for my friends. In form, *Jobs for Philosophers* is a collection of book reviews and the occasional manifesto, with the small peculiarity that none of the manifesto-issuers or books reviewed actually exist (except the first one, which is *Jobs for Philosophers* itself). A series of sources appear, including myself, all reviewed from yet another and incompletely specified authorial point of view. Sometimes the putative authors are multiple, even entire putative movements, as in the manifesto reprinted here. (So do not be jarred by the plural voice: it's really just me again.) The whole book, then, is a literary conceit to allow a sweeping re-vision of philosophy's possibilities, without the scholarly hyper-development and fortification often expected. The book presents itself as "a manifesto-in-disguise for a style of philosophy that does not exist (yet) but *should*" . . .

are offered a variety of theories of "nonanthropocentrism" in which the claim is to transcend anthropocentrism in thought, reconnecting with ancient and native worldviews, perhaps, or drawing on the most modern developments in ecology and even physics, to reinstall humans within a larger natural world.

This we could call *philosophy de-anthropocentrizing itself.*

It will be our first contention that no such project has a hope of succeeding even in its own terms: that is, even apart from the question whether a de-anthropocentrized perspective can make any difference in the world, de-anthropocentrizing the world in thought alone is not possible anyway, not in a world so thoroughly anthropocentrized in all of its aspects—philosophical and most emphatically in every other way too. A thoroughly humnanized language; the commercially colonized imagination; even the physical settings in which the question of post-anthropocentrism comes up—all of these inevitably give our supposed post-anthropocentrisms a profoundly and necessarily anthropocentric cast, though often enough, and naturally enough, well below the threshold of awareness.

It will be our second contention that this very dependence of thought on its "environment"—on its architectural, aural, even physical setting—cuts both ways. On the one hand it precludes even the self-supposedly freest thinker from leapfrogging the culture in thought. On the other hand, it immediately and just as emphatically opens another avenue for a de-anthropocentrizing process: to begin to de-anthropocentrize that very architectural, aural, even physical setting so as to *bring thought along.* We cannot de-anthropocentrize thought somehow in one stroke and by itself, but we can (begin to) to de-anthropocentrize the world as a whole, especially by remaking those very dimensions of the world usually thought almost beneath notice (and therefore quite literally not noticed) by those of us so committed to a dialectic of thought alone.

It is therefore our central contention that tomorrow belongs to the designers. Tomorrow belongs to those who are beginning to remake our ways of living, yes, and eating, building, celebrating, keeping time, sharing a world with other creatures. We offer here a philosophical prolegomenon to this work, then, and more: a philosophical claim to it, or its claim to philosophy. Here lies a different kind of invitation to philosophy, a different kind of philosophical dialectic and task: "breaking the spell of the actual" not in the service of some already-theorized or theorizable post-anthropocentric alternative, but precisely in the service of *finding our way to it* . . .

I. Philosophy Cannot De-Anthropocentrize Itself

Would not a true "environmentalism" require recognizing the dependence even of our thought upon its environment—upon its setting? What then of the setting of a new ethic *for* the environment itself—posited within a world that is profoundly anthropocentrized, in fact so profoundly as to hardly even be noticeable?

Even the very terms in which we put our ethical questions are suspect. We are told—indeed we are offered as a starting-point, a definition—that "environmental ethics is concerned with the moral relations that hold between humans and the natural world." So the called-for arguments, the sought-after "foundations" and "groundings" for such an ethic, are supposed to address all and only humans, "us," on behalf of "the natural world."

Environmental ethics is therefore invited to begin by positing, not questioning, a sharp divide that "we" must somehow cross, moreover taking that "we" unproblematically to denote all humans. But to invoke such a divide is already to take one ethical position among others. Historically, when humans said "we," they hardly ever meant to include all other humans. "We" might be the tribe, its domestic animals, its associated wild guardians, even the living mountains and land—all fundamental to the community, so fundamental in fact that if one were displaced the entire community died. Even in medieval Europe, "we" still meant a "mixed community," including at the very least a wide range of other animals. Look at the buildings: pigs and horses lived in the house.

Thus the starting-point assumption that all of "us" must now rethink "our" relation to all of "it," all of "nature," might even be the core of the *problem.*

Then there is the matter of physical setting. Take even the very academic offices and seminar rooms in which we talk and think about these matters: the *actual* "ground" of environmental philosophy. No (other) animals are allowed in our buildings, and even children are rare. Talk about "impacted" ground! We have no ground at all—or, if you like, our ground is only the maximally "impacted," prestressed concrete maybe—yet here is where we presume to stand. For all of our talk about "grounding" environmental ethics, *the actual "ground" of our philosophy is not ground at all.* Our offices and classrooms plagued by increasingly loud blowers, impossible to shut off, unopenable windows and doors, as if the designers deliberately set out to frustrate thinking or any sense of communion or awareness, especially in academic settings. Given this kind of setting, it is not surprising that only adult, rational, discursive, technological creatures stand out for ethical philosophy—so even children and certainly animals are problematic philosophically, ethically. When philosophers say things like "I do not see that animals count ethically," we should take them absolutely literally. They do not *see* animals . . . Well, they don't. But then pretty obviously the answer is to go look. Why take a radical and self-validating inattentiveness as something that needs *refutation?*

How much does the entire conceptual apparatus of environmental ethics owe to its arising on thoroughly ungrounded ground? The historian Roderick Nash, trying to speak through an interpreter to a Malay hunter-gatherer, could not even find a word for "wilderness." "Finally, in desperation, I asked the interpreter to ask the hunter how he said 'I am lost in the jungle.' An exchange occurred at the conclusion of which the interpreter turned to me and said with a smile that the man had indicated that he did not get lost in the jungle."[1] So perhaps it is only because we *do* get lost in the jungle that we need a language for lostness—but then it is in *that* language that we presume to "do" environmental ethics! It is no surprise that we are still lost, even more lost than we were before.

From this perspective that annoying old habit of localizing ethical principles or even whole philosophical systems is essential for clarity. Mary Midgley points out that existentialism, for example, is above all an *urban* philosophy:

> The really monstrous thing about Existentialism is its proceeding as if the world contained only dead matter (things) on the one hand and fully rational, educated, adult human beings on the other—as if there were no other life-forms. The impression of desertion or abandonment which existentialists have is due, I am sure, not to the removal of God, but to this contemptuous dismissal of almost the whole of the biosphere—plants, animals, and children. Life shrinks to a few urban rooms; no wonder it becomes absurd.[2]

Yes—but again: it is not that life has shrunk to a few urban rooms *because* one is an existentialist; rather, one is an existentialist at least in part *because* life has shrunk to a few urban rooms. Take Camus's famous lines delineating "the absurd":

> Strangeness creeps in: perceiving that the world is "dense": sensing to what degree a stone is foreign and irreduc-

ible to us, with what intensity nature or a landscape can negate us. . . .[3]

Might not "strangeness creep in" precisely because one has hitherto lived a life in which all stones were tamed, maybe even pulverized, so that confronted with even so simple and ordinary a thing, in nature for once, we find it threatening, "negating"? "At the heart of all beauty lies something inhuman," says our friend, and this nonhumanity emerges for him as *hostility*. "The primitive hostility of the world rises up to face us across millennia." When in fact we might wonder whether it is mere nonhumanity ("*in*humanity" is a loaded term), unfamiliar only to one who has been immersed so long in mere humanity that the human seems to constitute the entire universe. What a surprise, what a shock, what a *threat*, when there turns out to be more.

Humans have always appropriated land for homes, farms, cities. But the traditional patterns always also allowed a space for wildness, indeed lived within it. Beyond the city walls lay unpredictable encounters with wild things, including other humans. Hans Peter Duerr shows that for the medievals the boundary between wilderness and civilization was permeable and often-crossed, like a low fence. In the country, at least, invitations to the wild lay at every turn. Strange animals roamed there, and at night the vast panorama of the skies opened up. Even the blossoms of the yew tree under which one might fall asleep were mild hallucinogens. An afternoon's nap actually could turn into a trip to the Venus Mountain.[4] But now the animals and the yews and even the vastness of the night are gone, and the Venusberg is the stuff only of opera. Is it a surprise that "wild" philosophy has turned just as operatic?

So again: from *here* we expect to be able to articulate and develop a philosophy that decisively transcends anthropocentrism? To the contrary: It is no surprise that in the largely urbanized and technological environment where nearly all of our philosophical discussions take place, "nonanthropocentrism" remains merely an abstract and "alternative" position, a dimly imagined and essentially just verbal placeholder. We do suspect that a genuine "nonanthropocentrism" characterized other cultures and alternative practices. But they are also cultures and practices that themselves stand at a huge and perhaps unbridgeable distance from the world within which we are trying to envision them. Actually we cannot even describe them except negatively: they are *not* anthropocentric, we say. "Nonanthropocentr*ism*" is just a label. Once again, then: mightn't we be in the impossible position of attempting to explicate a sort of ethics of which only the vaguest outlines *can* emerge, for us, now?

Once human-centeredness—the "anthropo-" part of anthropo-centrism—is identified as the problem, it is natural enough to imagine that we can leverage ourselves into nonanthropocentric alternatives by embracing, perhaps, "biocentrism" (where all life becomes the "center" or source of value and the focus of moral consideration and action) or maybe "ecocentrism" (where ecosystems as a whole take this place). This way of thinking in fact is so familiar that it has become the structure of innumerable introductions and textbooks in environmental ethics. Once again it is often attempted with enormous good faith and hope. Still, though, it too bears the signs not only of the armchair but also of the wholly human-centered settings upon which, whatever its ultimate intentions, it still depends. The very idea of a "center," for one thing, invokes a logic of inclusion and exclusion, for if there is a "center" there is also a periphery, and there will be Others beyond the pale. If we then ask who or what stands at the center of the center, as it were—who or what is the reference-point for the whole "expanding circle," where the expansion starts—it turns out to be "us" again, the wholly human sphere, and within the human sphere the individual person, conceived in the old familiar ways. Even the most expansive forms of "-centrism" posit as their innermost circles the supposedly secure and familiar sphere of the (human) self. Whereas one might have thought that a kind of *multi*centric inclusiveness—in which "oneness" would precisely *not* be the goal—would have to characterize a real alternative.

Animal Rights? But the usual, supposedly nonanthropocentric argument is precisely the one just alluded to: the arguments appeal to specific parallels—cognitive, sensory, social, and so forth—between (other) animals and *us*, the intended conclusion being that since we have rights, we are logically compelled to *extend* such rights to them. So who after all is the "center," the point of reference, the real pivot of the argument here?

Once again, too, the entire argument for animal rights takes place against a background of what Ben Marcus labels "self-validating reduction."[5] One effect of factory farming chickens or veal calves, or of using physically restrained chimps for drug experiments, is to terrorize, cripple, and debase the animals to the point that the pitiful creatures that result do in fact seem to be utterly implausible candidates for anything but human use. Even people who work with those animals may find it impossible to feel any serious concern for them, and conversely people who speak up for them will indeed seem to be speaking sentimentally, and also may in fact know the animals less well. After all, we are not just speaking up against the treatment of particular animals now, but also and perhaps most fundamentally against the debasement of the species:

the refusal to honor the autonomous potential of such creatures and the
ultimate destruction of the very possibility of autonomy or spontaneity.
Only thus can we bring into focus the deliberately undertaken process
of turning certain animals *into* creatures who have no serious claim on
us. But therefore, in a world in which that process is nonetheless a fait
accompli, we are left to speak for what might have been, not so much
against the suffering and violation of this particular animal but for a
vision of an appropriate life for this *kind* of animal. Inevitably it *is* a
matter of speculation, sentiment, indirection. The old ways of speaking for (or, indeed, with) other animals vanishes, and we are left with
only philosophical talk, speculative and nostalgic. Then those ways of
speaking too are driven toward more and more general and perhaps
also "principled" statements, arguments from ethical theories, carrying
less and less actual force and invoking a set of possibilities at a greater
and greater distance. Thus one might pessimistically see the appeal to
animal rights as the last line of defense for many animals—and a tragi-
cally weak line at that.

   Even the philosophical appeal to something called the "intrinsic
value" of nature might be seen as a desperate rhetorical device rather
than the inauguration of a new relation between humans and the nonhuman world. It may be that the urgency with which intrinsic value is
now so liberally spread around is only another sign that the *instrumentalization* of the world has reached a fever pitch. *The very distinction
between means and ends, or "instrumental" and "intrinsic" value, itself
may be another feature of the anthropocentrized world:* another mode of
technological rationalization, in short a reduction of the multilayered
depth of nearly every thing to the purely available, ready-for-use-and-
discard kind of object we are now offered at every turn. The conception
of the "intrinsic" in turn as necessarily *un*connected to other things is
just as reduced on the other side: as if the depth of things could not lie
precisely in their connection, in their "ecology." Yet these are the very
terms in which most of environmental philosophy conducts business,
categories that seem to almost all of us to be given features of reality,
logical necessities. Perhaps then it is once again a mere placeholder, a
form of almost inchoate resistance to instrumentalization that ought not
to be taken so literally—but no, we are nothing if not literal. . . .

II. A Philosophical Designer's Mandate

An impasse, then? If a thoroughly anthropocentrized world irresistibly
confines and shapes philosophy after its own image, are we utterly trapped

in its web? Is there is nothing whatever for environmental philosophy to do, if we cannot think our way all the way out of anthropocentrism with our existing tools and within the environments that we now occupy?

It could be so. That environmental philosophers have a "job" at all is not a given. On the other hand, very large questions open here about the dynamics of change not just in philosophy but in general. Postmodernists, for their part, insisting on the radical dependence of thought on its context, mistrust any grand designs for social change; much of their analysis instead is directed against the uses of grand ideas, philosophical and other, as instruments of oppression or social rationalization. In the merely modernist and so-called vulgar Marxism that inspires much of this analysis, meanwhile, the emphasis shifts all the way over to "material" elements, to the "means of production" and the patterns of human relations they create. Philosophers either ought to make themselves relentless critics of everything existing—or join the working class, go unionize the factories.

But to continue in these schematic terms: surely a purely materialist model of change is just as oversimplified and, if you like, "unecological" as the original. Marx famously claimed to have stood the Hegelian dialectic on its head (he actually said, "feet")—ideas do not drive material changes, he declared: material changes drive ideas—but in fact neither Marx nor Hegel need to be simply flipped over. One-way linkages between clearly demarcated causes and effects do not characterize cultural phenomena (or indeed *any* phenomena). So the question is emphatically *not* whether ethical ideas are cause or effect in cultural systems, as if the only alternative to being purely a cause is to be purely an effect. Causation takes place in complex, interdependent, and evolving systems with multiple feedback loops.

So the truth is that we are not trapped at all. We are only at an impasse from that philosophical point of view that takes the relation to ideas to the world to be one-way, so that the dependence of thought upon the world and the consequent demise of the philosopher as independent and world-shaping *subject* essentially undercuts the very possibility of philosophy itself. This is the Hegel that Marx claimed to have turned upside down. Arguably the original is as "vulgar" as the reverse. With everything invested in one grandiose point of entry, with philosophy insistent on somehow securing an independent place to stand and move the world, the reassertion of an interdependent world of flow, with no independently grounded kinds of standpoints, inevitably comes as a disaster. As for *us*, however, we merely take this newer and more ecological model of mind to open up the possibility of philosophy in a different key. We seek instead a workable mode of world-reconstruction that is also, looked at in a long-term and multilateral way, a mode of thinking as well.

The very rootedness of thought within the "given" world creates a profound kind of leverage that we would never have if thought floated free. In a web of interrelatedness, even quite distant and small changes eventually touch every other element of the system. In place of a single, exalted entry-point, the real world offers us innumerable small ones. Change is mediated and equilibrated and integrated with all of the other dynamics of the whole—ultimate consequences and effects are unforeseeable, one tinkers with such "levers" as we can create, or as life offers, as a kind of *experiment*—but change is the underlying given; or *flow*. Even a small deflection upstream can change the direction of a whole river.

Ideas of course make a difference—only they have no automatic primacy. They too flow with the whole. The central question is strategic: where we can work to the best effect. Environmental philosophy, we suggest, has hitherto had the wrong answer. Vastly overinvesting in the ideal as such, philosophy essentially abandons the actual world to be remade willy-nilly by road-builders, moviemakers, interior decorators, software writers—by builders and designers, in short, often quite literally, with their own agendas and reference points. It is therefore precisely on the level of building and design that we choose to work. If our cities and workplaces and homes systematically cut us off from nature, if the land is no longer wild, if we cannot "see" animals—if all of these forms of anthropocentrization engender and sustain the anthropocentrization of thought itself, the opposite is also the case: We can begin to de-anthropocentrize thought by de-anthropocentrizing the world itself. Here then is our specific starting-point, our specific point of entry: we propose to undertake the reconstruction of *thought* through the reconstruction of *experience* through the reconstruction of the immediate world of experience itself.

III. What Is to Be Done?

There is a kind of designer who undertakes a conscious and continuous series of small but systematic changes in the some aspect of the shape of the everyday world. Modest enough, barely "philosophical" at all according to the usual Platonic standards, below the usual disciplinary radar, the project is nonetheless audacious in its own terms, specifically in *its willingness to undertake open-ended transformation*. And could not we see this, after all, as philosophical, only in a different key? Not to mention necessary? . . .

Stewart Brand—inventor, designer, founder of the *Whole Earth Catalog* and too many other other books and projects to even begin to list—poses a fundamental question in his book called *The Clock of the Long Now*:[6] How can our culture learn to take care for the long term? A grave disconnect is in progress, Brand tells us. We look ahead a few years, maybe, or a few decades—at best our own lifetimes, maybe just to the next quarterly report—while we lay waste to the world around us and leave the mess to our children and great-great-grandchildren. How can we stop so compulsively treating the Earth as if there were no tomorrow?

Now here is a real problem, arguably one of the deepest and most desperate problems of our time. No doubt it seems to demand a "revision in our way of thinking," as some philosopher is sure to put it, and thus to invite a new theory of time, a new metaphysics, or the like—as if the problem originates in our way of *thinking*. Brand, however, is a practical man, a designer on all scales. His type of solution is *cultural tinkering*, sometimes even of the tiniest specifics. The scale of the possible effects, however, is breathtaking.

Even such a simple and seemingly irrelevant matter as how we notate time—is this a mere detail after all? If we notated only hours, say, but had no way to remind ourselves of days or weeks or years, we would not be surprised to find ourselves with an even more spectacularly shortsighted view of things than we already have. A kind of analogue to this spectacular sort of practical self-limitation may have been behind the "Y2K" problem, otherwise perhaps inexplicable in its near-sightedness. Late twentieth-century entury computer programmers built the entire computer infrastructure around programs that recorded time in only two digits: 89, for 1989 for example, or 93, for 1993, while one would have thought anyone could see that this practice was unsustainable past the year 1999, because a two-digit computer program will not read 00, 01, and so on as next in line but rather as the beginning of the sequence. The result was that, at multiple-hundred-billion-dollar cost, the world's computers had to be reprogrammed to track the years in more digits.

In the end it mostly worked, the "Y2K problem" was solved in a cliff-hanger, and the doomsayers returned from the hills. Yet, Brand says, we have not learned the whole lesson. We have solved the problem temporarily, yes. The same problem will recur in the year 9999, though—the Y10K problem, as it were—when time must switch from four digits to five. If we took a *ten-thousand-year view* we would even now be writing the years in five digits. Not 1954 but 01954. Not 2003 but 02003. The past and the future, which we are accustomed to see at such a distance from us, then come closer. The year 2050 seems very far from 2000, but 02050 is almost adjacent to 02000. Dates that now stand out with a certain bold distinctiveness—1066, 1945—return to a bigger flow: 01066, 01945.

We could of course keep adding placeholders. Write 02003 as 000002003, and the leftmost counter would only turn over when the galaxy completes its next rotation. Add another and the leftmost counter would turn over when life has doubled its current tenure on Earth. But these scales stretch time so far as to make it inhuman. We remain with the question: What is an appropriate scale *for us?* Elise Boulding proposes two hundred years, the seven-generation idea. For Brand this is not long enough either. Ten thousand years, the life span of civilization so far, would be a worthier goal: not so long as to be humanly unimaginable, but long enough to bring the flow of earth history into focus.

Welcome, then, to "Clock of the Long Now" of Brand's title. He and his collaborators aim to create an embodied sense of a "Long Now" in something like the way that the Apollo photographs of Earth from space provoked a sense of the "Big Here," making themselves icons of global awareness out of a more parochial time. Those photographs made many of us *see* for the first time that we were living in too small a "Here": the "here" of the self; or of our town; or of our friends; and even of our nation. Enough benefit right there, Brand says, to justify the $25,000,000,000 Moon program. After Apollo the "Here" became the whole Earth. Now the question is: What could likewise make us *see* our current parochialism in regard to time? How could our "Now" become bigger—longer—than today or this week or this business quarter or my life?

The crucial step once again is *to approach our nearsightedness as a design challenge* rather than as an invitation to rethink our philosophical categories. It really does take a photograph, an iconic object, a different notational system. It takes, say, a new kind of clock. Imagine for instance a clock that has only a second hand—to show it is running—and then a hand that shows what century you are in. Think of the spaciousness of *that* view, and the freedom it embodies from the shackles (literally) we have learned to make of time itself. As in: the wristwatch that tells time in seconds (and now often in fractions of seconds), for instance, and so puts life on a hair-trigger—always late for the next meeting, but still with a few seconds to jam something else in between. This is a Short Now, a Miniscule Now, a Vanishing Now. It is also a cultural choice, a practice, a technology. And it is changeable in just the same terms.

Imagine a clock that ticks once a day, chimes once a century. Imagine some such clocks being enormous, so big you can actually go inside, watch them run, perhaps help wind them by your very presence. At the times of chimings and Great Turnings, imagine ceremonies, elaborate preparations and checks, a little like the moon voyages, perhaps, and intentionally as iconic. The clocks would not only tell time on the ten-thousand-year scale but also would be ten-thousand-year responsibilities of humankind: they would have to be built to last that long, longer than the pyramids so far, and keep accurate time too, through all sorts of possible perturbations—nuclear winters, meteor impacts, and on and on—but at the same time could not operate or be powered in such a way as to be utterly impenetrable to those who might have to repair or recalibrate them. Transparent, permanent, participatory.

You can see immediately that building such a clock poses all manner of deep design questions. How do you build a complex device that will remain transparent to the utterly unknown people who will inherit it—who will eventually be as distant from us as those of our own ancestors who created the first civilizations? How can or should it display information? What information? How can or should it be powered?

Such clocks have been designed. Decisions have been argued and made, prototypes have been built—one chimed in the new millennium—and enormous clocks are being planned for the high deserts, environments good for permanence. Those involved include the musician Brian Eno and Danny Hillis, famous as the designer of the world's fastest supercomputers, now the designer as well of, in effect, the world's slowest computer. Related projects have been launched, such as Ten Thousand-Year Libraries, an attempt to create means of passing down what the geoscientist James Lovelock calls "start-up manuals for civilization" in "conspicuously durable" forms, all too aware that even now the loss or destruction of massive amounts of information, indeed whole cultural legacies, is a real possibility (nuclear war; the degradation of all electronic storage media; even deliberate burnings of national libraries, which the Serbs undertook as recently as 01992 in Bosnia). Brand reminds us that only one copy of ancient classics—*Beowolf,* the works of Lucretius, Tacitus, the plays of Euripides—made it through the Dark Ages ("even with the heroic continuity of the Catholic Church, the skein of culture was reduced to fragile wisps")—and vastly more has been lost forever. Let it not happen again. This too is a ten-thousand-year responsibility. Such libraries could anchor a range of further "attention-lengthening" projects, such as time-mail to the future; "responsibility records," studying delayed effects of specific controversial decisions; long-term scientific studies; warnings from the past (for example, periodic reminders to the governments of the day where nuclear wastes are buried—a 500,000 year responsibility, actually, which itself ought to give us pause); and linguistic preservation (two-thirds of the world's spoken languages are at risk of disappearing entirely, our own cultural form of endangered species). Information can be passed on to the distant future in all manner of ways. "Hide forest-losing statistics and reforesting advice inside virgin forests. Bury information on global warming inside glaciers. Seed uncleared minefields with data on who exactly planted the mines."[7]

Brand and his cohort we now dub *post-anthropocentrizing cultural tinkerers*. Post-anthropocentrism here is a *project* (thus post-anthropocent*rizing* tinkerers, not post-anthropocen*tric*, as if they were already beyond anthropocentrism); tinkering is their *method*. Nothing less than the *culture* itself is the field of play. Philosophers as the designers of tomorrow.

Consider next the peculiarly humanized construction of the "our" and the "we" that we noted in foundational statements like "environmental ethics is concerned with our moral relations to the natural world." Suppose that we re-approach this too as a design problem: here as a question of architecture, interior planning, city layout. Indeed the peculiarly humanized construction of the "our" and the "we" is quite literally a question of *construction*. So suppose that we ask, on the level of design, how we could begin to construct a more inclusive and/or "mixed" experience—"mixed" in the sense of including more than humans, not so insistent on species lines, more particular to a specific place and time, to the flow of the land and the local community of life.

The answer is by making it possible once again for humans to encounter the more-than-human on a daily basis, and vice versa: that is, by making it *physically* possible—easy, compelling, in the end necessary—to have a constant and consistent sense of living within, of being a part of, a larger living community, recovering modes of everyday life and practice that bring with them a mixed community from the start. Building neighborhoods for instance that allow us to coexist with other animals, that honor existing migration patterns, maintain and recreate feeding spots, preserve breeding grounds and burrows and dens, redirect human paths elsewhere—sharing the land, in short, rather than imposing our own patterns on it as if it were otherwise merely "empty."

A step further and we can think about designing not just for coexistence but for encounter, for interaction. More than mere "live and let live," here we seek to enter into relationship. Plan human paths, then, that *meet* other animals'—at the borders of their and our more individualized spaces. The philosopher-farmer Wendell Berry highlights "the phenomenon of edge or margin . . . , one of the powerful attractions of a diversified landscape both to wildlife and to humans." "Margins" are places where domesticity and wildness meet.

The human eye itself seems drawn to such margins, hunger-
ing for the difference made in the countryside by a hedgy
fencerow, a stream, or a grove of trees. These margins are
biologically rich, the meeting of two kinds of habitat.[8]

Certain plant and animal communities may be necessary; relative
quiet; dark at night. A certain scale is needed too—Berry speaks of the
traditional landscape's conjunction of small fields and their wooded
borders—and thus also space for both sides in unwanted encounters
to back off.

A step still further and we can seek to create spaces that *enrich*
connection. Spaces, for instance, to which many different creatures are
drawn, partly to enjoy each others' company in turn. Spaces that enable
better communication, perhaps with shareable objects or projects: joint
music-making, say, as when musician Jim Nollman paddles out into in
Puget Sound in a canoe rigged up with underwater speakers and invites
the orca to jam, some nights for hours, in what turn out to be musically
precise ways. "What we invent is neither human nor orca. Rather, it is
interspecies music. A co-created original."[9]

More inviting questions, then, for the philosopher as post-
anthropocentrizing cultural tinkerer: What kinds of "margins" does such
music-making require? What kinds of places and spaces does it take to
talk with the dolphins or the owls, as the aboriginal shamans did? What
kinds of practices—of attention, self-purification, invocation? These are
answerable questions—with work.

Philosopher-designers such as Ian McHarg and Christopher Alexander and his colleagues work out the patterns of building that define the
most humanly and more-than-humanly vital of our cities, neighborhoods,
and houses, subtle patterns, sometimes, that underlie the attraction even
of small but "enchanted" natural places in the very midst of the city,
such as layered (gradual, phased) access and the presence of water and
animals. Alexander and his colleagues plead for "site repair," for building on the worst parts of a piece of land rather than the best, so as to
repair and improve the poorer parts while preserving the most precious,
beautiful, and healthy parts. They design "positive outdoor space": that
is, technically, places partly enclosed by buildings and natural features
so as to have a shape of their own—courtyards or partial courtyards, for
example, as opposed to the shapeless outdoor space so familiar around
the squarish and irregularly placed buildings of our suburbs and cities.
They propose interlocking "city-country fingers" to bring the open
countryside within a short walk or bicycle ride from downtown. Wide
viaducts over major highways to keep migration corrdiors open.[10]

Imagine still more along these lines. Houses more open to the winds: how dramatically different when the breezes and the winds are always there, the sound, the feel, the smells, sometimes even the tastes—all the senses but sight, all the senses usually somewhat diminished in a sight-centered world. (For some religious traditions the winds are the world's very breath—think of the ubiquitous prayer flags in Tibet—and the breath in turn the most intimate name of God himself. To say nothing of more prosaic matters such as obviating the need for constant air-conditioning . . .) More gardens everywhere. Here a mixed community is already close to the surface. The tomatoes and cucumbers and collards become part of "us," they form a community with its own needs, and the gardener stands inside or alongside, not outside, that community as well, along with the neighbors who plow and advise, the friends and soup kitchen that get the extra food, the racoons who rummage in the compost pile, the horses whose manure fertilizes, the insects who make their homes among the vegetables and consume their more destructive cousins. Correspondingly "they" become the various threats: other plants ("weeds," though lovely enough in their own rights), the groundhogs and deer that take more than they need or trample more than they get, the hornworms and cutworms and mites, the kids down the hill who lob baseballs into the corn. Even in this simplest and most modest of ways we already see the transformation of something fundamental. Species lines no longer determine our allegiances here; rather, our alliance is to one multispecies community and against various others who emerge as invaders and disrupters. A mixed community, a working landscape, a multicentric world.

Some of us might even teach ourselves once again to eat from the land. Ceremonially, this time, perhaps, so as to save wild things from overharvesting. We might promote the growth of more edible plants in wilder (ungardened) lands as well. "Design with Nature" already names a major architectural movement, very much with the emphasis on the "with." The philosopher-possibilizer Calypso St. James and his colleagues[11] propose a form of post-suburbanism that sets aside certain places as quiet zones: places where automobile engines and lawnmowers and low-flying airplanes are not allowed. Once again it would be possible to hear the birds and the winds, and to live in the silence. If bright outside lights were also banned, one could see the stars at night and feel the slow pulsations of the light over the seasons. Instead of another ten thousand suburban developments all the same, in short, a little creative zoning could make space for increasingly divergent styles: experiments in recycling and energy self-sufficiency, for example; or again mixed communities of humans and other species; or "ecosteries" on the model of the old monasteries; and other possibilities not yet even imagined.

For a final set of examples, let us return to the question of time-keeping, this time on the scale of the year. Natural rhythms lies close to the surface here. The year itself is the earth's journey around the sun. The month is named for the moon. The week's seven days are named for the seven celestial wanderers known to the ancient geocentric world (Saturday for Saturn, Thursday for Jupiter, Sunday for Sun, etc.). Native Americans honored all the moons with their own evocative names: "Long Nights Moon" or "Popping Trees Moon" in December; "Harvest" or "Fruit" Moon; the "Frosty Moon" of November, "Sap" or "Awakening" Moon in March. The ancient Near Eastern civilizations, all dependent on and acutely aware of the growing cycles, held their great festivals on the Solstices and Equinoxes—Litha, Mabon, Eostar, Yule—and also celebrated the points midway between.

Dimly and at a distance, then, our own great festivals draw us back to the old cycles of light and dark, the seasons and the stars. Christmas, Christianity's (re)birth festival, at Winter Solstice, the rebirth of the light. Hannukah, the Jewish festival of light, at the very moment that the year gets the darkest: the twenty-fifth of Kislev, in the Jewish lunar calendar: the waning of the moon closest to winter solstice: thus the day of the darkest moon and the shortest sun; the day the Macca-bees reconsecrated the recaptured Temple in Jerusalem, chosen because this was the day that the Hellenizers desecrated it, which in turn was chosen because the twenty-fifth of December was already a Roman holiday—the birthday of the Unconquerable Sun. The return of the light. Easter—Eostar—Passover—Spring Equinox: resurrection, escape from bondage, as the earth bursts into new life, maple buds swelling in the still-wintry wind. May Day is the following midpoint day, halfway between Spring Equinox and Summer Solstice, anciently called "Beltane." Ancient "Samhain," midway between Fall Equinox and Winter Solstice, became All Saints Day—its eve, All Hallows Eve: Halloween. The death festival, as the leaves fall and the darkness descends. No light without dark, no life without death.

Thus we propose that the best job of all for the post-anthropocentrizing cultural tinkerer is to create, or reclaim—to *re-philosophize*, if you like—celebration. Suppose that we take it on ourselves to re-root our festivals explicitly in the actual rhythms from which they sprang, and to elaborate new nature-centered festivals and practices where presently we have none. We mean *festivals*, too: not simply "vacations," literally empty time, time not committed to something else. No—something more like "holidays," true communal celebrations, literally "*holy* days," except not "holy" in the usual religious sense: rather, special days, festive days, collectively shared ritual times, like we already have in Thanksgiving and Halloween, but now with their natural and in a certain sense "pagan" origins recognized (re-*cognized*) and deepened. The very term "pagan" derives from the Latin for country dweller. Suppose that, experientially, it really is that simple. The country: that is, places where the cycles of light and dark are still present to the senses, where growing seasons matter, where the moon can still overcome you walking out the door. Where pumpkins ripen by Samhain, where lilies bloom for Eostar, where the long, long days and long, long nights can be felt. In such places, the old festivals are still new, still the right gestures, every year.

And why not some *new* holidays while we are at it? Already at New Year's many people all across the country venture out, before dawn, to count birds for the Audubon Society. Let us now institutionalize "Bird Count Day." Imagine weeks of preparation by eager schoolchildren learning to identify birds. Imagine the hopefulness of the observers that a rare bird might come their way, like amateur astronomers hoping to discover a comet. Imagine "Star Nights" on which all lights everywhere are turned out, not just in the dark/quiet zones: these could be timed to coincide with meteor showers, eclipses, occlusions. The poet Antler recalls Emerson's epiphany—"If the stars came out only one night in a thousand years, how people would believe and adore, and preserve from generation to generation, remembrance of the miracle they'd been shown"—and imagines the scene:

> Whole populations thronging to darkened
> baseball stadiums and skyscrapertops
> to sit holding hands en masse
> and look up at the billion-year spree
> of the realm of the nebulae![12]

Except, actually, it is there every clear night. What we need are the festivals to teach us to see it.

Coordinate other festivals with the great animal migrations: whales, salmon, hawks, warblers. We might move New Year's back to the Spring, where it was for the entire ancient and medieval world until 01582 when Pope Gregory XIII moved it to the dead of winter precisely to break the "pagan" connection. (There's the counter-theme: the two-millenium-old assault on paganism as a profoundly, necessarily *urban* phenomenon. Streetlights and noise are only the latest weapon.) We might set aside nights each month on which we simply pay attention to the Moon. *Real* Monday (Moon-day), so to speak. We might have a night each month on which all newcomers to this Earth are introduced to it, a kind of baptism into the living community that is the Earth.

Imagine how powerful, how connected, could be a culture that once again systematized and practiced such responses—that once again pays attention. No longer furtive and readily forgotten impulses, departures from the consensual, rationalized patterns within which we now think we live; now the communally shared, ever-deepening pattern of the month and the year and of one's life itself.[13]

IV. Concluding Dogmatic Clarification

The proposals just sketched are but a few possible possibilities among many. Much along these lines and others is already being done. Of course the details are arguable. Maybe a ten-thousand-year clock is not the best investment for cultural visionaries to make. Maybe environmenalists ought to be building bridges to fundamentalist communities rather than embracing pagan holidays as a mode of Earth celebration. It could be. But to argue on this level is to engage these projects in their own terms—a welcome engagement!—while it is those terms themselves that we aim to defend here.

The challenge we need to meet here—briefly and dogmatically as it may be—comes from another direction. It is a challenge to de-anthropocentrization itself as an alternative (to) environmental philosophy.

Mustn't we have a substantive non- or post-anthropocen*trism* in mind, after all, in order even to have the sense of "post-anthropocentrizing" direction drawn upon by Brand, Alexander, St. James, and all the rest? The preceding proposals, it will be said, only seem to succeed—even seem to be *relevant*—because we are covertly committed to a theoretical vision of an alternative, only it is a vision that is unacknowledged, left implicit, and insulated from scrutiny or criticism by the simple expedient of leaving it only hazily articulated. It will be argued that all such proposals are in fact *applications* of necessarily preexisting principles and commitments, and the real task of philosophy is to articulate and evaluate these. This is why philosophy remains a separate and necessary activity. Tinkering is not its line. Philosophy meets a loftier and logically prior need: to *guide* all such changes, all such projects.

Indeed this is a pivotal point. Environmental philosophy's attempt to de-anthropocentrize itself rests precisely on this claim to the priority of abstract explicitness and argument. On the "applied ethics" model, there is no other honest and fully self-critical method. From our side it is also possible—in fact, tempting—to simply cede the honorific "philosophy" to the "applied ethics" model. Even the most radical among this prolegomenon's coauthors do not object to a certain amount of environmental-ethical theorizing, though understood, as Inge Anderegg puts it, mainly as a form of conceptual art. So why fight over the name? Let them have it. Or perhaps we should continue to use it too, but without feeling the need to defend ourselves, and in the meantime just get on with the real work.

Some of us cultural tinkerers have made that choice. Yet to the present coauthors it does not seem quite decent to lay claim to philosophy itself without an accounting of our side of the argument. This is why we have proposed a critique of "philosophy de-anthropocentrizing itself," and why we have outlined a systematic alternative strategy—all framed as a *philosophical* prolegomenon to our work. Only the question of method remains to be addressed. Is the application of necessarily pre-existing principles and commitments after all the only possible method for practical philosophy?

It is not. A sense of direction is not at all the same as a sense of destination. Destination is ultimate—it does and must claim the status of first principle—but direction is *local*. We awaken, as it were, within the belly of the beast. We can see only a few moves ahead of us. We propose to make those moves. The further or different moves that will then become visible, the possibilities that will then open up, we cannot now say.

True, then: the proposals above have implicit, general goals and commitments. In fact often enough we have already made them explicit already. To re-create a sense of participating in "longer Nows," for instance, and to re-create the experience of a multicentric world. Alexander and his colleagues aim to make them precise and specific enough to guide city planners and architects. But these are not offered as "applications" of a prior, principled "given." No "ism" motivates and justifies them once and for all. Rather, they are *ventures*. Their function is dialectical: to take one or a few brave steps (why should *we* be so cautious when all the rest of the world is throwing caution to the winds?) in what currently seem like reasonable directions. We await the results: they alone can truly guide the next steps. Our mode is and must be experimental, exploratory. De-anthropocentrization so conceived, so far from being a mode of mere "application," is *itself a mode of thinking*—indeed, we argue, the only mode of thinking available to us.

It is not a paradox to design for undesigned spaces: these are merely spaces that humans do not control and that plants and animals and children are free to make and remake as they see fit, as they will.

Likewise we aim to open up means and settings for cross-species music-making, say, but do not claim that we know what will emerge in those spaces over time. Perhaps exactly what we would expect. Perhaps nothing at all. Perhaps something we cannot now even imagine. The venture itself is the key. Jim Nollman, for instance, jamming with the orcas: do not call this "applied" environmental philosophy, some kind of animal liberation perhaps. Nollman is not somehow Saving the Earth. He is not even saving orcas. He is *joining* the orcas, with grace, with skill, in an open-ended way. Enough to hope, and work, for just that.

We are advised that this is a more strenuous answer than we need have attempted. More defensible, or anyway more polite, might have been to allow that some hazy nonanthropocentrism actually does guide us, but that presently we can glimpse it only in the barest outline, all broad strokes and no details, so that it becomes our task to progressively fill it in. It would turn out then that we practice a kind of "applied philosophy" after all, but with so much of the real work still lying on the side of the slow fleshing-out of whatever it is we are "applying" that we had still best stress the practice and not the theory. The half-formed and initially vague goal of enabling a larger-than-human experience becomes progressively more specific and fleshed-out as we carry it into the world and begin to design more mindfully.

It is well-meaning advice. Perhaps we are indeed on a firm path, however poorly marked here at the trailhead, and the signs will grow more definite as we head resolutely into what now appears to be much more confusing and unclear. Perhaps. We are happy to embrace the self-constituting and self-defining character of this process, the space it offers to the kinds of cultural tinkerers we have aimed to highlight and enable. An ethic and also an etiquette are implicit in it—precisely inasmuch as it *is* a process, a kind of wilderness exploration of its own, with its own delicacy and preconditions—and so in some ways it really does approach the kind of light-footedness with which we want to insist that our post-anthropocentrizers must move. Yes. But for all this we cannot embrace even so attenuated an "applied nonanthropocentrism." The more strenuous view turns out to be the only honest one, at least for us. For (again!) it may turn out that even our limited sense of direction right now is a mistake.

We cannot claim that the long-term outcome must be describable as nonanthropocentric at all. And the problem is not merely that "nonanthropocentrism" is a wholly negative and thus virtually empty description. Even its wholly indefinite definiteness is in fact beyond us—thank god. For we may not arrive at a nonanthropocentrism even in this schematic sense. Maybe we will discover that a sort of human-centeredness is after all necessary and natural—the problem being rather with its hegemonizing, its tendency to devalue and reduce other "centers" to dim reflections of itself. Or maybe we will recover some dimensions of humanness itself that will somehow make even anthropocentrism itself a beautiful thing from a larger point of view. Maybe we will even come to abandon this entire Earth as a child might abandon a toy, and step into a cosmic perspective that renders even the most radical of "environmental ethics" far too narrow a perspective. We cannot say. We do not possess foresight on that scale. Only time will tell—or maybe not even that. Maybe instead even of Brand's Long Now we will arrive at a sense of timelessness, or a different conception of time entirely. Instead of ten-thousand-year clocks we may need no clocks at all, clocks with no hands, time-free zones . . .

We cannot know. Anything is possible. It is no good lamenting our lack of ultimate foresight—as if *we*, anyway, would actually *wish* first principles to be so pinned down that all we can do is fill in the details anyway. Talk of celebration—we celebrate the open-ended world. The very depth of the Earth, of the whole living world, that we environmentalists and environmental philosophers sometimes fleetingly sense—might it not in part be precisely this lovely and infinite openness?

Notes

1. Roderick Nash, *Wilderness and the American Mind* (New Haven: Yale University Press, 1982), p. xiv.

2. Mary Midgley, *Beast and Man* (Ithaca: Cornell University Press, 1978), pp. 18–19.

3. Albert Camus, *The Myth of Sisyphus* (New York: Vintage, 1955), p. 11.

4. Hans Peter Duerr, *Dreamtime: Concerning the Boundary Between Wilderness and Civilization* (Oxford: Basil Blackwell, 1985), p. 30.

5. See the review of Aner Benjamin Marcus's *The Hidden Possibilities of Things* in my *Jobs for Philosophers* (Philadelphia: Xlibris, 2004), chapter 3.

6. Stewart Brand, *The Clock of the Long Now* (New York: Basic Books, 2000).

7. Cited or invoked pages of Brand's book include pp. 5, 8, 28f, and 100–02.

8. Wendell Berry, "Getting Along with Nature," in *Home Economics* (San Francisco: North Point Press, 1987), p. 13.

9. Jim Nollman, *Dolphin Dreamtime* (New York: Bantam, 1987), p. 148.

10. Ian McHarg's classic is *Design with Nature* (Garden City, NY: Doubleday, 1969). Christopher Alexander, et al.'s is *A Pattern Language* (New

York: Oxford University Press, 1977). On windows, see sections 239, 159, and 107; on "site repair," section 104; on water in the city, sections 25, 64, and 71; on "accessible green," sections 51 and 60; on "holy ground," sections 24, 66, and 70.

11. See chapter 2 of *Jobs for Philosophers*.

12. Antler, "Star-Struck Utopias of 2000," *The Trumpeter* 9 (1992), p. 180.

13. The argument here follows my *Back to Earth* (Philadelphia: Temple University Press, 1994), chapter 6.

Chapter 7

What If Teaching Went Wild?

I

Officially we acknowledge that of course we are animals, that of course we are living beings among other forms of life on a vast and still largely unknown planet, and therefore that of course we are putting ourselves as well as much of the rest of the living world in danger as we appropriate and consume more and more of that world for our own ends. Whether we actually believe or *feel* any of these things in our heart of hearts, however, is quite another thing. Many environmental thinkers have argued that by and large we still do not.[1] In the philosophical and religious tradition, think for instance of the pervasive influence of Platonism and Christian Neo-Platonism, according to which true reality is perfect and unchanging, and "this" world (with the word "this" always a form of derogation) by contrast deficient, degenerate and degenerating, unreliable and ultimately unreal. It is of the very essence of God—of sacredness, divinity, intrinsic value, say it how you will—to transcend "this" world. The implications are drawn very clearly in the old church-camp song:

> This world is not my home, I'm just a-passing through.
> My treasures are stored up somewhere beyond the blue.
> The angels beckon me from Heaven's open door,
> and I can't feel at home in this world anymore!

This paper is based upon an enactment at the 2002 Meeting of the Philosophy of Education Society in Vancouver, BC, and subsequently appeared in that meeting's proceedings: Scott Fletcher, editor, *Philosophy of Education 2002* (Urbana, Illinois: Philosophy of Education Society, 2003), pp. 40–52. A response by Dilafruz Williams, "Reconnecting Body and Mind with Earth," follows (pp. 53–56). A revised version of this essay appeared in *Canadian Journal of Environmental Education* IX (2004), pp. 31–49, and abridged versions elsewhere.

Or think of how automatically we use the word "animal" to mean *other* animals—how natural it still seems to be to speak of "humans" and "animals" in the sense of humans *versus* (other) animals. A roomful of adults, directly asked "Are you animals?" knows the right answer, but most young children, up through elementary ages, deny it. I think the children are truer to the underlying cultural messages. This world is *not* our home; we are *not* really animals; and what goes around . . . well, goes *away*, won't come back to haunt us.

Consider also how thoroughly humanized are most of the spaces in which we live and work. Few other creatures show up in them, except maybe a few potted plants or a very limited range of thoroughly domesticated animals. The shape of those spaces itself has been rigorously geometrized, unlike the more organic shapes of natural things and spaces, and often highly simplified (blank walls, square rooms). "Our" spaces are also usually and insistently filled with wholly human sounds (radio, TV, sometimes even our own voices). The result of all of this is to convey, perhaps again primarily subliminally, a sense of the world itself as profoundly human-centered.[2] What lies outside this cocoon is "coded" (as anthropologists would put it) as insignificant, and probably vaguely threatening too. Young children are again a good indicator: the darkness and quiet of the night, for instance, once a kind of vast and soothing entry into more-than-human realities, has been so insistently eradicated that many children now are unable to sleep without a light or without TV or radio in the background (increasingly this is also true of many adults) and are uneasy, or worse, in the possible company of wild animals.

Given these views of our place in the world, it is no surprise that we have come to the cusp of environmental crisis. A civilization committed to disconnection, whose denizens deny their own animality, who do not see themselves as part of larger living systems, who do not know in their bones that what "goes around" will eventually come *back*, is likely to end up in trouble sooner or later, probably sooner. It is this sense of disconnection that makes it possible for us to so ruthlessly exploit Earth, this that reassures us (again, often below the cognitive level, on a level more unspoken and visceral) that we ourselves are not threatened by the degradation of larger living systems. It is otherwise an almost inexplicable fact that we are so willing to foul our own nest: it seems that only a basic refusal of acknowledgment that it *is* our "nest" could explain it. Indeed I would argue that, considered philosophically, this insistent kind of felt disconnection is not the root of environmental crisis but, most fundamentally, is the very crisis itself.

II

All of this sets a clear agenda for change. We must rediscover ourselves in connection with the rest of Earth: we must reacknowledge ourselves as animals, come to *feel* ourselves as parts of larger living systems after all. The task of environmental education, then, very broadly speaking is address our disconnection, reverse it, to re-situate us, to welcome us home. That is the urgent agenda.

The practical question is How? But this question, it seems, usually does not detain us for long. We all know how teaching is supposed to go. An environmental education movement is already well underway—there is even a nearly forty-year-old academic journal in the area[3]—and there are model curricula, standard courses, and reams of course materials. The usual courses offer thorough introductions and in-depth explorations of many aspects of the ecological crisis, along with good doses of natural history, evolution, maybe even local ecology projects. It may well seem that environmental education has (already) "arrived."[4]

But there are reasons for worry. Much of this I have spelled out in another place,[5] so I offer only the briefest summary here. The implicit general model of education in environmental education, as in most areas of education—almost always just assumed without question, just taken for granted—is what the critical philosopher Paolo Freire archly labeled the "banking" model, or what is colloquially dubbed the "mug and jug." Teaching is supposed to be information-transmission; the teacher is transmitter; talking is the primary mode—usually the only mode in fact. One way or the other, we *tell* students they belong to the Earth. We aim to fill them up with information that backs up this point. All of this is done honorably, often admirably well, and on an increasingly large scale. And (we might well ask) that's what teaching *is*, isn't it?

All of this has its critics, well known to philosophers of education. Critics such as Freire, John Holt, Ivan Illich, and many others have assailed its essential passivizing and disempowerment of students, and its reduction of life to "information."[6] Much of the criticism can be linked to analogous though less dramatically made points in John Dewey's philosophy of education, especially Dewey's insistence on the necessity of active learning and the urgency of integrating school/learning and life, rather than separating school from what he called the "great common world" either physically or intellectually.[7] All of these criticisms apply to environmental education on the standard model just as much as to any other kind of education. In fact, some of the critiques arguably apply even more strongly to environmental education than in many other cases. After all, for one thing, environmental education is about *nature*, and therefore archetypally is about the "great common [not just human] world," so that to try to teach *this*, of all things, in the classroom, as another book subject in its own separate curricular and thoroughly human-centered architectural niche, is (to adapt a line of Dewey's) to make the very place where children are sent to discover the Earth the one place in the world where the Earth barely shows up at all. One of my students recently put it poignantly: "Our current system does not emphasize our connection to the natural world. We are supposed to read about natural wonders, but at the same time are discouraged from experiencing them."[8]

Some years ago my friend Bob Jickling set up a conference on "Environment, Ethics, and Education" at Yukon College in Whitehorse, Yukon. In the lovely Canadian spirit of acknowledgment of indigenous First Nations, the event opened with a morning-long visit by a number of local tribal elders, speaking of how they teach their own young. In discussion a member of the audience asked about the possibility of elders coming into the schools to speak of these things. The general response was that it did not and would not work. The setting was too artificial—neither elders nor students felt (or were!) at home; the students "asked too many questions," they didn't know how to listen (to their elders, to each other, to themselves, to the birds . . .); and, most crucially, students could not join any ongoing work (the hunt, food preparation, celebration) in the context of which real learning could take place. Everything was reduced to an episodic encounter or "presentation," and to words. And none of this is surprising. School *is* an artificial setting; talking and presenting and questioning are its favorite methods; ongoing work has no place there. The elders, in their typically understated way, were therefore telling us that our schools cannot teach love for the Earth. Not because we cannot make the words part of the curriculum, but because precisely by doing so we obscure and undercut what the words actually mean. The worry (to put it generally) is that importing the usual modes of teaching into environmental education risks reproducing the very disconnection from the larger world that was the problem in the first place.

In environmental education there is an additional problem, familiar to all of us. Naturally the most accessible kinds of information, the most teachable as well as the most "newsworthy," and the stock-in-trade of every activist desperate to shock the rest of us into response, is information about dangers and disasters. Just think of how the environment (perhaps we need to say the Environment with a capital

"E") usually shows up in the media: massive fish kills here, air pollution there, radioactive power plant wastes, global warming, more species on the brink, and on and on. The net effect of piling up more and more of this sort of information about ecological crises is, ultimately, to overwhelm us, perhaps young people—students—especially. Early on we tell them (my third grader for example already knows it very well) that the world they are inheriting is diminished, dirty, in danger. Again and again we drive the point home. I find that today's college students are the best-informed I have ever known about environmental dangers. They are also the most deeply pessimistic: numbed, evasive, despondent. This too, I am afraid, is a product of doing all too good a job of (a certain kind of) environmental education. I take it that it is also not a good thing.

III

These thoughts naturally leave us confused and discouraged. If it is true that environmental education, after all a natural and well-intentioned response to a serious crisis, turns out to be ineffective at best and maybe self-defeating as well—what then?

I have argued in other places that there are constructive and indeed enormously appealing ways to reconceive education as a whole, and environmental education in particular.[9] The general idea is that the real work lies at the level of *social* "reconstruction": that is, the social context of school itself needs to be rethought and rebuilt, so that school's tasks and projects fit naturally into the "great common world," so that they join a larger dynamic that gives them purpose and appeal. For a spectacularly prosaic but very useful analogy, think of Driver Education in American high schools now—one of the few classes that students are truly eager to take, because driving manifestly enables them to take their place in a larger personal and social practice, shared by parents and peers, already familiar in all manner of ways, and a practice that further enables their own growing independence and adulthood. Ironically enough (as it may seem) this could be a model for environmental education as well. Looked at from this point of view, I propose, the task not so much of environmental educators per se but of all environmentally concerned citizens is to create the kinds of larger social/environmental practices and meanings that will make specific kinds of environmental learning—the specific sorts of things schools actually are good at—compelling and attractive in the same ways.

Imagine, for instance, a society that celebrated the passing of the first warblers, say—or hawks or salmon or whales—or that like the Audubon Society did a one-day annual bird count, everyone out listening and looking, or maybe turned out all the lights once a month to watch the stars or the latest comet. Such a society, for one thing, would engage "nature" first in the mode of celebration and connectedness rather than in unease or fear or distance. Moreover, and crucially for education, such a society invites "environmental education" almost as a rite of passage, a way of taking part in the great flow of life and its associated festivals. School cannot create environmental consciousness out of whole cloth: *that* is a matter of remaking the whole society, and it is then within *this* that school finds a role—a limited role, but correspondingly a role that it can effectively fulfill.

Still, this is a long-term vision, not a story that offers much to those of us who want to teach right now. At least in the short run, most of us teach (and philosophize about teaching) in the normal settings: that is, inside, and usually inside buildings made specifically for teaching purposes; with a large number of people, usually younger, led by one or a few older people through something like a "curriculum." School and society are what they are, and unless we pull out of them entirely, this is still the setting within which we must work for change.

My aim in this chapter, then, is to speak to this very setting. I do not believe that we are reduced to just making the usual motions. The question I wish to pose is, can teaching "go wild" *here*, even in this least promising of settings? A certain amount of the traditional information is no doubt necessary. But what else? Rather than abandoning the usual, how could we really push its envelope?

The answer I propose is that even in so thoroughly humanized and academic a setting as a classroom—or even (God forbid) a professional convention—we *can* work toward and embody a radically different practice and philosophy of (environmental) education. Even—and maybe to some degree *especially*—within the conventional spaces and modes of teaching, it is still possible to unsettle our deep-felt sense of disconnection from the world, and to begin to reconnect. Much else must be done to really come "back to Earth," of course, but I will argue that even in the conventional spaces we can make a constructive contribution to this process after all. And the same may also be true in reverse. It may just be that environmental education in this wilder key can open up unsuspected possibilities for conventional classrooms and methods generally. At any rate, I now want to propose some very specific and practical teaching strategies along these lines for your consideration.

IV

Wherever we are, first of all, there we are. Even when the astronauts leave Earth, they take not only the air and the water and the fire with them, but also, crucially and inevitably, themselves. Maybe our search for wildness should start right here: with our very own selves.

The very first challenge, then, odd as it may be to say it this way, is to notice that *we ourselves are actually present*, inevitably, in body as well as mind—or rather, as my Eastern colleagues would say, as body/mind, one integrated being. It is the body part that is all too often forgotten. Officially, in classrooms, we are supposed to be just minds, after all; the body fades away, becomes mere background, maybe at times a minor annoyance, but if it emerges into attention it can only be as distraction or embarrassment. Correspondingly, though, I want to suggest that bringing the body back into the picture creates just the right mix of discomfort and provocation to serve our pedagogical purpose.

It is not hard to do, in actual practice. By way of beginning I might ask a class or audience to form small groups of three or four. Then, as soon as the chairs are all moved and people have settled in with each other, I ask them to pack themselves—the same group—into half the space. Get people to push right up next to each other, practically on top of each other, inside the usual cultural "personal space"—at least enough to genuinely become aware of others as bodies, after all: as animals, as embodied beings.

Now I ask each person to look closely at their own hands. With my Critical Thinking classes I make this a ten- or fifteen-minute project, all by itself, and even ask students to write a report.[10] For present purposes, a few minutes are enough—enough to notice the pores, the skin cells, indeed the skin itself as one vast, supple organ; the scars that tell stories of the past; the mechanics of the hand, like its grasping function and the famous opposable thumbs; the webbing between the fingers that recalls our kinship with the ducks; the hair that recalls our kinship with the apes. Lest anyone miss that last message, in the background I project some images of ape hands compared to humans, or little lizard feet. Finally, I ask people to look at *each other's* hands in the same way—and again to take some time with this. The contrast between hands is often fairly striking, and is one way for people to

notice things about their own hands that otherwise are so familiar that
we take them for granted: the uniqueness of the shape and length and
orientation of the fingers, maybe, or the individuality and complexity
of the lines in our palms.

Even this simplest of little projects, I find, perceptibly changes the
feeling of the room, already loosens up and gives shape to a new kind
of energy. A context in which animality is acknowledged and *welcomed*
seems also to be more comfortable, both intellectually and also literally,
physically. And something else remarkable has happened too. People are
actually *holding hands.* In younger classes there may be a certain amount
of tittering about this (though far less than if you directly ask them to
hold hands—this way of doing it leads them into it before the usual
defenses and categories kick in), but it seldom lasts long. In older audiences I sometimes wonder out loud whether some of the people present
may have known each other for years, but without once ever touching,
at least in this sort of deliberate but simply "present" way.

It is a lovely new dimension. In any case what tends to grow on
people, younger or older, as they sit and continue to hold hands, are
the basic animal things: warmth, first of all, and pulse. The warmth of
another live, animal being. Pulse in turn leads to thought of the animality of rhythm itself—of how fundamental is the heartbeat, say, to the
ways we feel music in our bodies. An old choral teacher of mine told
me once that the monks and choirboys who sang the earliest polyphony
kept time by, well, holding hands. In this way they apparently managed
to synchronize their heartbeats, and then could keep absolutely precisely
to the beat of the music. This may also explain why so much of that
music in sung *andante,* about sixty beats per minute. Think of the beat
of the drums at Native American dances. It too is the pulse, the very
heartbeat of the dancers.

Now people may let go of others' hands, pull their seats a little
bit apart. Even so there is a remembrance of embodiment that remains,
something people carry away and think about. A number of students
over the years have told me how much "the hand thing" meant to
them: both looking at their own hands, and others', and recognizing
the similarities to nonhuman hands; and also holding others' hands, in a
way quite different than the one or two ways in which our culture allows
people their age to hold hands now. Indeed, I suspect that touching
like this is taboo in our culture partly precisely because we are reluctant
to acknowledge our own animality (and/or that we have so reductive
a view of animality that turns it all into sexuality, and an insistently
reduced sexuality at that). Many things, it seems, may be usefully and
memorably unsettled here.

V

Of course we do need more than ourselves to "go wild." Soon enough we need the presence of the more-than-human world. Here again certain means of subversion and reversal are ready at hand.

The first of these is very simple: open the blinds, and whenever possible, open the windows. Do this in a dramatic way, noting as you do it that it is sure peculiar that we are asked to teach and learn about the natural world in spaces more and more cut off from it. I am constantly struck by how inattentive we are to the structure of physical space generally, and, as teachers, to classroom space. A visiting Martian anthropologist would surely be amazed by our practice of teaching young people about their belonging to the world in rooms that are as enthusiastically as possible sealed off from anything but themselves, even to the extent of keeping the blinds closed and windows shut—if we are so lucky as to have windows at all. Since we do seem to have this practice, however, we can at least take it as an opportunity for a persistent, explicit, and dramatic challenge. "Silhouette" the usual practice, as it were, instead of letting it recede into the taken-for-granted background, and hence make it a subject of critical thinking itself. Open the windows, in short, and talk about it.

Teaching outside is a natural next step. This usually takes more work. "Going outside" on campus depends on suitable spaces. As every teacher knows, just sitting in the grass on the Quad tends to lead to entropic classes. The space has no natural focus, friends and other students are always walking by, and classes tend to drift into passivity and distraction. These are all remediable problems, however: what we really need are more workable outdoor classrooms. After some years of agitation, some of my students and I have succeeded in persuading our administrators to build an outdoor amphitheater specifically for teaching purposes: built into a hill partly below ground level, well-shielded from passersby, seating in semicircles so that the space focuses the mind rather than distracts. Outdoor space also has a "shape" and can be attended to for learning or other purposes. At Elon we also have access to a former church-camp Lodge and twenty-acre wooded grounds about a mile from campus, to which classes can bicycle or drive (walking both ways takes too much class time), either on the spur of the moment or by prearrangement.

Back in the classroom, hopefully with natural light and air, I propose that we need more "natural" things around us. I have formed the habit of picking up little rocks or other small tokens (striking twig formations, feathers, sometimes the skull of a bird or small mammal that places itself in my path) from the mountains or woods or shores I visit. These surround me now at my desk: Others are in my car, others my children inherit. The contrast to all the other artifacts around me always provokes a useful remembrance. My pens and keyboard and journals bear the signs of artifactuality: they are simple, geometrically regular, have an eyeblink of a history that I know and that I knowingly live within. My little rocks and crow skulls and trilobite fossils speak of other things. The rocks speak for example of tectonic upheavals and volcanism, eons of water and ice and fire. Their shapes are not human-made, their histories are measured in millions of years, not industrial or manufacturing half-lives.

So I take rocks or other such items into my classrooms. Often I offer each student such a token. Perhaps a small rock from the nearby beach, as I did for everyone who attended my talk at the Philosophy of Education Society conference. Bring in a variety and let people pick those that call to them. Then invite them to think about, maybe even to investigate, that rock's history. What is it made of, how and when was it formed. Ideally, then, even this littlest of things becomes a link to a much bigger history, a much bigger story, a visible, ever-present, almost ritual reminder that the Earth is bigger than we are, that we live at the intersection of vastly different kinds of stories.

I have a small meteorite that I sometimes carry around with me too. To me it represents a sort of "next step" in this thinking-through-rocks, framing even the ancient stories of Earth's rocks in terms of still longer and larger stories. Since Earth is geologically a live planet, almost all terrestrial rocks are much younger than Earth's full age, 4.5 billion years or so. They have been melted and crushed and remelted, maybe many times. Meteorites, by contrast, are virtually timeless. Some come from the Moon or Mars, which are not geologically active but once were, so their rocks are roughly contemporaneous with the older of Earth's rocks. Most, however, come from the asteroids, which were almost always too small to be geologically active, and so date back to the very beginning of the solar system itself. Here, I hold in my hand a 4.5-billion-year-old rock. In fact, certain very rare and precious meteorites may come from comets captured by our sun but originating in *other* solar systems, in the coalescence of gas from other supernovas—so they are the only physical material we have, that we can hold in our hands, that is older than Earth and our solar system itself.[11]

On the other end of the scale of permanence and evanescence, it is a nice complement to bring in, say, flowers. Sometimes I hand around a bowl of daisies, pansies, nasturtiums, and the like, along with my bowl of rocks, and ask everyone present to pick one of each. The color, the softness, the fragrance of the flowers all immediately appeal. I ask everyone to breathe deep the smell of their flowers (and the rocks too, for rocks too often smell). And then maybe to think a little more about this matter of smell, too. Unlike what we see or hear, what we smell or touch or taste does not stand at a distance. What you smell is already part of you, is physically inside you. When you smell the flower, the flower comes into you. Same with the rock: when you touch a rock, the rock touches you back. Holding rock or flower, in this sense, is like holding hands with the world, except that with the world itself there is no way to let go. In this sense we are all, always, literally in "communion" with the larger world.[12] At least this is one quite concrete way of thinking about the interconnection of all life with all other life and with the whole world, necessarily at at every moment—and it is, for sure, a rather unexpected way of thinking about flowers!

Take some nice deep breaths just for the air. Now think about that air. Where has it been? We breathe in and out 450 cubic feet of air every day. When not inside our own lungs that very same air has been inside each others', in and out of other rooms, down around the corner, at the beach, up and down smokestacks and tailpipes, and just about everywhere else too. Air is not neutral stuff: it carries vast numbers of spores, tiny insects and other life forms, electrical charges, varied chemicals—even, once again, tiny fragments of other worlds in the form of meteorite dust. The air in every breath is one more link, ultimately, with the entire universe. So we arrive again in a similar place. The philosopher-magician David Abram proposes that we no longer say that we live *on* the Earth, but rather that we live *in* it—for we do, we live at the bottom of the sea of air that is the atmosphere, and are in constant intercourse, in every literal sense of that word, with the whole of the world with every breath we take.[13]

Taste is the other sense that requires actual physical incorporation. No way to taste anything without taking it into ourselves—without taking it, literally, in "communion." So all food, for one thing, is a kind of joining or connection (or, if you think about subsequent stages, cycling). Only it is hard to remember this with the sorts of things we eat every day. For the sake of awareness it is much more useful to eat something *un*familiar—once again, something a little unsettling, something you will remember eating for quite a while. Having reached this point, I therefore invite my students or audiences to eat their flowers. After all, there they are, holding a flower; it will not last long anyway; and I take care only to bring in edible kinds.[14] Eat your flower, I say. Always an interesting moment. Usually about half of the crowd will try it—more if younger kids, fewer if adults. I eat a few myself just to demonstrate that it is possible to do so and live. I do not insist. The important thing once again is the new idea of what it is to eat something—not merely some kind of nourishment, understandable solely in terms of the self and its physical needs, but a kind of incorporation, taking the world inside ourselves, "intercourse" once again. Indeed I have friends who are not vegetarians for this reason: eating flesh, on their view, is one form of communion with animals.

This way of putting naturally invokes a religious or sacramental dimension. I consciously follow the pattern of Christian "Communion": passing the bowl, taking and eating as a form of affirming and indeed ritually recreating "oneness in body." But the intent is not blasphemy—though I admit to skirting the edge. Appropriating such cultural symbols is a useful, if edgy, teaching method. This very theological sort of unease opens up something that otherwise might not be reachable. Both the rock (which I invite people to carry away and keep, on the desk or in a pocket, as a kind of reminder) and the flower, loved for its beauty and fragrance and then consumed, serve as ritual reminders of community or oneness, sacramental reinvocations of the living Earth and one's relationship to it. And Oneness with Earth, I would argue, is the *original* communion—both fundamental to our own lives, every single one of us, and at the origins of humanity and life as such.

VI

On the face of it it seems impossible to commune with the other wild creatures in classrooms. After all, they're not here. And we wouldn't care to invite bears or vultures or orca into "our" spaces even if we could. Even the "biospheric egalitarianism" of which some radical environmental thinkers make so much does not imply that we somehow do not need our private (to self, to family, to species) spaces.

Still, the story I am telling does not yet include the wild creatures, and in some ways they are the most crucial of all: They are the ones with whom we (perhaps especially young people) can most readily and immediately identify—much more naturally than with, say, a meteorite—and they are the ones who animate and electrify a landscape or a dream. Surely we need them too, yet it is not clear how to invoke them.

There are some useful thought-experiments that offer at least a first step. Try, for instance, to think of some familiar and specific aspect of "our" world from the perspective of specific other animals. Pigs, say. As the saying goes, it matters a great deal to the pig whether or not the world is Jewish. In a somewhat similar vein, a North Carolina fast-food chicken restaurant chain has lately mounted a billboard advertising campaign featuring lovable cows urging you to eat more chicken. As a vegetarian I find this remarkable, since you would think that no meat producer would want to so prominently highlight the fact that a massive number of deaths, of cows *and* chickens, is the premise of meat-eating as such. I would have thought that the blood, as it were, is way too close to the surface here—but evidently not for the advertisers. It seems that even here we need a little more imaginative work, putting ourselves truly into the animals' places and not just as an amusing billboard gimmick.

Speaking of freeways, my favorite examples are the turkey vultures so ubiquitous along Eastern highways. What do they see in the roads? It turns out that they see what we see: a quick way to travel (the big highways create favorable winds and lots of heat columns to ride) and plentiful cheap food (roadkill). Puts *our* highway driving in a slightly different light, doesn't it?

Still, again, we speak here only of thought-experiments, not the presence of real animals, and so seem to hit a dead end. Is there anything else to be done? I believe that there is. I suggest that there are wild animals right here next to us after all (that is, besides ourselves), though typically overlooked or, when not dismissed as beneath notice, often feared. I speak of the *insects*.

Most of us may already recognize that there are "bugs" all around us most of the time. Even as I type, right now, a small spider keeps appearing and disappearing around one of my stacks of papers and books. There are ants on the floor and the occasional ornithopter-like mayfly softly buzzing by (I just changed the storm door screens yesterday, so there were many opportunities to come in). For my part I welcome the company, mostly, but even when the company is emphatically *not* welcome they persist anyway. A month or so ago I was flying from Los Angeles to Chicago on one of those huge Airbus-type planes, row forty or something, way in the back, in the middle of a row of nine seats, thinking about some of these things, and just as I got to thinking about insects, who should I notice inching along the side of my tray table but a little pillbug. Or maybe the actual causality was the other way around. Thirty-five thousand feet up in the sky, anyway, streaking along at six hundred miles a hour—even here there are bugs.

Ordinarily we might think nothing of all this insect life right around us, or just find them annoying (we get "bugged"—a revealing phrase, that). Only a small mental flip, though, and they may emerge in quite a different light. Consider what it is like when you think you are alone and then discover that someone else is with you, perhaps even watching you. Hegel pointed out long ago that self-consciousness does not and cannot arise when we are alone, but only and necessarily when we are with others: we see ourselves for the first time from another point of view. Couldn't something quite similar be true when we recognize that even as we sit in our wholly human-defined space, pursuing our intellectual agendas with single-minded passion, there are right around us other awarenesses, with other agendas, aware of us even if we are not aware of them? A spider, say, thus emerges as another form of awareness, another presence, a co-inhabitant of what we thought was "our" space, an independent being from whose point of view we can perhaps come to see ourselves in a new way. We become self-conscious in an unexpected way, cast in an unexpected light.

The probable presence of insects thus makes possible a real perspective-shift, not just another thought-experiment. I invite my audience now to look around, right where they are, in search of whatever insect life they may find. Do not move them, I say, certainly do not harm them: Just see who's around. When they are really likely to be present, it is not at all so hard to look at things their way, to take their point of view (and the questions are natural: "Where would they be? What are they doing? . . .").

All of this is prelude to the last card I play. I begin with a self-revelation. As it happens—perhaps not so coincidentally—I myself am a insect, in fact spiderlike though technically not a spider. My totem being, one of my primary more-than-human identifications, is a Daddy Longlegs (Harvestman). Daddy Longlegs come around me, turn up on my body and almost always in my tent in the mornings when camping out, whether the "bug-proof" netting is closed or not. I see myself as lanky, heading toward the impossible gangliness of Harvestmen; and besides I am a Daddy. . . . well, it all works out. Enough to say that some kind of affinity seems to be operating here. I go on to remind people that we Daddy Longlegs are completely harmless to humans (all that stuff about venom is nonsense, though maybe useful); we do not bite, do not make webs, and so on.

Now I tell the group that I have in fact brought in some Daddy Longlegs, right into this room, and released them right before people came in.[15] "You never know: Perhaps there were no spiders here after all, so just to be sure I brought some in myself." Sometimes one or two will show themselves at this point in the talk, and I can invite them down onto my hand or shoulder. In any case the group's challenge is to find the rest. So this is not an experiment, I say. We are not just trying to take the viewpoint of a spider in theory, but in *fact*. They are here, they know where you are even if you do not know where they are, and I want you to try to find them and make their acquaintance. Also eventually I want to escort them back outside (should it really be true that I brought any in). Look for their spindly legs sticking out from underneath chair frames or behind curtains or . . . well, where? Where would you go in this room if you were a spider?

It should be very clear that I am not speaking of bringing spiders or other insects into the classroom as exhibits, in bottles or tanks, appropriated and confined for our scientific or merely curious inspection. This is a philosophical experiment, not Show and Tell. The aim is to attend to how it changes our sense of this space when we discover such Others *already* present, co-inhabiting this space we were so sure was only our own, elusive but *independent*, on much more equal terms. The more-than-human world is not merely a safely controlled, distant object of study, but is all around us (in addition to *being* us) all the time, even so close as the spider that may at this moment be under your chair or laying eggs in the corner. Looked at in the right way, this can be an enchanting thought, and I have seen groups of young people take to it with enthusiasm. Adults are sometimes a little slower, or more mixed, but for all of us, somehow or other, it opens a new sort of door in the mind.

VII

What is it to "go wild"? One beginning of an answer starts where we just left off: It is to have a sense—quite literally a "sense"—that we co-inhabit this world with a diversity of other forms and shapes of awareness, of "centers" of dynamic change, right here and now. It is to recognize that even the shape of our own awareness (e.g., our own animality), often eludes us. Wild is that unsettling sense of otherness, unexpected and unpredictable and following its own flow, but still a flow that is in some not-quite-graspable way, ours too.

And so, I propose, teaching can "go wild" after all, even in the most conventional sorts of settings. I want to reiterate, still, that what I am proposing here is intentionally restricted to the specific question posed in section III. I am not proposing a curriculum—I have ideas about that, too, but again that is for elsewhere—or indeed anything so systematic. These activities are instead a way of unsettling and subverting the usual and, if you will, "hidden" or "implicit" curriculum, and right where it lives, right in the most traditional settings.[16] I want to insist that this sort of wild subtext needs to be a necessary part of any environmental teaching—and, perhaps, of any teaching at all.

As to teaching itself, what is radical about my argument is an invitation in a somewhat different direction. Everything I have described is easy to do, at least from the point of view of resources or preparation or training. The strain, such as it is, is on the conceptual side. To pull off most of these things in a classroom—let alone at an academic conference—requires that we take up the role of teacher itself in a rethought way. To reinvoke animality for others you must first be comfortable with your own. To be willing to speak your totem with others, not to mention handling spiders (or whatever the analogue for you might be), you yourself must experience the human/other-than-human boundary as more permeable than our culture teaches us it is. To be willing to move into "religious" space, for example by consciously invoking something like a "communion" model, you must be willing to walk certain lines that are not entirely comfortable, perhaps even to contemplate becoming a modest kind of spiritual innovator in a culture that tends to like its spirituality fixed and safe. To be willing to remake the very space of a classroom, to invite a kind of more-than-human wildness into a space that started out so neat, bodiless, wholly anthropocentrized, and in control, you must be attentive in a bodily way to the very shape and feel of space itself.

All of these, in short, require of the teacher a different kind of presence than the all too familiar fact-purveyor. And so, surprising as it may be (or not), the invitation to environmental education in this key can end up spurring a re-vision of what it is to be a classroom teacher *tout court*. I think this is a lovely implication, myself. Environmental philosophers have long suspected that environmental ethics has the potential to remake all of ethics—so perhaps it is not so surprising that the same should be true of the relation between environmental education and education proper. Wildness tends to ramify—which is why the tradition looks on it with such unease, and why, right now, we need it so very much.

Notes

1. A discussion that begins with Lynn White's classic article "The Historical Roots of Our Environmental Crisis," widely reprinted, for instance in Richard Botzler and Susan Armstrong, *Environmental Ethics: Divergence and Convergence* (New York: McGraw-Hill, 1998), a collection that includes a number of commentaries and related views as well. See also Paul Shepard, *Nature*

and Madness (San Francisco: Sierra Club, 1982); Daniel Quinn's *Ishmael*; and my book, *Back to Earth: Tomorrow's Environmentalism* (Philadelphia: Temple University Press, 1994).

2. See my article "Non-anthropocentrism in a Thoroughly Anthropo-centrized World," *The Trumpeter* 8:3 (1991).

3. *The Journal of Environmental Education* is now at volume 38.

4. For a somewhat fuller characterization, see my article "Instead of Environmental Education," in Bob Jickling, editor, *Proceedings of the Yukon College Symposium on Ethics, Environment, and Education* (Whitehorse, YT: Yukon College, 1996). An abridged version of this article appears as "Deschool-ing Environmental Education," *Canadian Journal of Environmental Education* I (1996).

5. Ibid.

6. The canonical references are Paul Goodman, *Compulsory Mis-Education* (New York: Vintage, 1962); Ivan Illich, *Deschooling Society* (New York: Harper and Row, 1970); Paolo Freire, *The Pedagogy of the Oppressed* (New York: Sea-bury Press, 1974); John Holt, *Instead of Education* (New York: Dell, 1976); and more recently John Gatto, *Dumbing Us Down* (Gabriola Island, BC: New Society Publishers, 1992).

7. In "School and Society," for example, see Martin Dworkin, ed., *Dewey on Education* (New York: Teacher's College Press, 1959).

8. Kevin Dunn, in a paper for my Philosophy of Education class, Spring 2002.

9. See "Instead of Environmental Education," and *Back to Earth*, chapter 8. I work out this theme more explicitly in "Teaching on the Edge," chapter 7 of *Jobs for Philosophers*.

10. "What can you tell about this person just from looking at their hand—Sherlock Holmes style, as it were? Where has this hand been? What is the person's occupation? How dry is the weather? . . ."

11. Robert Hutchison and Andrew Graham, *Meteorites* (London: The Natural History Museum, 1994), passim.

12. On this theme, see David Abram, *The Spell of the Sensuous* (New York: Pantheon, 1986), especially chapter 7.

13. Ibid., and also Abram's essay "The Perceptual Implications of the Gaia Hypothesis," *The Ecologist*, Summer 1985; reprinted in A. H. Badiner, ed., *Dharma Gaia: A Harvest of Essays in Buddhism and Ecology* (San Francisco: Parallax Press, 1990).

14. And raised without spraying—always an issue when you are eating a plant product that is not normally a food.

15. I hasten to add that there are safe areas for arachnophobes. Insect phobias are interesting in relation to my overall theme, but a theme for later—and people do not learn well if preoccupied or uneasy.

16. On the notion of the "hidden curriculum," see Illich, *Deschooling Society*, op. cit., and Elliot Eisner, *The Educational Imagination* (New York: Macmillan, 1985), chapter 5.

Chapter 8

Galapagos Stories

Evolution, Creation, and the Odyssey of Species

> It had never occurred to Shevek that life could proliferate so wildly, so exuberantly, that indeed exuberance was perhaps the essential quality of life. . . .
>
> —Ursula K. LeGuin, The *Dispossessed*

I

Less than half of the American public believes that humans evolved from earlier species of animals. Ask the question in certain ways and less than 10 percent agree. But the percentage is probably even lower in—of all places—the Galapagos Islands. Look a little beyond the main streets of the Galapagos's few fishing-and-tourism villages and you find Jehovah's Witness churches everywhere, along with the Catholic churches you would expect, and, within hailing distance of the Charles Darwin Research Station in Puerto Ayora, Seventh Day Adventists. Catholics are at best partial evolutionists, Adventists are literal creationists, and Witnesses deny that evolution produces new species. The Galapagenos themselves, living among the animals that have become evolution's very icons, are not Darwinians at all.

The citadels of science here at home are not so secure either. A Texas Tech University biology professor is currently being investigated by the Justice Department for refusing to write medical school recommendations for students who deny Darwinian evolution. There seem to be many. On the field trip I accompanied to the Galapagos in January

"Galapagos Stories: Evolution, Creation, and the Odyssey of Species" appeared in *Soundings* LXXXVI (2003), pp. 375–90.

2003—a small group of university biology students led by a evolutionary biologist colleague—several students maintained a quiet but clear dissent, learning the concepts but not taking them to heart.

Out in the Galapagos, meanwhile, science—and, it seems, evolution itself—march on. A legendary research project run by Peter and Rosemary Grant has tracked changes in the beak sizes of isolated populations of certain Darwin's finches since 1973. There have been long years of drought, others of virtual floods. The island's vegetation responds, the mix of seeds available to the birds varies dramatically—and then, very quickly, the average beak size in finch populations shifts too. Birds with beaks slightly less suitable to the immediate seed supply are slightly more likely to die off. When the rains come, the survivors reproduce prolifically; and so, much more quickly than Darwin expected, the characteristics of the species themselves measurably shift.

Science writer Jonathan Weiner details the Grants' work in his intriguing study *The Beak of the Finch*. Weiner ends with a look at the Creation-Evolution controversy from the point of view of his protagonists. As you would expect, they have no patience for creationism. The Grants tell of meeting Jehovah's Witnesses who find their work fascinating but never make the connection to evolution. "On an airplane," says another researcher, "I talked for an hour with someone about what I do, and never once mentioned the word *evolution*. . . . You just talk about what happens, and how you can study what happens: changes over many generations. . . . My fellow passenger was growing more and more excited: 'What a neat idea!' Finally, as the plane was landing, I told him that this neat idea is called evolution. He turned purple."[1]

I believe there is a clue here to the current cultural impasse over evolution—and, more important, an unexpected hint of a way beyond it. Certainly there are obtuse and closed-minded creationists. No doubt there is more than enough obtuseness all around. But something else is going on in this story. Here are people who "ask intelligent questions" and are thrilled by the picture of life's dynamism that emerges from the Grants' research. If this kind of genuine and informed excitement can be flummoxed in the end by a single word, isn't it just possible that the real problem is with that word? More specifically, might we need to rethink the rhetorical and conceptual cast currently put on the term "evolution"—to some degree by *both* sides? Could it be so hard to find a language that leaves the appreciation and fascination intact without invoking the same tired old polarization at the end? In all of his massive tome *The Origin of Species* Darwin uses "evolution" a grand total of once.[2] One of the Grant group muses about the possibility of doing the same thing today. Might a culture-wide analogue to that conversation on the plane—minus the ending—be possible for us? Why not? What would it look like?

II

The first Darwin's finch I saw in the Galapagos announced itself by landing on my hat. This is the iconic animal, I thought. See one of these and the whole story comes immediately to mind: how a few stray ur-finches once blew to these islands, and how in time, on different islands with their different endowments of flowers and seeds and insects, the distant descendants of those original immigrants developed different beaks—in some cases, radically different beaks. Much is explained in this way that otherwise must be left puzzling, such as why species on islands like the Galapagos so markedly resemble species on nearby landmasses such as, in this case, Ecuador and the Americas generally. There is both difference and resemblance, just as Darwin predicts.

Darwin's explanation in turn is simple, elegant and, at least on the logical level, unassailable. Variation, he points out, is naturally present in all populations. Most of these variations are heritable: that is, they can be passed on to one's offspring. But environments are not neutral with respect to them. When not every individual, no matter how endowed, can survive, those with even the slightest advantages will pass on their genes a little more successfully than others. Thus, Darwin concludes, over the generations even the most radical change is possible.

That such changes occur is not in question. Genetic, physical, and behavioral changes in populations can be created in laboratories in this way and have been verified in various other settings. Quite obviously too, humans have been remolding animal and plant species for millennia, as Darwin points out at length in *The Origin of Species*. This is "artificial" versus what he labeled "natural" selection. Pet lovers see its results daily. Here are genuinely new species, created more or less by design.

The contested question is whether natural selection can—or actually *did*—create entirely new species on its own. For the savvy modern-day creationist, it turns out, accepts natural adaptation within the "fixed limits" of existing species or families, drawing the line instead at the emergence of entirely new species or "kinds." Darwin's finches are still *finches*, after all, our creationists point out. They were not somehow transfigured into eagles or lichen or mosquitoes. Though Weiner subtitles his book on the Grant research "Evolution in Action," the actual changes are hardly that dramatic. We are not talking about anything like new species here. In fact, in the thirty years of data so far, relatively small changes have oscillated back and forth. The net effect has been no change at all.

Still, it is a rather stunning admission on the creationists' part, understandably not much advertised. To say it again: evolution of a sort actually does happen, according to at least some creationists, only it has no power to alter a species beyond certain pre-set limits. Nature has a certain adaptive creativity of its own, though limited, after all.

Even this small hint of a *rapprochement*, though, is fragile and apt to collapse back into contention. Here the conceptual ground is uncertain and full of pitfalls—rather like the Galapagos themselves, in fact, littered with ejecta from volcanic eruptions, sometimes covered by dense undergrowth, and criss-crossed by lava tubes with the disconcerting habit of caving in. An embarrassment on the Darwinian side is that biologists have never been too sure how to classify those Galapagos finches. The criteria for new species cannot be said to be crystal clear. At times those finches have actually been categorized as one species with a variety of subspecies—the young naturalist Darwin's own first guess, in fact. Later it was fourteen or eleven or (now) thirteen separate species, sometimes with pathetic names like *Geospiza incerta* ("ground finch, who knows?"), ornithologist John Gould's name for a variety he eventually folded in with another in the course of distinguishing thirteen species total, though not the thirteen currently most widely accepted. To make matters worse, they also regularly cross-breed. Is it so clear that they are truly distinct?

On the other hand, if evolution's critics are going to allow natural selection to explain variation within species, including such things as dramatically different finch beaks, how much further is it to entirely new species? That admittedly fuzzy definition of "species" cuts both ways. Maybe it is unclear enough to allow for legitimate disagreement over whether the Galapagos finches are really distinct "kinds" or not, but the very same uncertainty implies that there is no insuperable barrier to cross, no dramatic and obvious border between subspecies and genuinely new species. As the genome mappings begin to yield their results, we learn by what tiny proportions our genes differ from our near relatives. Measured by degree of genetic divergence (about 1%), humans are no further from chimpanzees than Galapagos ground finches are from Galapagos tree finches.

III

Sensing an advantage here, the argumentative Darwinian may go in for the kill. Evolution, it is argued, must be a purely physical, "dumb" process that simply takes advantage of whatever beneficial random mutations happen to occur. Its long-run results only *appear* to be intelligent, only look *as if* they were designed. It is easy to be misled—so easy that for most of human history, all of us were. When, in 1802, the theologian William Paley laid out the argument that the young Darwin at first found so irresistible—that the universe can only be understood as a giant sort of artifact, reflecting the glory of the Artificer—he spoke accurately for the science of the time, which everywhere told the same story about the genesis of order. But science has been transformed in the ensuing centuries. Darwin's great discovery was not the fact of evolution. That was already known, though not widely accepted. Rather, Darwin's great discovery, as evolutionists are prone to put it, evolution's *mechanism*, the physical processes that drive it. The "blindness" of the whole process is crucial—think of Richard Dawkins's evocative title *The Blind Watchmaker*—because if evolution in any sense "knows where it is going," then we are back in the realm of purposiveness and (seemingly) conscious intention. A mechanical process has none of this intentionality: the possibility of direction or design does not even come up. What Darwin really showed is that even the most exquisite adaptation is possible without any design at all.

There is a certain ferocity in this argument, though, not to mention a blind eye to mechanism's own cultural and conceptual baggage. For the idea of mechanism comes with its own overtones and associations. It is a *metaphor*, after all, not a pure description: and a metaphor whose imaginative world is all nineteenth century and industrial, invoking factory machinery and repetitive, lockstep motion. Pictured in this way, species adapt by themselves. No ultimate Machinist is necessary, but the process of adaptation itself must be wholly automatic. You cannot suppose any intention or foresight in the process. There is simply the rising and falling of endless generations of creatures, most of which perish without issue or with relatively fewer issue while the randomly generated better-fitted individuals come, ever so slowly, to dominate the gene pool. Adaptation is, as it were, just cranked out.

Mechanism, however, is not the only available metaphor. It may be that we have made ourselves so hypersensitive to any hint of intentionality in evolution—so insistent that evolution must be "blind," without conscious purpose—that we have blocked any possibility of also recognizing or acknowledging the *intelligence* of the process. On this point the defenders of (a certain kind of) science have, arguably, painted themselves into so extraordinarily small rhetorical and conceptual corner that it is no wonder that so many nonscientists balk. Species *respond*, after all, to life's challenges and opportunities—not consciously, not necessarily even purposefully, but surely in a way that we can describe as "intelligent" in an exact Websterian sense: "having the power of meeting a situation, especially a novel situation, by successful adjustment." Life has certain powers that the rhetoric of mechanism seems unable to accommodate.

Even the "blindness" metaphor doesn't really work. People who are literally blind do not somehow lack all capacity for direction. Often they are preternaturally responsive in other-than-sighted ways. Wouldn't it be sensible to ask the same question of an allegedly "blind" evolutionary process: To what *does* it respond, rather than to what it doesn't?

"Mutation" is a metaphor too. Darwin himself had no idea what produced the novelties on which natural selection is supposed to operate, and was so vexed by this problem that he resorted to increasingly desperate (and increasingly non-"Darwinian") hypotheses every time he revised *The Origin of Species*. It was only resolved by the rediscovery of Mendel's genetics in the early twentieth century, prompting the resurgence of evolutionism now known as the "Neo-Darwinian Synthesis," according to which the source of variation and novelty is mutation and other random errors in the combination and replication of genes—sheer, unaccounted-for, purposeless variation once again.

But why not use words like "play," or "improvisation," or "spontaneity" for the very same process? The point is that genes are not prone to sitting still. Change happens without obvious or traceable causes. Almost all of this spontaneity is entropic and heads off in degenerating directions. Only occasionally, rarely, but just often enough, some unexpected and dramatic adaptation arises too.

In short, there is some *space* in these seemingly technical and merely neutral terms, once a certain metaphorical side is recognized. There is some breathing room, even a way to begin to speak of something very like, well, creativity itself, within the very belly of the Darwinian beast.

Much the same can be said in a more complex case: the explanatory use of the concept of "genetic drift." When species diverge without any clear adaptive reason, "drift" is one possible Darwinian explanation. This too is part of the Galapagos story, for island species are uniquely susceptible to "drift." When these islands emerged from the sea, seven hundred miles from the nearest mainland coast, they were barren lava, cooling under the equatorial sun. All the life that is here emigrated, originally, from somewhere else. In the new environment, cut off from their relatives and facing new demands and opportunities, the new immigrants (or, more accurately, those immigrant populations not regularly replenished by more immigrants of the same species) gradually diverged from their ancestors. The Galapagos evolved four different kinds of mockingbirds, for instance, and (once had) thirteen different kinds of tortoises, mostly in nonoverlapping ranges.

Darwinians may describe this process as "adaptation" to specific new environments, a reasonable term if meant as a description not just of an organism's existing relation to its environment (it's "well-adapted") but of a *process* (adaptation is something that species *do*). "Drift" is invoked to explain seemingly nonadaptive divergences. The suggestion is that these divergences may ultimately trace back to statistical variation. Any small group of immigrants will diverge slightly from the general population from the start, for one thing, just by the normal vagaries of sampling. In any case, subsequent mutation is essentially a chaotic process and may go in myriad different directions. Over aeons, even absent any significant environmental divergences, two separated populations will almost certainly come to differ dramatically enough to count as separate species.

Once again, though, a small shift in language, a slightly different story-line, might fit the facts just as well but at the same time would give life, so to say, a lot more credit. Suppose that we describe "drift" instead explicitly as "creativity" or, once again, "improvisation." Again, we need not suppose that an individual or species consciously creates or improvises such changes. The very point of the "drift" metaphor is that nothing in the outer environment compels the change in question—so that if you really do view organisms as utterly at the mercy of external factors, all you have left is to view them as "adrift." But rather than therefore viewing such change as utterly undirected because none of the usual environmental controllers can be invoked, we could take precisely this as the occasion to recognize and celebrate a self-generative creativity in life itself. It is not that nothing whatsoever is happening, but rather that what is happening is more internal, more subtle and spontaneous.

Recent studies even suggest that a population's rate of gene-mixing and mutation increases when that population comes under stress—when, in short, there is a need to speed up the rate of change. Bacteria do it in laboratory cultures; animals do it by cross-breeding. Once again, we need not suppose they do this intentionally. Nonetheless a distinctive kind of responsiveness seems to be at work. The capacity for a certain efflorescence of form may be a deep-lying element of life's own endowments.

Out in the Galapagos you encounter species where neither the term *adaptation* nor *drift* really captures the panache of the actual type of creature in front of you. One species of booby has feet so blue they look utterly impossible, unreal. This is the same bird that dive-bombs straight down into the waves from eighty feet in the air to catch fish. Sometimes you can watch a whole flock feeding at once; the *pow-pow-pow* and the white flashes of bird after bird hitting the water are both exhilarating and bizarre. Or the ubiquitous Sally Lightfoot crabs, a creature of the black lava shores, dark greenish brown when juvenile but maturing to a flaming red. You can only describe that blazing color as a kind of beacon, almost a *dare*. It is possible to argue that there is no selective disadvantage in this. Our Galapageno guide alleged that fully grown Sally Lightfoots have no predators: the shells are too thick, he said, though we saw some that had obviously been eaten. Maybe the gulls would get them anyway. But why help? Anyway, even if their color has no selective disadvantage, this hardly explains why they actually *are* red, of all colors. And why *that* red, of all reds?

IV

Competition, according to popular Darwinism, is the prime engine of evolution. Here too, however, a different way of telling the story is possible—different terms, different resonance—and, once again, more room to move.

Darwin envisioned nature as a series of fixed niches or "offices," particular ways of using the resources of (or making resources of) a particular kind of place. Some animals eat certain specific plants, certain other animals eat those animals. Darwin also supposed these "offices" to be limited, both in number (since there are only so many ways of surviving in a particular place) and in capacity (since only so many individuals can make use of a particular niche). Drawing on Thomas Malthus, Darwin then concluded that since the generative capacity of all species vastly overshoots the carrying capacity of the land, individual survival, not to mention successful reproduction, is always a struggle, a battle that not all can win.

In this picture, evolution proceeds because certain variants drive out their competitors in the great struggle to survive. The official term is "competitive replacement." This is natural selection at its most dismal, what the ecological historian Donald Worster calls the "somber, tragic specter of Malthusian scarcity and contention."[3]

Arguably, however, competitive replacement is *not* the main story of evolution in a place like the Galapagos. On initially uninhabited islands, with many of the usual competitors absent or barely represented (terrestrial mammals, for example, which have no way to survive a 700-mile ocean crossing), new immigrants do not have to prove themselves against an already crowded field. Quite the contrary: initially the field is empty. Immigrants arrive to a wide-open arena of possibility. In the Galapagos, the tortoises moved onto the hillsides and into the calderas and became grazers. Some started eating so high up the cacti that the cacti evolved into trees. One iguana species took to the water, the only marine iguana in the world. Penguins arrived, and adapted themselves to stay—of all places, on the equator.

This is no kind of "replacement" at all, but the exploration and exploitation of new niches. Darwinians speak of *adaptive radiation* and *evolutionary divergence*. We could also call it *species creativity*.

The more arguable point is whether the "somber, tragic specter of . . . scarcity and contention" is the most accurate story anywhere. For it is seldom true that the number of ecological niches is strictly limited. Organisms are just as likely, and probably better advised, to find a new way to make a living—taking advantage of a new or altered trait to make a resource of something previously unused, creating new places for themselves, new niches, rather than displacing existing species already utilizing existing niches. We might as well say that *all* species *always* arrive to wide-open possibility. The laws of creativity—improvisation and diversification—are fundamental laws of evolution too. Coexistence and mutual dependence take their place alongside, and often enough overrule, competition and mutual extermination.

Darwin's Galapagos encounter with adaptive radiation was crucial to his conversion to an evolutionary point of view. Even on the level of mechanics, his theory of competitive replacement—and indeed, natural selection itself—was offered as only one evolutionary dynamic among many. Many modern Darwinians, it turns out, are "pluralists" too. Steven Jay Gould and Richard Lewontin argue that a species' overall design and structure may influence its evolution much more than natural selection.[4] This "European" kind of Darwinism, as they call it, has a striking resonance with the creationists' distinction between change within a species (basically, variation within a fixed overall structure) and the emergence of a new species or "kind" (a new structure)—though Gould also proposes that a profusion of new kinds can arise by other means in rare, short, but explosive evolutionary saltations. Darwinism, anyway, has evolved.

All the same, species creativity somehow always recedes into the background when the evolutionary picture is being painted in broad strokes. Darwin and Darwinians still mostly allow adaptive radiation and evolutionary divergence to be eclipsed by the image of "nature red in tooth and claw." Worster attributes Darwin's own captivation by the competitive model partly to his Victorian frame of mind, partly to the constant, miserable struggles in his own life (for professional recognition for example, and even to get up in the morning). The pattern continues in our own time, partly out of inertia, partly because we still have neither taste nor eye for the subtle and the slow. Predation makes for better television. But none of the reasons are internal to the evolutionary point of view itself. Nothing actually compels us to make competitive replacement alone paradigmatic.

Another story is emerging. *Co*-evolution and mutualism, the elaboration of complex webs of interdependence between different (often *very* different) species, are the new watchwords. We are learning to see an invitation to creative coexistence even where we first learned to see only head-to-head competition. Ethologists show us even the jungle (think of the overtones we have attached to *that* word!) as a cooperative and mostly peaceful community. Considering life as a whole, predation is almost vanishingly rare. Nature is certainly not "red in tooth and claw" to a hyacinth or a redwood tree. A contemporary Darwinism not only can but must insist that nature mostly works in other ways.

V

Walking across a bare Galapagos lava flow one blazing noon, my student Rachel DellaValle momentarily forgot Darwin's famous title and spoke not of the "Origin" but of the "Odyssey" of species. A lovely slip of the tongue, truer to Darwin's spirit, perhaps, than many modern Darwinisms. Etymologically the word "evolution" means *unrolling*, as of a scroll, or the *unfolding*, as of a story. Life is a continuous project. Creation is still going on. Even the legendary tameness of the Galapagos's animals invites you to a larger story. The gregarious little finches, the nesting boobies and iguanas you can walk right up to, the sea lions who hustle over to swim with you—here you feel invited to something that elsewhere is only a dim part of our species memory, to a genuinely co-inhabited world, to a *shared* odyessy. "Tameness" is not really quite the word, either. It is more that a kind of trust, a feeling for co-inhabitation, for fellow-traveling so to say, is part of these animals' very wildness.

Embracing that shared odyssey, embracing life's delicate, exuberant, continuous adjustment and improvisation in each place—embracing, could we even say, *evolutionary creativity*—we have begun to glimpse a Darwinism in a very different key. At the same time, it is a Darwinism that situates creativity, indeed even more emphatically, in the processes and entities of this world rather than in an external Source. Its theology, if you could call it that, is all "immanentist." Intelligence and creativity have to be pictured as inherent in life itself. A lovely image, and one that surely speaks to at least part of contemporary Creationism's appeal, the wish to honor creativity in the world. Nonetheless the fundamental Darwinian challenge to that very kind of Creationism remains. Creativity is possible *without design*. The spectacularly and intricately beautiful world we know is possible without a Creator. Indeed: to honor it most fully might *require* recognizing and affirming its own self-creation.

Thus the very concept of "creation," too, acquires—even demands— a certain metaphorical space. Those whose stake in "creativity" is not quite so fixed on divine design would do well, like the Darwinists I have been addressing, to put more emphasis on spontaneity, improvisation, play—on nature's own creativity, in short, rather than outside design. How this will sit with the biblical literalists remains to be seen—but perhaps we may also wonder if they are the necessary future custodians of (so to say) the creationist impulse. A better question would be: What sort of theology would a recognition of life's own self-regenerative creativity require? Meanwhile, for an interesting test of just how scientific "scientific creationism" actually is, we could explore how far Creationism itself might, well, *evolve*.

Certain practical debates also take on a different hue against the background of "the odyssey of species." Legally it may or may not be arguable that refusing to write medical school recommendations for students who do not believe in evolution is unfair discrimination. We might get further by noting that the term *evolution*, especially coupled with "believe in," massively raises the ante of a question that we could more constructively address in the terms suggested here. The essential thing is to "believe in" life's *responsiveness*, its self-regenerative, improvisational fluidity. A pesticide or antibiotic that kills 99 percent of the offending insects or bacteria will still leave a few to reproduce—variation within species will see to that—and therefore soon enough you have a totally resistant population. This is why we are losing a higher percentage of crops to insects than before the widespread use of pesticides. This is why effective antibiotics are becoming ever more specialized and expensive and ever more temporarily effective, and why some strains of bacteria are now resistant to all known antibiotics.

Must we affirm the right of students to be recommended for medical school if they feel compelled (theologically, one supposes) to deny even these most basic dynamics of life? I do not think so. Never mind theology: we are talking about the preconditions for minimally competent medical practice, or minimally effective crop protection—though frankly I think it ought to offend us theologically too, to so spectacularly underestimate life. It certainly offends common sense and our hopes for health and for a livable environment. Maybe to go to medical school you needn't "believe in" a mechanistic or indeed any sort of Darwinian explanation for the origin of species. You *do* have to understand—it is no longer acceptable, intellectually or practically, to deny—that they, like we, are on an odyssey, and that this fact has implications.

Darwinians in turn, however, are not necessarily the sole future custodians of the "odyssey of species" either. It may even be that the coming debate will not feature creationists as Darwin's chief antagonists at all. "Secular catastrophism," as Vine Deloria labels it, is the thesis that the history of Earth is one of multiple, radical upheavals—comet impacts, massive eruptions, and the like—producing multiple and radical biological saltations as well.[5] Catastrophism's arguments somewhat parallel contemporary creationists': they point out certain inconsistencies in Darwinism, and certain recalcitrant data, such as jumbled and off-the-scale sedimentary layering, which suggest an Earth with a briefer and more unsettled past than now currently believed. Deloria points out, however, that all of this is invoked by creationists only to try to discredit Darwinism, after which the whole subject is dropped. In truth the same data sit poorly with creationism too. Merely to invoke "creation," especially multiple times, explains nothing, not to mention that a God with such a penchant for the half-hearted though spectacular destruction of living experiments would be more than a little perverse. Darwinians, meantime, according to Deloria, resist catastrophism for all the wrong reasons: partly out of loyalty to the uniformitarianism of the Founder, now truly a historical relic, and most of all because it sounds to them like Genesis all over again. Which it isn't—the creationist story actually is not catastrophic *enough*.

But life's spectacular recoveries after multiple disasters are a puzzle for evolution too. One of the original difficulties for Darwinism reappears: there was not enough time. Catastrophism, in short, may require natural creativity on a scale unimaginable to both Darwinism and Creationism. Life's challenges have truly been Odysseus-like—or Herculean, maybe, depending on your favorite Greek. This also is the upshot, Deloria says, of traditional peoples' story-preserved memories of early Earth history. Only the wily, persistent, impossibly vigorous survive, and even that is something of a miracle. We are left, as usual, with more questions than answers. At least we can say that a better sense of the very openness of the whole issue—a recognition that as yet the fundamental questions have barely even been posed in the right terms, let alone answered—would be wise all around.

VI

One root of the opposition to Darwinism has been a long-standing cultural stake in denying human continuity with other animals. Conceivably it even underlies the resistance to an immanentist image of God: we do not want to think ourselves *that* closely linked to the rest of the world. To recover any kind of environmental sanity, however, we need to develop precisely a deep sense of shared inhabitation, a love for the Earth as our home, as the generative matrix of all that we love. A sense for the shared odyssey is now our compelling need.

Here, unfortunately, it is the creationists' turn to resist for the wrong reasons: because they too have been led to believe that creative intelligence cannot be found in nature itself, because they too picture nature "red in tooth and claw," because outside of creationist orthodoxy they have not been offered a unified vision of life on Earth that speaks to the heart. But none of this is any sort of "given." That some of these reasons must be laid partly at Darwinism's own door is true, also unfortunately, but it is not the end of the story. It is only an opportunity, once again, to tell a better story. We must find a way to carry on in very different terms.

At Salango on the Ecuadorian coast, in the region from which many of the Galapagos' first life-forms emigrated, anthropologist Richard Lunniss and his staff laboriously document the unique cultures that flourished locally from 4000 BCE or so until the Conquest. Lunniss's whole theme is that culture cannot be understood out of place. Ceremonial sites, song and clothing, the layout of houses—none of it makes sense except in the context of wind and wave, the melodic contours of the local birdsong and the visual contours of a coastline dominated by ragged and rapidly eroding sandstone promontories and peninsulas. Gradually you begin to see how deeply Lunniss's work is linked to Darwin's. The evolution and diversification of human culture is part of the odyssey too. Human life, considered both biologically and culturally, is also part of the Great Flow. The creative radiation of one kind of finch into fourteen has its structural analogue in the stunning diversity of human cultures in Ecuador's geologically and ecologically diverse landscape.

Lunniss's aim is to reconstruct one place's cultural history, while recognizing that even his way of telling that story is also a product of that very place, a place to which he, like those he studies, has given his

life. And so, for the last time, my theme too: we need more of that
sense of embeddedness, that humility in the face of the immensity and
variety of the story we all live within. We need to regain a sense of how
much of a story it all still really is, how much the nuances of our words
and the resonance of our underlying, half-articulated images still matter.
To speak of "spontaneity" changes none of the facts of "mutation." To
speak of "species creativity" changes none of the facts of "drift." Yet
everything is still different. The mechanistic language we have learned
to insist upon is no more neutral or objective or nonspeculative than
the language of "responsiveness"—it is only, right now, more familiar.
Likewise, the language of "creation" is no one's monopoly. The moment
may even come when we can say that we are all creationists now. The
question is, what sort of creationism could that be? What sort of creativity is actually at work beyond and within us?

At least we can say this: We do all belong to this Earth. We are all,
both in human time and in evolutionary time, in flux and flow *with* the
Earth as well as with each other. This is the kind of story that we—all of
us, officially Darwinian or Creationist or Catastrophist or whatever—now
desperately need: a story that celebrates life's dynamism and creativity,
and therefore invites our recognition and love in response; and a story
that requires us to rejoin the larger living world on terms that are not
entirely our own. Told in certain ways, I have tried to suggest, some
of the stories we already tell are actually, achingly close to such a story.
They have the capacity to grow bigger. To give them the chance may
be the real task of the present moment.

Notes

1. Jonathan Weiner, *The Beak of the Finch* (New York: Vintage, 1994),
p. 297.

2. Admittedly the very last word, though. Charles Darwin, *The Origin
of Species* (New York: Penguin, 2003), p. 459.

3. Worster, Donald, *Nature's Economy: A History of Ecological Ideas* (New
York: Cambridge University Press, 1977), p. 213.

4. See Stephen Jay Gould, and R. C. Lewontin, "The Spandrels of San
Marcos and the Panglossian Paradigm: A Critique of the Adaptationist Pro-
gramme." *Proceedings of the Royal Society of London, B 205* (1979): 581–98.

5. Deloria, Vine, *Evolution, Creationism, and Other Modern Myths* (Golden,
CO: Fulcrum Publishing, 2002).

Chapter 9

Eco-Philosophy in Space

I. Beginnings

Apollo 8 reached lunar orbit on Christmas Eve, 1968, its three-member crew the first Earthlings ever launched beyond our planet's gravitational well. Awestruck by the beauty of the distant Earth, they argued with Mission Control about diverting precious time and film to take a picture. Finally they took one as a kind of afterthought.[1] The rest is history. That photograph of Earth in its fragile beauty helped to inspire the nascent environmental movement. Truly having stepped outside of Earth for the first time, we could look back on the home planet and see it as a whole. Stewart Brand famously opined that that one image was worth the entire $25,000,000,000 cost of the Apollo program.[2]

Yet even with that image on our movement's flag, environmentalism remains resolutely Earth-bound. How can we support space programs, we keep arguing, when we do not even know how to live appropriately on this Earth? And yet perhaps, just possibly, the question of space deserves a bit more of a look. Deep space exploration frames not just the Earth as a single whole but the entire solar system, or even larger wholes. Profound challenges to established ways of thinking are likely to arise once we begin to recognize ourselves not merely as Earthlings but as, maybe, "Solarians," or, as it were, plain cosmic citizens. Might even the very vision of an Earth-centered ethic itself, so recently and so laboriously won, begin to seem incomplete and parochial in its way? What then? Moreover, doesn't environmental philosophy have its own distinctive contribution to make to this most momentous of reconceptions, as humans begin to probe worlds beyond Earth in earnest? If the exploration of space may transform environmental philosophy, so

This essay was written in 2005 and circulated among friends and colleagues, revised a few times, but not published until now. There are hints of its themes in "Second Comings," Chapter 4 of my *Jobs for Philosophers* (Xlibris, 2004).

environmental philosophy may—and must—also transform the exploration of space.[3]

II. Escape Velocities

The space program is a human project, pursuing all-too-human goals not only in the crass sense—planting the flag on the Moon, say, or mining asteroids—but subtly too, as when scientists see in Moon or Mars certain previous phases in Earth's own geological or (possibly) biological evolution, and hence justify space exploration on the grounds that we will thereby learn more about ourselves. There is also the persistent argument that space-based technologies benefit everyday life back home. Still, all the same, whatever else may be said about space exploration, one basic feature is that it insistently forces upon us a larger-than-human perspective—in fact, a *vastly* larger-than-human perspective. For environmentalists, still struggling to inch our fellows even just slightly out of an anthropocentric point of view, achieving such a philosophical "escape velocity" is no small thing.

Apollo 11 planted the flag, of course, but the largest TV audience in history tuned in for something far more primal: to share the first direct encounter with another world. The first few landings were in relatively safe and consequently flat and featureless places—no one knew what it would be like to land a spacecraft with so little margin of safety so unimaginably far from home—but once the basic skills were down, they started going to really wild places: edges of craters, up into mountain ranges, down into the canyons of Hadley Rille. Fewer people have seen these photos, but they are as stunning as any landscape photography from Earth—*more* stunning, maybe, for the setting is, after all, Moon.[4] The nationalism, even the anthropocentric self-congratulations ("giant leap for mankind"), gain their power from this primal fascination, not the other way around.

The momentum continues. Mars has been orbited and mapped for decades, and the rovers now on its surface can be followed move-by-move on the Web. Vast reservoirs of Martian water (ice) are known. An earlier mission took a photo of Earth and Moon together from the Martian surface—a perfect complement to Apollo's world-historical Earth-from-Moon picture.[5] The outer gas giants have had close flybys, and now even their moons attract attention: the Cassini Saturn mission swung around Earth once and Venus twice to reach the ringed planet, along the way landing a probe on the dynamic and perplexing surface of Saturn's moon Titan. Several spacecraft have left the solar system entirely.[6] Asteroids, comets, and all sorts of matter and other forces traverse even the so-called emptiness of "space" itself, which physicists tell us is more a matter of relative density than the old Newtonian uniform-but-unoccupied Cartesian "space" anyway—pure "space," strictly speaking, does not exist.

Just in the last year or so, hundreds of planets, some of them potentially Earth-like, have been discovered in other solar systems. Farther out lie vaster and unimaginably different kinds of objects: black holes, neutron stars, and other galaxies, billions of them, to the edge of the universe itself.

Philosophically too, all of this may end up carrying us very much further than we thought we were going. In Hegelian terms, that photo of the Earth-Moon system from Mars arguably marks a whole new dialectical stage. Now we can begin to see previous opposites in their unity and connection. Looking at Earth from Moon we begin to think past anthropocentrism. Looking at Earth-and-Moon from Mars, we may begin to think past the very opposition between anthropocentrism and "nonanthropocentrism" itself. The whole distinction begins to seem Earth-bound. "Nonanthropocentrism" is just a negation, after all. As nascent "Solarians," seeing ourselves as one node of a much larger system, we may awaken to the need for a new, more inclusive, positive ethic.

How much of our existing conceptual equipment—how many of our moral and environmental categories—are up to the trip? We tend to assume, for example, that the mountains of Moon carry, or at least might carry, some moral weight. Mining Moon or asteroids, we want to say, might be just as ethically problematic as gold mining along Montana's Blackfoot River or strip-mining more mountain ranges in West Virginia. We should not be so sure, however, that we can explain why. The argument cannot be biocentric or ecocentric, for there is no life on Moon at all. J. Baird Callicott has argued that a Leopoldian land ethic is resolutely and necessarily Earth-bound, though he allows that a reverence-for-life ethic, though according to him impractical on Earth, might work elsewhere.[7] But what of lifeless places? When my daughter learned that the Apollo landing sites were left littered with debris—deliberately crashed landing modules, discarded experiments, footprints and tracks everywhere, all to last hundreds of millions of years—she was outraged. Surely she has a point. But exactly what values does trashing an utterly lifeless place violate?

A life-based or Earth-based environmental ethic cannot be the whole story. About at least some natural values we must tell a different story. It seems that in an absolutely literal sense space exploration opens us to what William James called the "Multiverse."[8] The point for the moment, though, is simpler: any perspective that might so insistently push us beyond both anthropocentrism and geocentrism is a perspective worth taking seriously. Already philosophers are unavoidably invited into space.

An extraterrestrial perspective may also reframe our thinking about wilderness. Mars has mountains three times the height of Everest. A passing storm on Jupiter or Saturn could swallow the whole Earth and barely notice. The rugged hills of Moon are both strangely familiar and yet *unearthly*. If "wild" means, in part, self-possessed, "untrammeled," or sublime, then surely all of this is paradigmatically wild too. Yet that term does not quite work either, and it is only partly because these extraterrestrial "wilds" are so far off the scale of anything terrestrial. We are concerned with "wilderness" on Earth partly because such places are under siege, places where the human presence is not only problematic but sometimes, arguably, ought to be excluded. Some environmentalists, it is true, are willing enough to extend these implications to other worlds. But the cases may not be analogous. When wild places really are in danger, staying out makes sense. That the same kind of restrictiveness applies to entire unexplored and unpressured worlds is not so clear.

More crucial may be the spirit in which we go. Aboriginal peoples, after all, were not trammeling the land in the first place, at least by the European standards that are usually implicit in this sort of discussion. Still, they often did alter the landscape and ecology in significant ways. Nor would most environmentalists claim that Thoreau or Muir, say, or the Romantic poets and painters, should have stayed away from Walden Pond or the Adirondacks or the High Sierra.[9] The human presence as such is not *necessarily* problematic. So we may not want to argue that humans ought not to go into space at all; at any rate, that is not somehow the only possible environmentalist view of the matter. Again, though, the deeper and more challenging point is that our usual normative and conceptual baggage—wilderness, biocentrism, and so on—might not be up to spaceflight either. The appropriate conclusion is at the very least *not clear*. In these thoughts, then, there is a certain "escape velocity" from the conceptual and ethical environment of Earth as well: not an escape from ethics as such—that had better be emphasized right away—but an invitation to rethink everything in a vastly different and larger context.

III. Toward a Cosmic Environmentalism

A more-than-Terran perspective also teaches that the very concept of "environment" itself needs dramatic rethinking and expansion.

Normally we picture "environment" as terrestrial, as the region of Earth's surface and what lies close beneath and above it. Deep in the Earth, though, is more life: giant deepwater worms at underwater vents, bacteria in rocks miles down.[10] Possibly there is more life "in" the planet than "on" it—and (since this life does not depend on atmosphere) therefore possible "in" other planets too.

Thinking about space invites us to look in the other direction: up. For starters, obviously, the entire system is solar-powered. No sun, not much of an environment. Moon cycles deeply influence life cycles as well—the tides, menstruation, migration, mating—and even the stars may have an influence. Every night when the sun goes down, the familiar blue-skied living "environment" opens up to the infinite universe—there all the time, really, just not visible during the day.

Earth's material environment is not self-contained either. Matter from other planets and even from beyond the solar system is continually arriving. In the 1990s we were greeted with the news that protobacteria had been discovered on Mars (announced by the President, no less, specially notified by NASA). This was not from materials brought back from Mars by spacecraft—"return missions" are still only a distant prospect—but from a piece of Mars found on top of the ice in Antarctica: from a meteorite, in short, blasted off Mars by eruption or impact, that found its way eventually to Earth and luckily to the ice cap, where it eventually floated up through the ice (rocks are more heat-absorbent than ice) and came to rest on the surface. Apparently it happens a lot: meteor-hunting on the ice is a sort of poor man's space program.

That the chemical formations found in those rocks were evidence of bacterial life turned out to be unclear. The larger point remains: we do not need to leave Earth to find parts of other planets and moons, asteroids and comets, even other stars. Outer space is already here. It continues to arrive. One hundred tons of Martian material is estimated to make it to the Earth's surface every year; pieces of Earth likewise annually arrive on Mars. Thirty to forty thousand tons of cometary and asteroid material also arrive yearly.[11] This is happening *now*; and it has happened constantly and spectacularly in the course of Earth's history, when interplanetary space was even more full of cosmic debris, comets, and so forth. Some scientists theorize that most of Earth's water—think of that absolutely immense volume of matter—must have come from comets. Some 300 meteorites have even been discovered that are older than 4.5 billion years and therefore predate the solar system itself.[12] We ourselves and everything around us are made of the materials of long-dead stars.

Matter is circulating on larger scales. "Environment" does not end at the surface of the Earth. But then why suppose it ends at all?

Of course there are always various provisional boundaries, much as one ecosystem can be distinguished from neighboring ones—but no absolute boundary. Ultimately we are coming to understand that all terrestrial ecosystems are linked into a greater and quite dynamic whole. By analogy, space exploration is now challenging us to recognize that the "terrestrial" may not be a closed system either. We may have still more geocentrisms to shed.

Life itself is very much at stake in a more open-ended understanding of "environment." Some theories of the origin of life even suggest that the first seeds of life—the amino-acid building blocks, or perhaps more advanced forms—arrived from space (this is the so-called panspermia hypothesis;[13] "pangermia" would be less sexist). It is not an ad hoc hypothesis: there are some classic arguments for it, for example that life showed up on Earth at almost the first moment it could—and at a time when Earth was being mercilessly bombarded by cometary material. Indeed possibly the universe so teems with life that Earth has not been seeded just once but multiple times—life's germs are floating around all over, it's not a one-time thing—so that whales, say, might have a different extraterrestrial origin from, say, trees. Some scientists argue that multiple extraterrestrial origins may help explain some of the radical differences between different lineages of life-forms on Earth.[14]

Ourselves too, perhaps. Extraterrestrial origin stories figure prominently in the cosmologies of aboriginal peoples around the world. Of course we come here to possibilities well outside of the current scientific consensus, though nonetheless only a natural extension of pangermic hypothesizing. I will say only this: consider how dramatically fresh and open a universe we glimpse if even for a moment we take seriously the possibility that the universe is not only already the scene of communicating civilizations, but that they may have played their role in the "seeding" of life, including human life, on earth, or even a role in human prehistory.[15] Here we at least catch a glimpse of what it might feel like to see the skies above us not as a spectacle, or as an unreachable and inhospitable realm, but more like a great open commons, the edges of our familiar biosphere only a local boundary and not some sort of ultimate limit.

Pangermia may be just what we environmentalists really are hoping for. Surely we believe in whole systems, in the interconnections of life, in the Great Flow? Surely we should want the narrative of life on Earth to fit into some larger picture, to connect to the rest of the universe? The implications, however, are unexplored. New challenges await us. If the universe teems with life, for instance, it may be that life *here* is not quite as absolutely unique and precious as we sometimes want to say. Lost species might be readily regenerated or reseeded; their loss would not be such a total disaster. Recovery would only require re-colonization, as it were, from an adjoining ecosystem.[16]

If life is rare in the universe, on the other hand, then maybe part of our calling is to spread life ourselves. *We* could become the pangermic seed-spreaders, cosmic Johnny Appleseeds. Restricting ourselves to a stay-at-home, sort-out-your-local-problems sort of modesty may in fact be downright irresponsible in the currently precarious state of things.[17] In this spirit, not just science fiction writers but seemingly sober scientists already speak of "terraforming" Mars: setting global warming to work on purpose, creating a thicker atmosphere to trap more sunlight, melt the ice, and release enough oxygen into the air that eventually Earth-based life-forms could live on the surface. Mars has enough gravity, some atmosphere already, and large amounts of water. James Lovelock (yup, the Lovelock of the Gaia Hypothesis) imagines hurling CFCs to Mars with recycled intercontinental ballistic missiles. Others suggest huge orbiting mirrors, new "supergreenhouse" gases, which understandably have not been a growth industry lately; or genetically engineered plants and bacteria tailor-made for Mars.[18]

To many environmentalists these very imaginings may confirm the spirit of domination they fear is already rampant in the space program so far. To imagine re-engineering an entire planet smacks of the ultimate hubris: some other choice words from my friends include "arrogance," "deep delusion," and "the myth of scientific supremacy." Some environmental philosophers have worked out objections within mainline ethical frameworks as well.[19] But surely, at the very least, the question needs much more extended attention. The project may not be quite so easy to dismiss. From a biocentric point of view it could even be argued that terraforming other planets is a sort of cosmic obligation—redescribed, naturally, maybe as "making another planet hospitable to life"—though of course, for some critics, this may just be another reason to question (that sort of) biocentrism (for instance, the very preference for living systems over the nonliving itself). And indeed these questions are being seriously and systematically debated already—but predominantly in science fiction: for example in Kim Stanley Robinson's massive Mars trilogy, where this debate is key to the whole three-volume story, and Frederick Turner's epic poem *Genesis.*[20] Again, though, a much more involved and sustained engagement by environmental philosophers is essential as well.

IV. "Mission to Earth"

Let us now consider some ways in which environmental philosophy may open up new perspectives on space exploration in turn.

Usually it is said that it would be a milestone—maybe *the* milestone—in human history were we to discover life outside Earth. We would discover, in the words of a classic book on the subject, that "we are not alone."[21] Our "long loneliness" would be over, Loren Eiseley wrote, especially if we find "men," as he so quaintly adds, in the stars.[22] The baldness of these assertions is striking even though we know very well where they come from: the still-dominant philosophical, religious, and cultural tradition that radically distinguishes humans (and still, sometimes, men) from the rest of creation. Kant was not the only thinker to hold that we could more readily commune with rational creatures in the stars than with our fellow creatures right here on Earth. Yet in the usual kind of space rhetoric this familiar kind of dismissal turns more radical. The rest of the living world simply *vanishes*. It is unnoticed, treated as inessential to the point of invisibility, taken for granted even as it remains, in truth, as essential as ever in sustaining our lives and everything around us, including the project of space exploration itself. How else could we even begin to imagine that we are "alone"?

To be sure, enormous new cultural and philosophical opportunities and questions certainly would arise if extraterrestrial life or intelligence show up: how to reconcile the new discoveries with old creation stories, for example, and what we might learn from alien civilizations who, arguably, are likely to be vastly older than we are. Wild new fears would arise too, no doubt. All of this would be absolutely fascinating and surely deserves far more philosophical attention. Given that a verifiable encounter with extraterrestrial life or intelligence has a greater-than-zero probability right now, and by some plausible accounts is a near-certainty in the long run, we could argue that it ought to be a major subfield of philosophy already.

Still, for environmental philosophers, this truly stunning "backgrounding"[23] of Earth itself must be confronted first. The whole point of environmentalism is that we are *already* "not alone." We are not by ourselves and never have been, and if we are feeling lonely, it is a loneliness that we ourselves (not humans as such, but a very particular form of human culture) have created and perpetuate. It is more like a form of blindness. By what right do we complain of loneliness when we live in a world so alive and alert that a kind of intelligence even shows up, as Robert Frost noted in a famous poem, in the mites crawling across the very pages of our philosophical or scientific tomes, perhaps those very tomes that complain so feelingly of loneliness? The fact is that we already live in James's Multiverse, and it is *right here*.

"Backgrounding" has effects in turn, of course. It makes domination and conquest possible, indeed barely even visible. Val Plumwood has made much of this theme, noting that even the word *space* itself "evokes *terra nullius* and a colonizing mindset."[24] How else is it that we can routinely describe a piece of land as "unoccupied" or "empty" when in fact it is teeming with life-forms and constantly traversed by all manner of more-than-human activities? Anyone who thinks that we would do better with other planets might consider the planners who knowingly sacrificed whole species, right here, in the space-exploration-based search for Life Somewhere Else. The Florida Dusky Seaside Sparrow, already endangered, was driven into extinction by the construction of Cape Kennedy: its marshes flooded to discourage mosquito breeding, or drained, or burned, or bisected by expressways built to make commuting more convenient for space work-ers. The last of those sparrows disappeared in 1989 when a windstorm knocked a tree into his compound at, of all places, Disneyworld.[25]

The original provocation for H. G. Wells's classic *War of the Worlds* was apparently a remark of Wells's brother's about the British invasion of Tasmania in 1897. "Suppose," said Wells's brother as he and H. G. walked through some especially beautiful Surrey countryside, "that some beings from another planet were to drop out of the sky and begin laying about them here!"[26] His point was that the British in Tasmania were virtually that alien—and, again, they were humans merely encountering another cultural and ecological system right here on Earth. Wells' horror story in turn shaped the twentiety-century's image of the extraterrestrial alien, and indirectly then a whole genre of stories about "contact." We know the characteristic themes: extraterrestrials who persistently fail to recognize human civilization, or who treat us as just another animal, or who come to use the planet for their own purposes (we become food, slaves, lab rats, cannon fodder, or . . .), or who do not even notice that we exist. The allegorical point is that this is how *we* have acted, right here on Earth. The alien monster is *us*.

Thus the critique. It applies not merely to the space program, of course: that is only one more melancholy case in point. There are all too many familiar examples of "backgrounding" right here on Earth. Likewise we may certainly undertake to *foreground* Earth, to bring Life Right Here back onto center stage, without reference to the space-age imagination either. Yet I want to suggest that there is at least one way to "foreground" the Earth that can be furthered precisely *by* the space-age imagination. Here, at least, the invitation is not to simply decry the space program and insist on an Earth-based perspective after all, but instead to use space exploration's own tools, and the genuinely new imaginative horizons it offers, to *bring us back* to Earth.

Some astronauts have proposed a systematic "Mission to Earth," and indeed NASA already classifies an impressive range of satellite-assisted earth science programs loosely under this heading.[27] What I propose is more like a *philosophical* "Mission to Earth," a mission to reclaim the sheer wonder of this Earth by using a view from space to re-approach it without the usual assumed familiarity that breeds inattention, or contempt. So: imagine arcing down in a burst of fire to our very own places, even to our own backyards, finally escaping the merely human claustrophobia of some tin-can starship with unutterable relief. You open the hatch. Now you encounter "wonderous strange" beings, enormous or tiny, amorous or ancient perhaps, intricately specialized or preternaturally adaptive, floating, flying, dancing. Any other day these would be just grasshoppers or rhinoceros or woodpeckers or tamarack, clouds and the fall foliage. But now: what a magnificent, stunning, unparalleled planet!

A preeminent whale researcher fills in the picture:

> When you listen over a pair of headphones to whales . . . in deep ocean, it's really as though you were listening from within the Horsehead Nebula, or some galactic space that is otherworldly, not part of anything you know, where the boat is floating. Once, on an early fall night, I was coming back from the Arctic, where I had been [studying] bowhead whales in a boat at sea. As we flew down across the Canadian Arctic, we were beneath an arc of northern lights, which were pure green and bell-shaped. We and the plane were the clapper of this bell, with the green light over us. And for the first time in my life I felt that I was in the position of the whale that is singing to you when you're in the boat and just listening to it. That's the kind of space that is somehow illuminated, depicted, made sensible by the hydrophones. It gives you a special impression of the sea. We all love the ocean's beautiful blue sparkle, but beneath it, down deeper, whales are moving with the slow drifting currents, whales that are great, gentle cloudlike beings . . .[28]

"Great, gentle cloudlike beings"—hauntingly intelligent in ways that we have barely begun to guess, both "alien" in a sense and coinhabitants of our very own world. Is this not a clearer view?

Imagine that we *do* find bacteria on Mars. Of course bacteria pervade Earth—between antibiotics and disinfectants we daily assassinate them by the quintillion. But on Mars? What treasures! What marvels of evolution! Or imagine that we find not only bacteria but also . . . Dusky Seaside Sparrows. What a spooky or divine riposte *that* would be—and, recognizing as much, might we not think differently (at least, have a startlingly new frame of reference) the next time an endangered species teeters on the brink?

In short, a view from space can at least sometimes give us the "space," almost literally, to see *this* world in a new light. Consider that even Lovelock's Gaia Hypothesis, which fundamentally shifted how we think of Earth, actually originated in his thinking about *Mars*. Consulting for NASA in the 1960s, one of Lovelock's assignments was to conceptualize instruments to search for extraterrestrial life. While most of NASA's thinking was moving toward specific chemical tests (later actually deployed on the first landers), Lovelock came to realize that a more telling and holistic test for life would be a distinctively off-balance atmospheric chemistry. *Then* he brought his new thinking back to Earth—the rest is history.[29]

V. SETI for Philosophers

We may carry these points farther by looking at the assumptions that currently shape the search for life, and particularly for intelligent life, beyond Earth—another crucial arena for eco-philosophical engagement.

The Search for Extra-Terrestrial Intelligence, or SETI, currently takes a very specific form. Astronomers search for, and sometimes send, messages using massive radio antennae directed to the stars. A surprisingly elegant epistemology underwrites this project. Even from a position of complete ignorance about what or whether ETIs actually exist, the radio-astronomical SETI project manages to suggest concrete conclusions about how to look for them.[30] Radio is the chosen medium because—so it is argued—it is the first interstellar communication medium *we* discovered, and therefore probably the most primitive and widely possessed. Radio messages could come at any of a infinite number of possible frequencies, of course, but an ETI deliberately trying to communicate with unknown others will presumably pick a frequency that any listening civilization will be likely to hit upon too, a frequency which must therefore be distinguished from others by some universal characteristics. Our radio astronomers therefore search for a message chiefly at the hydrogen frequency, 1420 Megaherz, because H is the simplest and most plentiful element in the universe and therefore supposed to be a natural "consensus point." And at 1420 Megaherz the search is for "alert" sequences like prime number sequences, which nature is not supposed to be able to produce on its own.[31]

Would the hydrogen frequency really stand out, however, for an utterly different kind of intelligence?[32] Is there any reason to think that

a million- or billion-year-old civilization would have scientific chemistry (and thus even have a concept of the "simplest and most plentiful
element") at all, let alone a chemistry like ours? Even other human
civilizations—even our own, in recent memory—have been impressed
by quite other elements. Alchemists surely would scan the universe for
signals at the atomic frequency of gold. Similarly, why should prime
numbers stand out—as if any other mathematics must make the same
peculiarities salient? Must another intelligence even begin counting with
1? Or count at all, for that matter?[33]

The medium of radio itself, meanwhile, is culturally and maybe even
biologically particular too. It is so salient a technology for us due to a
contingent set of historical circumstances—World War II, the dominance
of certain media corporations, and the like—as well as our predilection
for sound. The whole conceit of a radio message itself may be only the
latest of a long series of "messages" humans have already sent to the stars
(and/or to the gods?) such as the ancient monuments—the pyramids,
Easter Island's gaunt monoliths, Peru's twenty- or thirty-mile-long sand
paintings visible only from the skies—most of which are undecipherable
even to us. Meanwhile we are told of native peoples' knowledge of
other star systems that is only beginning to be replicated by astronomers.[34] Maybe lucky or vague guesses, maybe something more. Isn't it
possible—just remotely *possible*—that a 70-thousand-year-old civilization
such as the Australian aborigines' might have found other routes to the
stars, totally unimagined by us?

Radio astronomers have sometimes sent messages of their own, too:
all science, as it turns out, and often quickly discovered to be erroneous
to boot.[35] Once again, other contemporaries or recent ancestors might
choose or have chosen quite other kinds of messages; Bach, maybe, or
proofs of the existence of God, or the Pali Canon. Actually, we are send-
ing much of this already thanks to NPR. Every single TV transmission
sails out to the stars too, as they have been, at an increasingly furious
rate, since the beginnings of broadcasting. Our major electromagnetic
contribution to the universe, so far, is the like of soap operas and Richard Nixon's denials that he knew anything about Watergate. When an
alien "message" comes to Earth in Sagan's *Contact*, it consists partly of
a replay of the first human TV transmission—the extraterrestrials had
been listening and waiting—which happens to be Adolf Hitler welcoming the world to the 1936 Berlin Olympics.

All of this, finally, masks a still deeper conceit: that *we* are the
Earthlings (if any) with whom an alien civilization might want to communicate. What if it is actually the whales, say, who are communing
with the stars, already clicking and harrumphing their million-byte-long
"songs" out into the ether—these "great, gentle, cloudlike beings" who

have, from our point of view, no science at all? Or spiders, or redwoods, or . . . who knows? And of course, *this* kind of communication could already be happening, and could have been happening from the beginning, or perhaps even *be* the beginning, if somehow the "messages" had the power to rearrange matter itself.

Arguably, then, immense, poignant, but intriguing epistemological hurdles remain. How can we even begin to say what it would take to recognize an extraterrestrial "intelligence"? We might miss it even if we were face to face with it, so to speak; even if it were gesticulating wildly, like God in Nietzsche's mocking image, trying to get through to us. It is not merely that we in fact repeatedly miss just such "messages" from other-than-human creatures right next to us, but also that on the whole we do not even communicate that well with *each other*. Scientists who merely trained in different graduate programs have trouble making "contact," for God's sake, as manifest in the ongoing debates over SETI itself. Half the time people do not even recognize their *own* intelligence.

Here too philosophers might usefully follow where science fiction writers have gone before. Stanislaw Lem, for example, in his epic *Solaris*, imagines vast efforts to "contact" a gelatinous ocean on a planet in a double-star system that somehow manages to adjust the planet's orbit to maintain the right distance from both suns.[36] No "contact" is ever made—though at one point the spacefarers even bombard the ocean with bombs "to get its attention"—but the researchers who hover above the ocean receive strange visitors, suggesting that the "ocean" has somehow probed the humans' minds. What are the visitors? Jokes? "Presents," as one character suggests? Warnings? In Lem's unnerving little novel, *His Master's Voice*, a "message" actually does come from the stars, but no one can figure out what it means.[37] A series of ironic but all too human twists ensue. Certain religious cults recognize the message first, but for all the wrong reasons. Governments arm-wrestle to control it, with the usual arsenal of dirty tricks and assassinations. Hardheads from different scientific factions who are finally handed the message conduct nonstop internecine warfare behind the scenes while publicly maintaining a united front behind their own fixed and self-aggrandizing paradigm. Some partial decoding eventually is accomplished, issuing in what for a time seems to be a doomsday weapon. Finally they all give up; the message, now just a curiosity, is made public; and everyone goes home none the wiser.[38]

Here on the brink of a kind of despair, though, I think environmental philosophy may be able to offer some guidance, even hope. What we could call the Question of the Extraterrestrial Other ultimately puts before us everything: everything at once strange, unutterably strange, and yet at the same time possibly reachable, maybe even distant relatives (remember pangermia). If we might already be surrounded by meanings and "messages," then surely our task is nothing at all like separating out something meaningful from a million channels of noise, as in the radio-astronomers' project of trying to discern an intelligent message against the background of constant radio hiss from the nebulae. We should ask instead whether there is anywhere even such a thing as "noise" at all—pure, meaningless, mindless jangle. Quite the opposite: Maybe *everything* bears listening to.

On this point even so didactic a source as the psychologist John Baird (in a book beautifully titled *The Inner Limits of Outer Space*) slips into allegory:

> We really know nothing about how alien civilizations might wish to contact others. The messages might be hidden in radio waves, in the currents of the ocean, in the light from a nearby cluster of stars, or in the meowing of a housecat . . .[39]

Carl Sagan, reflecting on the limits of the technological SETI, even suggests listening to seashells.[40] He hastens to add that he means this only as allegory. Environmental philosophers, however, might not hasten quite as fast. I believe that these images and allegories suggest an alternative and much more inclusive vision of SETI itself.

In his re-vision of environmental philosophy, Tom Birch calls us to "universal consideration," to what the Zen tradition calls "mindful attention": to a less judgmental openness, a tentative presumption *in favor* of things, indeed in favor of *everything*, in place of our insistent presumption against most everything, reduced to silence or sometimes even destroyed by the aftereffects of our own refusal of attention or care. No longer can we prioritize the "consideration" question as the question of who or what "counts"—as if we could determine a priori, paradoxically prior to consideration itself, who or what merits consideration. No, says Birch: our method can only be to continuously "consider" everything. This is "consideration" in what he calls the "root sense": the process of actually, carefully, considering all things.[41]

The same argument can be made not just for who or what "counts" but for who or what is "intelligent," or could be communicating meaningfully. I therefore argue that universal consideration can be a model for, among other things, nothing less than a distinctively philosophical search for extraterrestrial intelligence. It brings with it exactly the requisite "etiquette." As I have written elsewhere:

> An open-ended world of multiple, diverse and always some-what opaque centers requires us to move with caution, at-

tentiveness, circumspection. Ethics is no longer constituted by a merely abstract respect, but demands something far more embodied: a willingness and ability to make the space, not just conceptually, but in one's own person and in the design and structure of personal and human spaces, for the emergence of more-than-human others into relationship.[42]

We speak here to the human relation to terrestrial others, so long devalued and backgrounded by practices and ideas all too familiar to environmental philosophers. There is no reason, though, that the very same considerations would not extend, with the very same force and for the very same reasons, to an openness to *any* kind of intelligence, however it may come before us, or might be invited or invite itself into communication. In a Multiverse in which we already know very well that we are surrounded by manifold opaque "messages," even the distinction between terrestrial and extraterrestrial matters little in the end. We are simply called to continuous, multidirectional receptivity. And what a lovely conclusion that is!

What we actually hear in seashells is our own internal "seas," the sounds of ourselves, so in an unintended (I assume) but elegant way, Sagan's offhand allegory about listening to seashells mirrors the necessary return to *this* world, and to ourselves. At the same time, we need not "return" in a way that precludes other worlds and other kinds of connection. Likewise, the primary message in the meowing of a house cat is surely from the *cat*, not some unimaginable alien communicating through the cat. The cat itself demands attention. Perhaps the cat really is literally an alien. Anyone who knows cats well occasionally gets that feeling (and the origin of the domestic cat is apparently a bit of a mystery). In any case, once again, the cat is a good model. It would behoove us both to learn to really pay attention to our cats (and, again, mites, whales, forests, each other . . .) and in exactly the same way and for the same reasons to practice open-ended attentiveness to all sorts of other kinds of intelligence, especially where we least expect to find it. Baird is right—we really know nothing about how alien civilizations might wish to contact others—but what follows from this is certainly not that we might as well abandon any serious attempt to listen. What follows is that we must try to listen, and seriously, *in every way we can*.[43]

VI. Eco-Philosophers in Space

Environmental philosophers, then, already can and should be space explorers in a sense. Environmental philosophy itself could be a mode of studied openness to all manner of unknowns. I want to conclude by going two or three steps farther. Even in a purely physical sense, I will argue, philosophers should go to space.

The first humans in space were what Tom Wolfe calls "fighter jocks"—military men who graduated from flying combat jets, often in Vietnam, to test pilots and finally to astronauts. Voyages were so wholly pre-choreographed that changing the schedule for anything had to be exhaustively argued over at Mission Control. Things eventually broadened out, a little, to include scientists (finally—on the very last Moon landing, a geologist), women, and now even the occasional politician, millionaire, rock star, or teacher. More than four hundred humans have gone into space so far. A few other life-forms have made it too—apes, dogs, fish, various insects, bacteria—but only as experimental subjects, or (sometimes literally) guinea pigs.

Now we are speaking of deep space missions once again: stations on Moon, trips to Mars. Humans are going into deep space, again and farther. But these missions lie far enough in the future that the entire existing astronaut corps will be long gone by the time crew selection comes around. Piloting abilities may no longer be so crucial, or even necessary at all. Indeed the very nature of the missions themselves is not yet defined—so this is the time that critical and imaginative rethinking can make the largest difference. The question arises anew: Who should go—and for what?

Poets—why not poets: people who above all are trained to put new kinds of experience powerfully into words? Musicians? Even—philosophers? Anyway *some* philosophers: flexible, imaginative, open and receptive minds. Imagine the training programs.

Many of the men who landed on the moon followed vanishing paths soon after. Several became evangelists—it was the only way they could find to speak of what they had felt. Alan Bean (Apollo 12) became a painter. Edgar Mitchell (Apollo 14) is one of the founders of the Institute for Noetic Sciences. When Buzz Aldrin (Apollo 11) was asked what it felt like to step on to the lunar surface, he reportedly was often so overcome he could not answer. Nepalese schoolchildren knelt with candles for a visit by Stuart Roosa (Apollo 14), for "a god had come to visit."[44] As Stephan Harding once put it, apparently a lot of the Apollo astronauts "got mooned." Here, then, there may be a need at least as great as any technical skill or operational information: to find new kinds of words or images for these fundamentally new kinds of experience; to bring them home to all of our fellows; in short to begin to *conceptualize space*. So surely conceptual thinkers—precisely as such—should *go* to space.

The thought of philosophers in space may be wild enough, but we can get wilder still if we begin to think of the trip mechanics. Why do we imagine, for one thing, that the only way to go to Mars, say, is send people round-trip? Why come back? Dropping people onto planets is a lot easier than getting them off again. Surely we could find suitable people willing to leave Earth for good, even for an enormously uncertain future—to be the first Earthlings actually to make a go at living elsewhere. Would this not take a kind of Thoreauvian-philosophical spirit? So again, why not *us*?

The entire nature of an interplanetary mission would have to be reconceived in turn. Rather than an intricately preplanned mission with everything exactly stowed for "deployment" and crew endlessly trained in rigid protocols, we would need to send jacks-of-all-trades with a lot of materials of all sorts; their job would be to set up camp and see what they can do. They can analyze materials on-site, roam the surface, improvise, rhapsodize. And other life forms must go too. The trip is too long to stow enough oxygen and water: an entire living environment must go, to regenerate the air, feed the crew, be fed by their wastes and exhalations, and keep them company. Imagine multispecies "crews," then, space-faring Midgleyean "mixed communities," mini-Multiverses, as Earth's—no longer just one species'—emissaries to the stars.[45]

We might also rethink the entire tempo of such a project. Certainly it is arguable that contemporary humans are not ethically or philosophically ready to go into deep space in earnest, even if it is becoming technically possible. It does not at all follow that we *never* will be ready. Maybe the necessary prelude to actual interplanetary voyages is to found preparatory institutions that will nurture the necessary eco-philosophical attitudes and practices, both in the culture at large and in the adepts who eventually will give rise (after many generations) to the first voyagers (or whatever they will then be called: pilgrims? aspirants? . . .). What's the rush? These new astro-monastaries (for why *not* religious language?) may even rise alongside the "eco-steries" already being established to realize and refine eco-philosophical ways of living right here on Earth, ultimately also across many generations.[46] What projects for eco-philosophers![47]

We are used to the image of astronauts heading off into the heavens in metal containers powered by distilled fossil fuels. This may only be an unbearably primitive first generation of space-faring vessels. Taking further the idea of life itself going forth to seed the cosmos, what if, just possibly, the vessels themselves were alive? Frederick Turner imagines just such a vessel in his epic poem *Genesis*.

This ship's a living tree turned inside out . . .
. . . a planetoid, a world;
Its barrelvault of heartwood, ten feet thick,
Protecting an environment of green
And leafy springtime branchiness within.

An immense hollow trunk, with great glassy sky-ports for the sun at one end; groves of trees growing inward; pastures, cows, rivers, birds.

The ship is named *Kalevala*, and smells
Of lemon trees and showers and cooking-smoke;
And like the clippers of the southern seas
Creaks when the press of speed is upon her, so
A music haunts its pinched harmonic sphere,
A sweet groan like the sound of sea or wind.[48]

The inner solar system is pervaded by "solar wind," massive discharges of particles from the sun that may be gathered by huge solar sails, now being tested on current deep space missions, and used to push a spacecraft along. So imagine that: massive wooden space-faring vessels, mini-Multiverses of their own, driven by *sails*, creaking along through space, and slowly, too, like the old clipper ships. Eco-philosophers, long nurtured by generations of evolving practice on Earth, as the crew. Back on the home planet, a practice of multidirectional attentiveness, alive to a universe of living and intelligent possibilities that do *not* end at the edges of the thin terrestrial envelope of life and intelligence we presently (are trying better to) know. In short, it might after all be possible to envision space exploration neither as a threat to nor a dialectical opposite of environmentalism, nor as some sort of unfortunate distraction, but as nothing less than *an extension of eco-philosophy itself*. Let us arise and go now . . .

Notes

1. Andrew Chaikin, *A Man on the Moon* (New York: Penguin, 1994), p. 110–13, 563. In its early years NASA was so uninterested in space photography that John Glenn actually had to buy his own camera in a Florida drugstore to take pictures out the tiny porthole of his epic 1962 flight.

2. Stewart Brand, *The Clock of the Long Now* (New York: Basic Books, 1999), pp. 133, 144. And that was in 1970s dollars. For a contemporary cam-

paign to provide every classroom in the world with a copy of this picture, see www.earthseeds.net.

3. Some philosophers have examined these questions. Eugene Hargrove organized a conference on "Environmental Ethics and the Solar System" at the University of Georgia in 1985, with participants from NASA, NOAA, and other political or scientific fields, as well as environmental ethicists, and published the proceedings as *Beyond Spaceship Earth: Environmental Ethics and the Solar System* (San Francisco: Sierra Club Books, 1986). As I write he is organizing another, "Space Science, Environmental Ethics, and Policy," for the Spring of 2007. *The Monist* published a special number in 1987 on "Philosophical Issues in Space Exploration" (70:4). Edward Regis's collection *Extraterrestrials* (Cambridge: Cambridge University Press, 1985) includes a surprising number of philosophers—also, a number of surprising philosophers, including Lewis White Beck, whose contribution is actually a 1971 APA Presidential address. Beck comments, though, that if his essay were not the Presidential Address it would be unlikely to be accepted by the Program Committee at all: "Our Association is not hospitable to cosmological speculations" (p. 3). A lot of the philosophical action, as I go on to suggest, takes place in science fiction.

4. Michael Light's collection *Full Moon* (New York: Knopf, 1999) offers a thrilling eyeful.

5. At http://mars.jpl.nasa.gov/mgs/sci/earth/. Moon in its size ratio to Earth—more equal than any other planet-moon pair in the solar system—is really more like a small sister planet than a mere satellite.

6. At http://photojournal.jpl.nasa.gov/jpeg/PIA00450.jpg is a picture of the entire Solar System taken by Voyager I as it passed the orbit of Pluto. It is truly hard to even begin to comprehend that we have access to such a view.

7. J. Baird Callicott, "Moral Considerability and Extraterrestrial Life," in Hargrove, *Beyond Spaceship Earth*. See also the essays by Geoffrey Briggs (NASA), William Hartmann (Planetary Science Institute), and Holmes Rolston in the same volume.

8. William James, *Essays in Radical Empiricism and A Pluralistic Universe* (New York: Dutton, 1971), p. 275.

9. A friend writes: "Species dispersal seems to be the ecological norm. How long does it take before exotics become natives? How different in kind is space exploration from the Polynesians setting sail across the vast Pacific?"

10. Thomas Gold, "The Deep, Hot Biosphere," *Proceedings of the National Academy of Sciences* 89 (1992): 6045–49. Bacteria even grow on the control rods in nuclear reactors.

11. As planetary scientist Christopher McKay puts it, Earth and Mars have been swapping spit for billions of years (Oliver Morton, *Mapping Mars* [New York: Picador/St Martin's, 2002], p. 312). For figures, see Paul Davies, *The Fifth Miracle* (New York: Simon and Schuster, 1999), pp. 220, 241.

12. Robert Hutchison and Andrew Graham, *Meteorites* (London: The Natural History Museum, 1994).

13. Fred Hoyle and N. C. Wickramasinghe, *Astronomical Origins of Life— Steps Towards Panspermia* (Dordrecht: Kluwer Academic Publishers, 1999).

14. Morton, *Mapping Mars*, p. 313.

15. For example, Robert Temple in *The Sirius Mystery* (Rochester, VT: Destiny Books, 1998) and Graham Hancock, *Fingerprints of the Gods* (New York: Three Rivers Press, 1996). These sorts of views are easy to ridicule, of course, and are enormously speculative at best. Still, barring the wild improbability that life only developed on one planet in the entire universe, there are likely to be billion-year-old civilizations well within striking range, and if so, the real question is why ETs have not visited more *frequently* (or perhaps, they have). For discussion of these points from a mainstream and technical perspective, see Brian McConnell, *Beyond Contact: A Guide to SETI and Communicating with Alien Civilizations* (Sebastopol, CA: O'Reilly, 2001), part I. Also energetic and enjoyable is David Grinspoon's *Lonely Planets: The Natural Philosophy of Alien Life* (New York: Ecco/HarperCollins, 2003).

16. Australian observers have sometimes been mystified by aboriginals' relative unconcern with extinct or endangered species, as if "lost" species could somehow regenerate. See Deborah Bird Rose, *Nourishing Terrains* (Canberra: Australian Heritage Commission, 1996), pp. 84–85. Rose comments: "A holistic world view, which situates life forms as part of living systems, will conceptualise loss in complex and non-absolute ways."

17. "Species redundancy" is how the space-colonization advocates argue for species expansion: see Bruce Grierson, "Beyond NASA: The Dawn of the Next Space Age," *Popular Science* 264 (2004): 70.

18. For an overview, see Martyn Fogg, "Terraforming Mars: A Review of Research," at http://www.users.globalnet.co.uk/~mfogg/paper1.htm and Oliver Morton, "Gaia's Neighbor," in *Mapping Mars*. Lovelock's book (with science writer Michael Allaby) is *The Greening of Mars* (New York: Warner, 1984).

19. Most notably Robert Sparrow, "The Ethics of Terraforming," *Environmental Ethics* 21 (1999): 227–45. For a NASA scientist's view, see Christopher McKay, "Let's Put Martian Life First," *The Planetary Report* XXI (2001): 4–5.

20. Kim Stanley Robinson, *Red Mars/Green Mars/Blue Mars* (New York: Bantam, 1993) and Frederick Turner, *Genesis: An Epic Poem* (Dallas: Saybrook Publishing, 1988). See Morton, "Gaia's Neighbor" for an account of parallel discussions on the fringes of NASA. An intriguing reversal is David Gerrold's (unfinished) series *The War Against the Chtorr*, in which aliens determine to transform Earth into something more hospitable to *them*.

21. Walter Sullivan, *We Are Not Alone: The Continuing Search for Extra-terrestrial Intelligence* (New York: Dutton, 1964; rev. ed., 1993).

22. Loren Eiseley, *The Immense Journey* (New York: Vintage, 1959), p. 162.

23. Val Plumwood's exactly-apt term: see her *Environmental Culture* (London: Routledge, 2002), pp. 104, 108–09. See also Catherine Keller, "Talk About the Weather," in Carol Adams, ed., *Ecofeminism and the Sacred* (New York: Continuum, 1993). I am indebted to Plumwood for this reference.

24. Personal communication. *Environmental Culture* is an invaluable source on all these themes.

25. Charles Bergman, *Wild Echoes* (New York: McGraw-Hill, 1990), pp. 51–54. Meanwhile the University of Arizona's Mt. Graham Observatory project is threatening the last habitat of the endangered red squirrel. The mountain is also sacred to the San Carlos Apache people. One of the telescopes on Mt. Graham was built by the Vatican for the express purpose of discovering ETIs—so that they can be evangelized. For one Apache view of this bizarre situation, see http://users.skynet.be/kola/mtgrah.htm.

26. See Wells, *War of the Worlds*, ed. Martin A. Danahay (Peterborough, Ontario: Broadview Press [2003]), p. 193 (Appendix A).

27. See http://science.hq.nasa.gov/missions/earth.html.

28. Quoted by Dianne Ackerman in *The Moon by Whalelight* (New York: Random House, 1991), p. 130.

29. James Lovelock, *Gaia: A New Look at Life on Earth* (Oxford: Oxford University Press, 2000), Chapter 1.

30. The original source is G. Cocconi and P. Morrison, "Searching for Interstellar Communications," in A. G. W. Cameron, ed., *Interstellar Communication* (New York: Benjamin, 1963). Another classic is Carl Sagan, *The Cosmic Connection* (New York: Dell, 1973).

31. You can now join the search yourself. From http://setiathome.berkely.edu/ you can download a search program and portions of our by-now voluminous data from space and let your PC do the searching while you sleep. Two million people currently take part in this, the largest, fastest, and cheapest distributed computing project ever created. See McConnell, *Beyond Contact*, chapters 1 and 9.

32. The arguments to follow are more fully developed in my "Radio Astronomy as Epistemology: Some Philosophical Reflections on the Search for Extraterrestrial Intelligence," *Monist* 71 (1988): 88–100.

33. Carl Sagan's protagonist raises similar worries in *Contact*, his intricate and surprisingly theological SETI novel (New York: Simon and Schuster, 1985). In the end, though, exactly the expected sort of message shows up.

34. The Dogon's apparent knowledge of Sirius's invisible companion star is the essential premise of Temple's *The Sirius Mystery*, for example.

35. See David Whitehouse, BBC News Online Science Editor, "A Cosmic Mistake," at http://news.bbc.co.uk/1/hi/sci/tech/353409.stm.

36. First published in 1961; reissued by Harvest Books (New York: Harcourt Brace) in 2002.

37. Northwestern University Press (Evanston, IL), reprint edition, 1999.

38. Most of NASA's own space-probe data is already unreadable and unusable, coded in defunct computer programs on degenerating magnetic tapes (Brand, *The Clock of the Long Now*, p. 87ff). We cannot even read our *own* radio messages from space. Voyager I carried a phonograph record out of the solar system—a "message" even my children, quite human and quite contemporary, would be hard put to decode.

39. John Baird, *The Inner Limits of Outer Space* (Lebanon, NH: University Press of New England, 1990), p. 135.

40. Sagan, *Cosmic Connection*, p. 224.

41. Tom Birch, "Moral Considerability and Universal Consideration," *Environmental Ethics* 15 (1993): 313–32.

42. In Multicentrism: A Manifesto," p. 95 in this book.

43. There are extended theological analogues to all of these issues. We learn from James Lewis's intriguing collection *The Gods Have Landed* (Albany: SUNY, 1995) how ready people are to interpret putative alien visitations as manifestations of god—and also how ready other people are to interpret putative manifestations of god as alien visitations (Jesus as extraterrestrial?). Then there are the theologians who debate whether Jesus's crucifixion on Earth could redeem ETIs—as if we have gospel for the entire Universe (Ted Peters, "Exo-Theology," in ibid.)—though Del Ratzsch points out (in "Space Travel and Challenges to Religion," *Monist* 70 (1987)) that ETIs might well require a different kind of salvation. Meanwhile the (apparent) silence of ETIs, so far, has striking parallels with the (apparent) silence of God. Bertrand Russell, when asked what he would say if God Almighty called him to task for his atheism, replied that he would ask God why He made the evidence for his Existence so poor. The more advanced an ETI is supposed to be, the stickier the analogous questions become. After all, radio is probably only the crudest of self-evincing communicative technologies. Presumably a really advanced civilization would long since have discovered more obvious ways of manifesting themselves: artificial modulations of a star's light, maybe, or, say, personal appearances. So where are they? A traditional religious answer to Russell's challenge is that God *has* made Himself evident, for example by putting in personal appearances—the parallel for ETIs is obvious. A pantheist answer is that the entire world is already a manifestation of God. It is a fundamental mistake to look for the occasional miracle when the world itself is already a miracle. The parallel for ETIs might be the suggestion that the order of the universe itself is somehow their doing—the theme, not surprisingly, of yet another of Lem's stories: see his "The New Cosmogeny," in *A Perfect Vacuum* (New York: Harcourt, Brace, Jovanovich, 1971). Likewise, Sagan's protagonist in *Contact* muses that "perhaps the sign of a really advanced civilization would be that they left no sign at all" (p. 99). Thus the theological argument may arrive in the same place as the argument in the text: all we can really do is practice the widest and wildest kind of attentiveness.

44. Chaikin, *A Man on the Moon*, Epilogue. This "mooning" deserves much more attention (and before it's too late) than anyone has yet given it. Why don't we have dissertations in philosophy or religion (even psychology) on such things?

45. Should we be so glad that Biosphere II failed? Maybe in the short run—who were we to think a self-sustaining ecosystem could be replicated so easily?—but in the long run "mini-Multiverses" may be the only way to go to deep space.

46. See http://www.ecostery.org.

47. I think here of the final lines of Plumwood's *Environmental Culture*:

Space colonisation is an extreme example of a rationalist project that misunderstands our nature as earth beings. Hyperbolised autonomy and the backgrounding of the earth create an illusory sense of detachability from the earth, and present as "rational" a project where every venture outwards further damages the earth we depend on. When we have learnt the true nature of our being as earth-dependent and have learnt both to cherish the earth and to go beyond it without damage, it may be time for us to try to leave for the stars—but not before. (p. 240)

I agree with this entirely. The new "monasteries" would have to be deeply engaged not just in preparing for space but transforming our entire relation to Earth. "But not before" could be the motto over their gates. Still, they would *have* gates . . .

48. Frederick Turner, *Genesis*, p. 94. Octavia Butler imagines a different kind of living space vessel in her *Xenogenesis* series.

Appendix

Anthony Weston
Complete Publication List

Books

A Rulebook for Arguments.
Indianapolis: Hackett Publishing Company, 1987.
Second edition, 1992.
Third edition, 2001.
Fourth edition, 2008.
Translated into Spanish, Portuguese, Italian, Greek, Korean, Russian, Japanese, Czech, and Braille.

Toward Better Problems: New Perspectives on Abortion, Animal Rights, the Environment, and Justice.
Philadelphia: Temple University Press, 1992.

Back to Earth: Tomorrow's Environmentalism.
Philadelphia: Temple University Press, 1994.

A Practical Companion to Ethics.
New York: Oxford University Press, 1997.
Second edition, 2002.
Third edition, 2005.
Translated into German, Japanese, and Portuguese.

An Invitation to Environmental Philosophy
New York: Oxford University Press, 1999.

A 21st Century Ethical Toolbox.
New York: Oxford University Press, 2001.
Second edition, 2008.

Jobs For Philosophers.
  Philadelphia: Xlibris Corporation, 2004.

Creativity For Critical Thinkers
  New York: Oxford University Press, 2007.

Creative Problem-solving In Ethics
  New York: Oxford University Press, 2007.

How To Reimagine the World: A Pocket Handbook for Practical Visionaries.
  New Society Publishers, 2007.

Articles

"A Pattern for Argument Analysis in Informal Logic," *Teaching Philosophy* 5:2 (1982): 135–39

"The Two Basic Fallacies," *Metaphilosophy* 15:2 (1984): 148–55

"Newspeak: The State of the Art," in R. C. and M. D. Lazar, eds., *Beyond 1984* (New York: Associated Faculty Press, 1984): 44–50.

"Toward the Reconstruction of Subjectivism: Love as a Paradigm of Values," *The Journal of Value Inquiry* 18:3 (1984): 181–94.

"Drawing Lines: The Abortion Perplex and the Presuppositions of Applied Ethics," *Monist* 67:4 (1984): 589–604.

"Subjectivism and the Question of Social Criticism," *Metaphilosophy* 16:1 (1985): 57–65.

"Technological Unemployment and the Lifestyle Question," *Journal of Social Philosophy* XVI:2 (1985): 19–30.

"Beyond Intrinsic Value: Pragmatism in Environmental Ethics," *Environmental Ethics* 7:4 (1985): 321–39.
  This essay subsequently reprinted in:
  Environmental Pragmatism, edited by Andrew Light and Eric Katz (London: Routledge, 1995).
  Environmental Philosophy: Critical Concepts, edited by J. B. Callicott and Clare Palmer (London: Routledge, 2004).

"The Socratic Philosopher-Citizen: Some Reservations," *Metaphilosophy* 17:4 (1986): 371–78.

"Toward an Inclusive Ethics," *Bowling Green Studies in Applied Philosophy,* vol. 8: "Values and Moral Standing" (1986): 36–44.

"Forms of Gaian Ethics," *Environmental Ethics* 9:3 (1987): 121–34. This essay subsequently reprinted in *Environmental Philosophy: Critical Concepts*, edited by J. B. Callicott and Clare Palmer (London: Routledge, 2004)

"Radio Astronomy as Epistemology: Some Philosophical Reflections on the Search for Extraterrestrial Intelligence," *Monist* 71:1 (1988): 88–100.

"Ivan Illich and the Radical Critique of Tools," *Research in Philosophy and Technology*, volume 9: "Ethics and Technology" (1989): 171–182.

"The Photographic Memory: A Note on the Commodification of Experience," *Journal of Social Philosophy* XIX:3 (1989): 3–11.

"Listening to the Earth," *Tikkun* 5:2 (March/April 1990): 50–54. This essay subsequently reprinted in Michael Lerner, ed., *Tikkun Anthology* (Oakland, CA: Tikkun Books, 1992): 55–59.

"On the Body in Medical Self-Care and Holistic Medicine," in Drew Leder, ed., *The Body in Medical Thought and Practice* (Amsterdam: Kluwer, 1991): 69–84.

"Uncovering the 'Hidden Curriculum': A Laboratory Course in Philosophy of Education," *APA Newsletter on Teaching Philosophy* 90:2 (Winter 1991): 36–40. This essay subsequently reprinted in Tziporah Kasachkoff, ed., *In the Socratic Tradition: Essays on Teaching Philosophy* (Lanham, MD: Rowman and Littlefield, 1998).

"Non-anthropocentrism in a Thoroughly Anthropocentrized World," *The Trumpeter* 8:3 (1991): 108–12.

"Toward a Social Critique of Bioethics," *Journal of Social Philosophy* 12:2 (1991): 109–18.

"Between Means and Ends," *Monist* Special Issue on Intrinsic Value in Nature, vol. 75:2 (1992): 236–49.

"Before Environmental Ethics," *Environmental Ethics* 14 (1992): 323–40. This essay subsequently reprinted in:
Environmental Ethics: Divergence and Convergence, edited by Susan Armstrong and Richard Botzler (New York: McGraw-Hill, 1993).
People, Penguins, and Plastic Trees: Basic Issues in Environmental Ethics, edited by Christine Pierce and Donald Vandeveer (2nd ed.; Belmont, CA: Wadsworth Publishing Company, 1994).

Postmodern Environmental Ethics, edited by Max Oelschlaeger (Albany: SUNY Press, 1995).

Environmental Pragmatism, edited by Andrew Light and Eric Katz (London: Routledge, 1995).

"A Liberatory/Laboratory Course in Philosophy of Education," *Resource Paper Series,* National Society for Experiential Education, 1992.

"Self-Validating Reduction: Toward a Theory of the Devaluation of Nature," *Environmental Ethics* 18 (1996): 115–32.

"Instead of Environmental Education," *Proceedings of the Yukon College Symposium on Ethics, Environment, and Education* (Whitehorse, YT: Yukon College, 1996).
This essay subsequently reprinted as "Deschooling Environmental Education," in *Canadian Journal of Environmental Education* I (1996).

"Is It Too Late?" in Anthony Weston, ed., *An Invitation to Environmental Philosophy* (New York: Oxford University Press, 1998).

"Universal Consideration as an Originary Practice," *Environmental Ethics* 20 (1998): 279–89.

"Risking Philosophy of Education," *Metaphilosophy* 29 (1998): 145–58.

"Environmental Ethics as Environmental Etiquette: Toward an Ethics-Based Epistemology in Environmental Philosophy" (cowritten with Jim Cheney), *Environmental Ethics* 21 (1999): 115–34.
This essay subsequently reprinted in *Environmental Ethics: Divergence and Convergence,* edited by Susan Armstrong and Richard Botzler (New York: McGraw-Hill), 3rd ed., 2002.

"Galapagos Stories, or: Evolution, Creation, and the Odyssey of Species," *Soundings* LXXXVI (2003): 375–90.

"What If Teaching Went Wild?" in Scott Fletcher, editor, *Philosophy of Education 2002* (Urbana, IL: Philosophy of Education Society, 2003): 40–52.
This essay subsequently revised and reprinted in:
Canadian Journal of Environmental Education IX (2004).
Green Teacher 76 (2005): 8–12 (abridged).

"Multicentrism: A Manifesto," *Environmental Ethics* 26 (2004): 25–40.
This essay subsequently reprinted in *The Trumpeter,* vol. 22:1 (http://trumpeter.athabascau.ca/content/v22.1/7weston. pdf).

Reviews and Short Pieces

Review of Thomas Schwartz, *The Art of Logical Thinking*, *Teaching Philosophy* 5:1 (1982).

"Medicine by the People," *Science for the People* 14:1 (1982).

Review essay, "On Finding an Ethical Voice: A Response to Sontag and MacIntyre," *Free Inquiry* 4:1 (1983).

"A New System for Non-Sexist Family Names," *Coevolution Quarterly* 41 (1984).

Review of Michael Taylor, *Community, Anarchy, and Liberty*, *Journal of Philosophy* LXXXII:8 (1985).

Review of Milton Konvitz, ed., *The Legacy of Horace Kallen*, *Transactions of the C. S. Pierce Society* XXIV:3 (1988).

Notice of Michael Crowe, *The Extraterrestrial Life Debate: 1750–1900*, *The Quarterly Review of Biology* 63:1 (1988).

"Unfair to Swamps: A Reply to Katz," *Environmental Ethics* 10:3 (1988).
This reply subsequently reprinted in *Environmental Pragmatism*, edited by Andrew Light and Eric Katz (London: Routledge, 1995).

"Interdisciplinary Teaching and the Nature of Philosophy," *APA Newsletter on Teaching Philosophy*, June 1989.

"Anna Fixx" (case study), in Michael O'Neill, ed., *Ethics in Non-Profit Management: A Collection of Cases* (San Francisco: University of San Franscisco, Institute for Non-profit Organization Management, 1991).

"On Callicott's Case against Pluralism," *Environmental Ethics* 13:3 (1991).

"Ethics Out of Place," *Environmental and Architectural Phenomenology* 3:1 (1992).

Review of Bryan Norton, *Toward Unity Among Environmentalists*, *Environmental Ethics* 14:3 (1992).

Review of Christopher Stone, *The Gnat Is Older Than Man*, *Environmental Ethics* 16:4 (1994).

Notice of Stephen R. L. Clark, *How to Think About the Earth*, *Ethics* 106:3 (1996).

Review of R. Murray Schafer, *The Soundscape: Our Sonic Environment and the Tuning of the World*, Environmental Ethics 18:3 (1996).

Review of Eric Katz, Andrew Light, and David Rothenberg, eds., *Beneath the Surface: Critical Essays in the Philosophy of Deep Ecology*, Environmental Ethics 23:3 (2001).

Review of Mitchell Thomashow, *Bringing the Biosphere Home*, Environmental Ethics 25:4 (2003).

Review of R. Bruce Hull, *Infinite Nature*, Environmental Ethics, 29:3 (2007).

Index

Aborigines, Australian, 174, 182n16
Abram, David, 13, 17, 93, 100–101, 141
Acampora, Ralph, 106n31
Afrocentrism, 97
Aiken, Conrad, 81
Alexander, Christopher, 38–39, 122, 126–127
Animals
  concept of, 57, 132
  and etiquette, 9–10, 78–79
  as fellow earthlings, 69–70, 170–173
  interaction with, 24–25, 36–37, 142–145
  rights, 114–115
  self-validating reduction and, 49–52, 57, 114–115
  see also bears, chimpanzees, dolphins, monkeys, vultures, whales
anthropocentrism, 2, 5–6, 11–12, 13–18, 20, 23–27, 33–34, 53–54, 56–58, 164–166
  and anthropocentrization, 109–130
  and multicentrism, 93, 97–99
anthropocentrization, 2, 15, 17, 23–27, 109–130, 132
  see also de-anthropocentrization
Antler, poem, 125
Apollo moon photos, 16, 119, 163
"Archimedean point" for ethics, 27–28
architecture, 109–113, 122–123
Armstrong, Jeanette, 81

Arras, John, 28
Audubon Society, 125, 136

"backgrounding" (Val Plumwood), 170–171
Baird, John, 176
Baudrillard, Jean, 55
Beak of the Finch, The (Jonathan Weiner), 150
bears, polar, 51
Bernstein, Richard, 30
Berry, Thomas, 12
Berry, Wendell, 37–38, 77, 121–122
Beston, Henry, 69–70
Bettleheim, Bruno, 48–49
biocentrism, 11, 98, 114, 166
"biospheric egalitarianism," 98
Birch, Tom, x, xii, 13, 58, 70, 77, 88, 94, 176
Blind Watchmaker, The (Richard Dawkins), 153
Borgmann, Albert, 6, 55
Brand, Stewart, 16, 109, 118–121, 126, 129
Bringhurst, Robert, 74
Buber, Martin, 94

Callicott, J. Baird, xiii, 35, 165
Camus, Albert, 112–113
Cape Kennedy, 171
celebratory environmentalism, 16, 124–125
centrism, 11–12, 33, 93, 96–99, 114
ceremonial worlds, 71–75

Cheney, Jim, x, xii, 9–11, 13, 25–26, 65–88, 95, 176–177
chimpanzees, 152
Chipewyan Indians, 84, 100
Christianity, 30, 53, 124, 131, 142
Christie, Gordon, 71
classroom, possibilities in, 136–146
Clock of the Long Now (Stewart Brand), 118–120
co-evolution
    in nature, 158
    of values and practices, 31–33, 35
comets, 167–168
communion, 142, 146
concentrism, 90–92, 98–99
Contact (Carl Sagan), 174
Creationism, 4, 19, 151–152, 159–162
creativity, in evolution, 155, 157, 159–162

Daddy Longlegs, 144–145
Darwin, Charles, 149–162
Darwinism, 19, 149–162
Dawkins, Richard, 153
de-anthropocentrization, 13–16, 109–130
Deloria, Vine, 101, 160
Dewey, John, 2–5, 34, 133–134
dolphins, 52
Douglass, Frederick, 46–47
Duerr, Hans Peter, 113
Dusky Seaside Sparrow, 171–172
Dryzek, John, 96

ecocentrism, 11, 98, 114
ecophilosophy and space, 163–185
Ecuador, 18, 151, 161–162
egoism, 5, 92
Eiseley, Loren, 170
Emerson, Ralph Waldo, and the stars, 125
"enabling environmental practice," 35–39
environment, concept of, 167–168
environmental education, 16–18, 131–147

"environmental etiquette," 9–11, 65–88, 94–95, 100, 176–177
environmentalism, cosmic, 166–169
epistemology, and ethics, 9–11, 60, 65–88
    ethics-based, 68–71, 74–75
ethics, epistemology-based, 66–71, 74–75
    originary stages of, 31, 34
    tasks of, 32–33
Evernden, Neil, 94
evolution, 19, 149–162
existentialism, 112
"expanding circle," 89–92
extraterrestrial life, 170
extraterrestrial origin stories, 168

factory farms, 8, 49–50
finches, Darwin's, beaks, 150
flowers, eating, 140–142
Frankenstein, 52
Freire, Paolo, 133
Frost, Robert, 170
Frye, Marilyn, 45–47

Gaia Hypothesis, 169, 173
Galapagos Islands, 18–19, 149–162
Geddes, Carol, 75, 80
Genesis (Frederick Turner), 169, 179–180
"genetic drift," as metaphor in evolution, 154, 162
Gill, Sam, 10, 71–72
Gould, Steven Jay, 157
Grant, Peter and Rosemary, 150–151
"grounding" environmental ethics, 111–112

Hallen, Patsy, xii
Harding, Stephan, 178
Hargrove, Gene, xiii, 181n3
Hearne, Vicki, 9, 78–79
Hegel, G. W. F., 116
"hegemonic centrism," 93, 96–98
Hester, Lee, 80, 84
His Master's Voice (Stanislaw Lem), 175

holidays, 124
Holt, John, 133
Hopi origin stories, 81

Illich, Ivan, 133
incompleteness, of environmental
    ethics, ix
indigenous worlds, 10, 71–75, 79–84
Inner Limits of Outer Space, The
    (John Baird), 175
insects, 144–145
intrinsic values, 1, 3, 66, 115
invitation, self-validating, 76–80

James, William, 12, 94, 98, 165, 170
Jenness, Diamond, 72
Jickling, Bob, xii, xiii, 134

Jobs for Philosophers (Anthony
    Weston), 65, 109, 163
Kant, Immanuel, 40n17, 170

Land Ethic, The, 34, 165
language, performative, 10, 67, 70,
    72–75
LeGuin, Ursula, epigraph, 149
Lem, Stanislaw, 175, 184n43
Leopold, Aldo, 34, 53, 57, 83–84,
    165
Lewontin, Richard, 157
Lopez, Barry, 52, 82
love, 61, 68
Lovelock, James, 120, 169, 173
Lovibond, Sabina, 28, 30
Lunniss, Richard, 161–162

MacIntyre, Alasdair, 28, 30
Marcus, Ben, 114
"margins," 37, 121–122
Mars, 20, 164, 167, 169, 172, 173,
    178–179
Martin, Calvin, 77
Marx, Karl, 30, 116
McHarg, Ian, 101, 122
Malthus, Thomas, 156
mechanism, as metaphor in evolu-
    tion, 154

Merchant, Carolyn, 96
metaphors
    in Darwinism, 153–154
    their necessity at ethics' originary
        stages, 33
meteorites, 140
Meyer, Leroy, 71
Midgley, Mary, 6, 24, 36, 68, 112,
    179
misogyny, 45–46, 51
"Mission to Earth," 171–172
"mixed communities," 6, 68,
    121–123, 179
modernism, 74
Momaday, N. Scott, 73, 81–82
monkeys, howler, 50–51, 61
Moon, exploration, 164–166, 178
multicentrism, 2, 11–13, 89–107
"Multiverse," 12, 94, 165, 170, 177,
    179–180
music, 9, 51, 61
mutation, as metaphor in evolution,
    154, 162

Naess, Arne, 101
narrative, 79–84
Nash, Roderick, 112
National Aeronautics and Space
    Administration (NASA), 167,
    171–172, 173
Neo-Platonism, 131
Nietzsche, Friedrich, 175
Nollman, Jim, 50–51, 61, 79, 96,
    122, 127
nonanthropocentrism, 2, 23–27, 33,
    113, 128–129, 165
Norton, Bryan, 34

Ong, Walter, 71
Origin of Species, The, 150–151, 158
Ortiz, Simon, poems, 83

Paley, William, 153
"pangermia," 168–169
Papago origin stories, 81
Parks, National, 55
Peacock, Doug, 77

philosophy, its prospects, 110–130, 172, 177–180
philosophy of education, 133–134
Platonism, 131
Plumwood, Val, xii, 13, 89, 92–93, 96–98, 101–102, 170–171, 184n47
pluralism, 15, 39, 69, 98
"post-anthropocentrizing cultural tinkerers," 121, 128
postmodernism, 74, 116
pragmatism, 2–4
Protestantism, 32

racism, 46–47
Ramirez, Tony, 71
Rawls, John, 27–28
Reconstruction (John Dewey)
in philosophy, 15, 34
social, 135
relativism, 30
rights, 7, 31, 41n23
and animals, 114–115
Robinson, Kim Stanley, 169

"sacramental practice," 73–74, 82
sacred groves, 53, 56, 76
St James, Calypso, 123, 126
Sagan, Carl, 174, 176, 177
Salango (Ecuador), 161
Sally Lightfoot (crab), 156
Schelling, Thomas, 45, 48
Search for Extraterrestrial Intelligence (SETI), 170, 173–177
seti@home, 183n31
seasons, cycle of, 124
"secular catastrophism," 160
Seed, John, 92
self-fulfilling prophecies, 47, 76
self-validating invitation, 61
self-validating reduction, 7–9, 45–64, 75–79
Sharp, Henry, 73, 84–85, 99–100
Shepard, Paul, 53, 73
Sinai, Mt, 56
Singer, Peter, 67, 89
Snyder, Gary, 77

solar wind, 179
"Solarians," 165
space exploration, and eco-philosophy, 19–20, 163–185
species, criteria for, 152
Stone, Christopher, 33, 102
stories, and narrative understanding, 79–84, 162

Tasmania, British invasion of, 171
Taylor, Charles, 28
Taylor, Paul, 24–25, 28–29
"terrformation," of other planets, 169
theology, 159–162, 184n43
Turner, Frederick, 169, 179–180

universal consideration, 13, 70, 77, 94–95

values, social contingency of, 4–7, 27–31
value theory and naturalism, 1
vultures, 143

wakan tanka (Lakota), 82
Walker, Margaret, 96
Walzer, Michael, 28
War of the Worlds (H. G. Wells), 171
Washoe, 78
Weiner, Jonathan, 150–151
Wells, H. G., 171
Whales, 172, 174–175
and self-validating reduction, 51–52
wilderness, 36–37, 54, 112, 113, 166
wildness, 145–146
Wolfe, Tom, 178
worldviews, 71–75, 79–84
Worster, Donald, 156, 158

Y2K problem, 118–119
Yukeoma (Hopi), 81

Zen, mindful attention in, 176
ZenLite Philosophical Expeditions, xii